SPIN CYCLE

SPIN CYCLE

How Research Is Used in Policy Debates
The Case of Charter Schools

Jeffrey R. Henig

Russell Sage Foundation · New York
The Century Foundation · New York

 # 1599218880

The Russell Sage Foundation

Library of Congress Cataloging-in-Publication Data
Henig, Jeffrey R., 1951–
   Spin cycle : how research is used in policy debates : the case of charter schools / Jeffrey R. Henig.
      p. cm.
   ISBN-13: 978-0-87154-339-4
   1. Charter schools—Political aspects—United States.   2. Charter schools—Government policy—United States.   3. Education—Research—Political aspects—United States.   I. Title.
   LB2806.36H46 2007
   371.01—dc22

2007030312

Text design by Suzanne Nichols.

RUSSELL SAGE FOUNDATION
112 East 64th Street, New York, New York 10021
10   9   8   7   6   5   4   3   2   1

Contents

About the Author

Jeffrey R. Henig is professor of political science and education at Teachers College, Columbia University, and professor of political science at Columbia University.

Acknowledgments

I owe an unusually large debt to others for their help in completing this book. The Spencer Foundation provided a grant that put the wheels in motion. Later, both The Century Foundation and the Russell Sage Foundation provided additional support for research assistance and to allow me some more time for writing. My thanks to all three, not just for the material help they provided, but also for the psychological boost that comes along with confirmation that at least some folks are interested in your project and would like to see it succeed.

Neil Eckardt, a doctoral student at Teachers College, was an excellent research assistant. He not only did what had to be done, he provided a valuable sounding board as well, checked me on some of my sillier notions, and contributed ideas and analyses of his own. Jonah Lieberman, like Neil a student in the Politics and Education Program, worked on a smaller segment of the research but was equally helpful, speedy, and easy to work with.

Numerous people took the time to provide feedback as this book evolved. Greg Anrig, Richard Kahlenberg, and Richard Rothstein slogged through the entire version of an earlier draft and provided extremely helpful detailed comments as well as the important general message that I needed to speak with a clearer voice of my own. Richard Colvin, Carl Kaestle, Hank Levin, Andy Rotherham, and John Witte each read and provided feedback on sections. Two anonymous reviewers for the press provided additional suggestions wrapped in nice words of encouragement. Several others gave me helpful commentary on closely related papers I was working on at the time and helped me develop my thoughts and arguments more clearly; these include Julian Betts, Rick Hess, Brian Glenn, Paul Hill, and Steven Teles. And along the way I picked the brains of many others. I'm very appreciative of those who consented to be interviewed and took the time to offer thoughtful responses. In a literal sense, this book could not have been completed without their help.

Anne Derbes and Bob Schwab, with their usual generosity, provided a great setting for writing during the summer of 2006. Finally, my wife, Robin Marantz Henig, who has been my writing coach for virtually all of my adult life, provided her normal and absolutely critical doses of editorial oversight, encouragement, and emotional sustenance.

To
Robin, Jessica, Samantha
What Really Matters

Chapter 1

The *New York Times*/AFT Charter School Controversy

August 17, 2004, was a warm day in Washington, D.C., the temperature in the eighties, the tail end of an unusually cool and wet summer, the time of year that political activists, public officials, and journalists sometimes refer to as the summer doldrums. For the rest of the year, most of the nation's political and policy attention is focused on Washington. Lobbyists, advocacy groups, media outlets, and congressional staff wait poised and ready to respond to whispers and rumors that might signal shifts in partisan fortunes or be exploited for political gain. Washington was built on a swamp, however, and, even in the age of central air conditioning, often oozes a humidity that induces lethargy and drives the lucky ones who can to escape to Rehoboth Beach and Martha's Vineyard.

With Congress out of session, the town seemingly half empty, and many of the nation's commentators reading beach novels instead of the day's headlines, the stage was hardly set for a raging controversy. The letters to the editor section of the *New York Times*, rather than buzzing with sharp debates about Iraq or Vice President Cheney, gave much of its attention (six letters) to responses to the passing of television chef Julia Child. "I recall that she once said that a person who didn't eat butter was a crank with limp hair," wrote Estelle Shanley of York, Maine. "Julia Child lives on in all our kitchens."

For charter school supporters, however, this was what one observer labeled "a day that will live in infamy" (Petrilli 2006). Those who did pick up the *New York Times* found, besides reflections on the loss of a culinary cultural icon, the prominent page one display of a story about charter schools. "Charter Schools Trail in Results, U.S. Data Reveals," read the headline. The article, by *Times* reporter Diana Jean Schemo, described a report released by the American Federation of Teachers (AFT) on the performance of charter schools, a rapidly expanding mechanism of education reform.

"The first national comparison of test scores among children in charter schools and regular public schools shows charter school students often doing worse than comparable students in regular public schools," Schemo wrote in her opening sentence. She went on to describe the findings as "buried in mountains of data the Education Department released without public announcement," implying that the Bush administration, which was a vocal and active proponent of charter schools, had tried to suppress the evidence.[1]

Charter schools are just one in an array of school choice options that have been breaking down the historical link between where one lives and the schools one's children attend. The most controversial of these are publicly funded school vouchers[2] that families can apply toward tuition at private schools. Vouchers are controversial because they are often linked to a general argument that private markets are superior to government as an institution for meeting social needs. Some school choice options, though, are wholly incorporated within the traditional framework of public school districts—among them, magnet schools,[3] interdistrict public choice,[4] and more liberalized transfer options. Charter schools generally are designed to straddle the line that traditionally distinguishes public schools from private. They are officially public schools, but the charter concept envisions them as being managed largely independent of government regulation.

Just a little more than fifteen years since the first charter school opened in Minnesota, there are now nearly 4,000 nationwide, serving an estimated 1.1 million students (Center for Education Reform 2007). The laws governing charter schools differ—sometimes substantially—from state to state, of course, but some general characteristics have emerged. Charter schools receive public funding on a per-student basis, are often responsible for achieving educational outcomes defined by their government chartering entity, and are subject to at least nominal public oversight. They typically are barred from charging tuition on top of the public per-pupil allocation, but are free to pursue other forms of supplementary support from donors, foundations, or corporate sponsors. Although they must observe certain baseline regulations, such as prohibitions on discrimination and the provision of safe environments, they are exempt from many of the rules and regulations that bind regular public schools to specific standards and procedures. This hybrid status, as we shall see, has made charter schools a special focus of attention and helped draw them into ideological whirlpools that raise the stakes surrounding the research into their actual form and consequences.

The *New York Times* article was as striking for its location as for its content. In the real estate of newsprint, the most valuable property is on the front page and "above the fold." The *New York Times*, too, is arguably the nation's premier print outlet, at least when it comes to catching the attention of national policy elites. With the best spot in the best paper, this was a story unlikely to be ignored.

Despite the summer doldrums, "all hell broke loose" (Petrilli 2006). Within days, proponents of charters and other choice-based and market-oriented approaches to school reform had launched a counterattack. Jeanne Allen of the Center for Education Reform, a Washington-based organization supported by conservative foundations, tracked down prominent researchers, many on their summer vacations, to see whether they would be willing to have their names listed on a protest ad. The full-page ad, which cost over $115,000, ran just eight days after the article first appeared. Rather than simply affirming a policy stance in favor of charter schools, the text[5] read almost like a primer on proper methodology for conducting research, taking the *Times* to task for failing to subject the AFT report to a more rigorous and skeptical review. At the same time, school choice proponents got busy placing editorials, providing supporters with talking points for discussion on television talk shows, issuing critiques on various electronic newsletters and blogs, and publicizing a report by Caroline Hoxby, a Harvard economist, which they claimed was much stronger methodologically and which they said arrived at the opposite conclusion: that charter schools were working very well indeed.

The experience strengthened the sense among some in the conservative community that the *Times* was an avowed opponent of market-based ideas for reforming schools and that they needed to be primed with a strike team for quick response. It was not long, however, before the rebuttals themselves were being subject to intense scrutiny—and to charges that the critics of the AFT report were hypocritically and selectively using the standards of social science to mask and advance an agenda grounded more in ideology than evidence. These charges and countercharges make this case a useful window into a troubling phenomenon. Despite high hopes about its potential to promote collective learning and a more informed democracy, research often seems to appear on the public stage in a swirl of political sloganeering that defies reason, fogs understanding, and runs the risk of reducing claims of scientific evidence to the status of Madison Avenue advertising claims.

The Issue and Its Significance: Collective Learning About Education Policy and Practice

Research and evidence have had an ambiguous role in informing public policy and citizens in the United States. On the one hand, the vision that the technical tools, expertise, and objectivity of social science might help in the pursuit of the collective good has had a powerful influence at critical points in American history. On the other, the nation's commitment to social science research has been sporadic, shallow, and at times cynically manipulative. Competing sides in contemporary policy debates typically match one another study for study, and muster equal indignation about their opponents' know-nothing refusal to bow to the power of the cold hard facts. Observers have to figure out how to get beyond the posturing. To disentangle evidence from assertion, they need sophistication in distinguishing the good studies from the bad. Observers must know which findings are compelling and which are only suggestive, which conclusions have general and transferable implications and which apply only in particular contexts and times.

The public, even the attentive public, depends heavily on the media to keep informed and to sort through competing claims. (The inattentive public settles for vague and symbolic allusions to research—if it cares about research at all.) Unfortunately, overworked and undertrained journalists often lack the time and expertise really to master the research methodologies in play. New media, too—various blogs, electronic newsletters, and Web sites—provide alternative channels, but these can be even more amateurish and unreliable than traditional outlets. Even journalists who have the training, experience, and inclination to dig deep are limited by editorial priorities, space constraints, and assessments of how much complexity their audience is willing to tolerate.

Against this backdrop, what are we to make of the fact that a relatively simple report, presenting publicly available data and addressing a policy about which many Americans remain unaware, was thought to warrant front-page attention? What are we to make of the fact that the subsequent debate has pushed methodological intricacies into the forefront of the public agenda? Is it a sign of the public's growing willingness to wrestle with the tough questions about social issues? Or is it just another illustration of the shallowness of our collective understanding—just one more case of claim and counterclaim substituting for reasoned analysis? Does the fact that social scientists are willing to speak out publicly and to work harder to get their findings more quickly into the hands of citizens and policy makers mean that they are finally coming down from their ivory towers and turning their skills to solving real problems in the near-term? Or does it reflect the further degradation of science, that its symbols have been co-opted and its prestige borrowed in service to base political interests and ideologically driven campaigns?

Sniping among researchers, of course, is nothing new. Nor is it, in and of itself, particularly alarming. Medical researchers publicly clash over the health risks of salt or fat in the diet. Climatologists tussle about the extent—or even the existence—of global warming (Revkin 2006).

Those who study stem cells argue about whether, as a Bush administration appointee to the President's Council on Bioethics once averred: "Every embryo for research is someone's blood relative."[6] In these instances, too, competing interest groups call on their own stock of favored studies and researchers, and claims about what constitutes "good" research seem manipulated to discredit those on the opposite side. Indeed, the phenomenon is so common that it appears to be part of the warp and woof of normal scientific exchange—the pluralistic clash of theories and methods that ultimately protects us from settling too comfortably into orthodoxies.

Some distinctions are worth making, however, between competition and warfare, between critique and attack. When it comes to school choice research, the boundaries have seemed at times unusually porous. Choice proponents charge their adversaries with employing bad science as part of a campaign to, as some put it, "pillory, marginalize, and suppress" their research.[7] Choice critics charge their opponents with "chicanery."[8] In one of several high-profile battles, the political scientists John Witte of the University of Wisconsin and Paul Peterson of Harvard engaged in what became a rather nasty exchange. Their battle, and mutual name-calling, eventually erupted onto the front pages of the *Wall Street Journal* (Davis 1996).[9] Characterizing the charter school debate overall, two researchers from the nonpartisan think tank RAND concluded that it "often appears to be driven by theory and ideology, with little information on how the reform itself is affecting students" (Zimmer and Buddin 2006).

Handled openly and honestly, even intense scientific disagreements have the potential to illuminate public discourse. The vitriol of charter school debate, however, seems to many observers to obscure more than it informs. "One of the more negative features of contemporary educational policy debates is the way in which a number of 'camps' have adopted a strategy of intellectual non-engagement and avoidance toward differing positions," wrote one observer, reflecting explicitly on the AFT study and the high-profile reactions to it:

> The martial metaphor of "camps" is deliberately chosen here, since the underlying logic of this strategy is one of opposing armies meeting on a field of battle. The essentials one needs to know in any debate, according to this view of educational policy, is who lines up with your army and who lines up against it—is the advocate of this policy friend or enemy? The substance of the argument made for or against a policy is largely immaterial. Indeed, it is better not to discuss that substance, since a discussion might reveal a weakness in one's own position, or worse, the strength of the alternative position. All that is important is whether or not the "policy" in question is part of your weaponry, and whether its advocates belong to your army. (Casey 2005)

When scientific pluralism morphs into political attack and counter-attack, more than civility is at risk. Scanning a field full of landmines, some of the best young scholars may turn to other areas of inquiry, choking off the supply of research in areas where it is arguably most needed. Even more troubling is the prospect of what we give up as a society if the boundaries between research and ideological warfare become so blurred that politicians, foundations, the media, and the public essentially conclude that there are no such boundaries at all.

A Puzzle

I was drawn into writing this book by a puzzle. I have studied and written about issues relating to school choice for nearly twenty years. In the beginning, I learned that this was a high-voltage topic. In my first book on the subject, I expressed wariness toward choice—particularly the more radical forms and more explicitly market-oriented arguments in its favor. However, perhaps because the book was less strident in its claims, less personalized in its review of others' studies, less black and white in its conclusions, I was not, as others were, immediately typed as belonging to one camp or another. As a result, I have for years been able to maintain cordial relations with researchers on each side of the debate, and been privy to the ways in which they talked about the issue and about one another. I knew the characterizations were harsh, and often reciprocal. In the earlier years of the debate, each camp also seemed to share confidence that time and solid evidence, once collected, would prove its views correct, and expose those of the other side as having been based on ideology.

Over time, I noticed a new dimension. In private discussions, the positions researchers staked out became less stark, more nuanced. Those who broadly favored choice became more willing, based on accumulating evidence, to admit that many examples of charter schools were no better than most traditional public schools, and that indeed some of them were worse. They became quicker to admit, too, that the strong claims made by voucher and charter school advocates were unrealistic, and that the poor test performance of many low-income and minority children depends on things that happen outside of school and cannot be attributed to poor teaching or unresponsive school bureaucracies alone. At the same time, many who raised the early alarm about the possibly destructive consequences of choice—its potential to resegregate schools by race and class and to draw funds out of an already depleted public school system—began to admit that some of their fears were proving overdrawn. They were seeing evidence that charter schools were not, as they had feared, catering to a white and well-off clientele, that many charter school founders and teachers were deeply committed professionals with clear records of serving disadvantaged populations, and that many in the charter school constituency were advocates of better and more responsive government, not of displacing the government with markets.

Yet—and this is what puzzled me—in their public pronouncements, some of the same researchers who seemed to be moving toward some common ground were as likely as ever to be quoted as representing sharply divergent views. This was partly, but not only, a matter of how they were selectively quoted by journalists and advocates. The resistance toward acknowledging a more nuanced and complex common ground was not revealed just in the popular press, however; it showed too in what the researchers themselves were writing. Whereas data and findings often provided weak and mixed pictures, these scholars' papers revealed framing and policy conclusions that often seemed to go further, to reinforce the polarized positions, to resist—as if it would be a sign of muddy-headedness or lack of confidence—staking out a reformulated understanding of the charter school debate that did not fit neatly into the pro- and anti- parameters in which the school choice argument originally was born.

What was going on? Was this a case, I wondered, of social scientists getting seduced by the shiny trappings of small-scale notoriety that come with getting one's name cited in a public debate? Was it a case of social scientists doing what so many people had asked them to do: coming out of the ivory tower and making sure the knowledge they were creating was translated into useful and effective forms of social change? Maybe there was a third alternative: that the root of polarization had less to do with the behaviors of researchers and more with the echo chamber of the overly partisan and ideologically polarized society into which their small bits of evidence were being introduced. Were researchers whispering tiny truths only to be shocked to hear them reverberate with a stridency and affirmativeness they had not intended? As I wrestled personally with this puzzle, I became convinced that the answer would have bearing on the prospects for informed democracy, and implications also for the way in which we should direct our energies in shaping social reform. But I was not precisely sure how. One of the few luxuries of being an academic is being able, often, to let one's personal puzzles frame one's professional investigations. Having the luxury to do so, I set out to see what I could learn.

The Evidence

This book uses different kinds of data and different forms of analysis to zero in on the issues at stake. A primary source of data is the set of thirty-six formal interviews I conducted with researchers, advocates, funders, and journalists. The twenty researchers I selected represented both sides and the middle of the spectrum in terms of their perceived placement on the pro- and anti-choice debate.[10] I also interviewed five advocates who were closely involved either with the AFT study and its reaction or with charter school politics more generally, five funders representing a range of foundations, and six journalists who covered the issue or could provide insights into newspaper decisions about what constitutes newsworthiness and how much detail about research could and should be included. I used somewhat different interview protocols for the four types of respondents (researchers, advocates, funders, and journalists), though some questions overlapped.[11] Much of the protocol was open ended in format, but in one series of close-ended questions respondents were encouraged to select among several options. These close-ended questions provide the grist for some of the more systematic comparison tables and figures presented in the book. All interviews were transcribed and subsequently coded using NVivo software. The coding was used to help identify underlying themes and to make it easier to sift through the interviews to find illuminating quotations I sprinkle liberally throughout the book. A few of the tables and figures presented rely on coding the open-ended responses.

A possible concern in a project like this one, where the topic is interesting precisely because it is politically controversial, is the extent to which respondents can be expected to be open and honest. There are considerable and reciprocal layers of mistrust and hostility in this area, a sense that "the other guys" are disingenuous, spiteful, Machiavellian. Both before and during this research I heard individuals worry aloud about the prospect that this person or that has schemed or might scheme against them—bad-mouthed them to others, scuttled grant proposals or journal submissions under the cover of an anonymous review, damned with faint praise a young scholar's tenure hearing.

I cannot claim to have miraculously cut through this fog of wariness to elicit consistently truthful and comprehensive answers. Certain factors, however, reduce the probability that I, and consequently you as reader, will have been the victim of deliberate and systematic misdirection. First, I offered respondents various levels of anonymity. They could ask not to be listed among those interviewed; they could request that the interview not be recorded; they could indicate that they did not want any identifying quotations to be used in the book; they could indicate that any identifying quotations would first have to be reviewed by them. As it developed, I encountered less skittishness than others had warned me to expect. Only two people I approached for interviews flatly turned me down; one other simply never answered email inquiries. Of those interviewed, only one refused to have the session recorded. In one case, logistical matters forced us to hold the interview by email. None of those with whom I spoke refused to have his or her name listed as an interviewee.

Although it is awkward to assert this claim, I believe that a second, less formal, set of factors increasing the likelihood of receiving honest answers has to do with the fact that I was the person doing the interviews. I had existing relationships with exactly half of the respondents before the project and in nearly half of those the relationships were fairly close. I do not know, but suspect, that some of those with whom I did not have a prior relationship checked with others who knew me before going ahead with the interview. Although this increased the likelihood of getting open answers, it had the added advantage of letting me test the atmosphere and tone of the interviews with those who had been strangers against those with my acquaintances. With very few exceptions, my sense is that even those respondents who started off with some guardedness for the most part settled into a reasonably relaxed and revealing mode of discussion.

Third, I structured the interview protocol to encourage confidence in my respondents by starting off with more concrete questions that drew on their direct expertise, and saving for the end those more explicitly about the intersection of politics and evidence. I do not doubt that some answers were self-serving or evasive, but most often the respondents appeared intellectually engaged in the substance of the discussion and interested in helping shed some light on the issue.

Despite the fact that many of those I interviewed gave me carte blanche to attribute their quotes, I opted to mask identities except when respondents referred to events in which they were directly involved and when knowing their identity is critical to assessing the credibility of the accounts (in these latter cases, the text attributes quotes to the individuals without additional citation information). Instead I have used short ID tags, labeling respondents with a letter indicating their general role (A=advocate;[12] F=Funder; J=Journalist; R=Researcher) and a number. I made this decision largely for logistical reasons; it would have been awkward to include some names while masking others, but there may also be an advantage, I believe. Precisely because of how highly polarized the debate is, attaching names to observations might incline some readers to reject or suspect some comments without wrestling with them fully. Occasionally, I identify some respondents as being broadly favorable or opposed to choice to highlight either patterned responses that do break down on predictable lines or—more commonly—that comments so often either are consistent across the group or exhibit paradoxical or idiosyncratic patterns.

The book does not rely on these interviews alone. I had innumerable informal discussions with researchers about the topics dealt with here. I also supplemented the opinions, beliefs, and experiences of my respondents with several more objective sources of data. As I delved deeper into the funding issue, I found it important to gather empirical information about actual funding practices, in both government and the foundation world. It was not enough just to look at who funded the important studies of charter schools, because that would leave matters unclear about how various funders' involvement in the issue fit within their broader portfolios of giving. I examined National Science Foundation grants and Department of Education grants and contracts. For foundations, I used Foundation Center data on private giving to explore the size and distributions of grants for education research, as well as those dealing more specifically with charters, vouchers, and school choice. More details on the data and methodology are provided in chapter 6. For now, suffice it to say that this approach led me to conclude that much of the important story had to do with what funders do instead of directly funding education, instead of funding research, and—when they do fund education research—instead of funding studies dealing specifically with school choice.

Although my interviews shed light on how researchers regard the media and how reporters regard education research, I found it important to collect some additional data with which to check these impressions and put them in a broader context. I analyze the broad scope of coverage of charters, vouchers, and school choice in five major newspapers, and examine more closely articles in the *New York Times* and *Wall Street Journal* that provide explicit discussion of research in these topics. This allows me, in chapter 7, to answer such questions as whether there is a difference in coverage between the purportedly anticharter *Times* and purportedly procharter *Journal*, and to systematically analyze how journalists present research and cite researchers.

A Brief Overview

Chapter 2 considers competing visions of the relationships among scientific research, mass democracy, and rational policy making. It contrasts an idealized vision of the policy sciences that has been influential at key times in American political and intellectual history to the cynical backlash that portrays research as little more than a weapon of manipulation and self-justification for partisan elites. It also raises the question of whether science, social institutions, and the public are up to the challenge of deliberative democracy and collective rationality. The idealized vision, however, is overly naïve in its aspirations for research, and overly cynical in its conception of politics.

Not every policy issue occasions the ideological engagement and polarization that has infused the charter school debate. Chapter 3 explains how the charter school issue came to be framed in terms of markets versus government, and how this in turn has raised the partisan stakes and made the issue so volatile and the stakes so high that little room is left for complexity, nuance, and contingency. This did not simply happen, it was in large measure the result of a deliberate strategy by conservative activists and foundations. Nor was it a phenomenon specific to charter schools. Rather, because of their popularity and political feasibility, charter schools became the arena in which a wide array of political interests chose to engage in a much broader war over privatization. Charter schooling need not have been framed this way, and in my judgment should not have been. However, in a manifestation of what is often referred to as path dependency, decisions made during the early 1990s continue to influence the course of research and democratic discourse today.

Chapter 4 presents in more detail the punch and counterpunch of the AFT charter school study and its critics, showing that this is not an aberration but an ongoing feature of the highly politicized debate around school choice and charter schools. The story here is a disturbing one for those who yearn for a more civil, thoughtful, and informed democratic discourse about important issues. At least as it plays out in the most visible public forums, research on charter schools appears to be not just inconclusive but fundamentally inconsistent, researchers appear to be not just offering contrasting methodologies and interpretations but also fiercely (and in highly personalized terms) challenging one another's motivations and competency. This image corrodes the legitimacy of research, reinforcing the impression that it is an extension of partisan wrangling, no different from public relations or lobbying, if in a slightly fancier garb.

Chapter 5 presents a partial antidote to depression, but underscores the puzzle that is at the core of this book. Despite the highly polarized uses of charter school research, I argue in this chapter, the enterprise of social science investigation is working much as what we would like to see. Although uncertainty and continued basis for debate remain, consensus has been tentatively reached on a set of findings that differ from earlier conjecture, are illuminating, and have the potential to lead to better policy. This convergence, however, has not led to a moderation of the way research is presented in public discourse.

Chapters 6 and 7 explore this puzzle in different ways. Chapter 6 zeroes in on public and private funding and the roles they may play in exacerbating the polarization of research. Support can be an important inducement for researchers to undertake certain kinds of study, and both its availability and conditions could play a role in polarizing the role that research plays in the public debate. Historically, conservatives argued that federal funding and large foundations have fueled a liberal agenda of expanding the public sector. More recently, liberals have argued that the Bush administration used federal funds to aggressively promote charter schools and private sector involvement in education delivery, and that a few core activist conservative foundations have orchestrated research on vouchers and charter schools with the deliberate intent to discredit traditional public schools and build momentum for them to be displaced.

Drawing on my interviews and quantitative data on federal and foundation funding, chapter 6 shows that though funding may be less of a substantial and direct force in charter school research than many imagine, the funding environment is an important part of the story, albeit indirectly, as much through what is not funded as through what is. Proponents of charter schools, expecting that the results would be favorable to their arguments, were influential in leading the government to collect the data that the AFT later used in its report. When their expectations were confounded, some changed their stance and argued that the data were fundamentally flawed as a basis of comparing charter schools to traditional public schools, and that the federal government ought not have been conducting such studies in the first place. Foundations in general are not especially keen on using their dollars for research per se, and many of the largest foundations have been reluctant to engage with the voucher and charter school debates. This strategic withdrawal, however, gives a smaller number of highly focused foundations more influence in promoting pro-market research than they might otherwise be able to muster. Even when they cannot influence the content and findings of research, both public and private funders have influence through the roles they play in affecting which findings get attention and how they are characterized in the public realm.

Chapter 7 focuses on the various institutions that communicate research to policy makers and the public. Those who believe that research is little more than a political weapon portray the major media as an echo chamber that magnifies disagreements among researchers, either by selectively presenting the evidence or by exaggerating extreme interpretations in pursuit of greater drama and compelling stories. I argue that the media do play a role in polarizing research, but that it is less intentional and direct than cynics imagine. News coverage of charter school research by the major print media is not extensive or deep, but neither is it ideologically skewed. The editorial stance of the newspaper, however, does appear to affect its overall presentation of research, primarily through how it allocates space on its editorial and contributing opinion pages. Electronic media, in the meantime, have substantially sped up the transmission of research, but often through channels that are more ideologically and politically defined. Scholarly journals, which could play an important role as arbiters of quality and significance, are bypassed or ignored, even more so in the education arena than in other areas of the physical, medical, and social sciences. As with funders, what the media do not do is in some ways as important as what they do.

Finally, in chapter 8, I return to the broader questions about the limits and possibilities of a more informed democracy. I do not try to revive the naïve vision of knowledge and research as incorruptible forces independent of and exogenous to politics and conflict. In a diverse and dynamic society, choosing directions for public policy necessarily involves making tough choices that create losers as well as winners. Agenda-setting and governance, accordingly, are irretrievably a focus of conflict, and making and enforcing decisions inevitably require exercising power. There are some irresolvable tensions between the needs of those who strive to maximize knowledge in a complex world and those who strive to make the best possible decisions despite disagreement and complexity. The different roles and values that animate researchers and politicians suggest that there will always be a pull and tug between science and governance. This is tolerable and probably even healthy, but systematic trends in the American political system—the echo chamber into which the charter issue was introduced—are exacerbating this normal tension, making reasoned, textured, pragmatic, and contextual analysis more likely to be drowned out against a background racket of ideological and partisan noise. Disentangling those that are endemic from those that are not is a challenge.

However, the degree and the ways in which conflict and power co-opt and distort research are variable. In the end, the tale told in this book is in some ways a hopeful one. Despite the high-stakes political maneuvering that has surrounded, and at times infected, the research enterprise regarding vouchers, charters, and school choice, I argue that the quality of research has improved, and that our prospects for mapping a policy route to better education have as a result also improved. Research and science do not have the answers to society's tough policy challenges, but they do have much they can contribute if properly constituted and properly understood. Even if it cannot steer democratic decision making, good research can inform it, save it from some misadventures, and in some cases set it on a more effective course. This is a less heroic but more realistic and sustainable vision of the role that research can play in democracy.

If the legitimate pursuit of policy-relevant research erases the boundaries between science and partisanship—indeed, maybe if it only appears that this is the case—the potential value of research will be eroded. There will be a social price to pay. However, though the institutions and values that sustain good research are under pressure and weakening, the evidence presented here shows that they are resilient and not without defense. We need to develop a more sophisticated understanding of what research can and cannot do, and we need to self-consciously nurture the conditions under which collective learning can thrive. That battle is important, but it has not been lost. I conclude the book with some proposals for modest reform.

Chapter 2

Informed Democracy: An Ideal and Its Skeptics

Mankind in a test-tube is the hope and aim of social science.
—Stephen A. Stephan (1935, 515)

In America, we need to have education reform based on science if we're going to make progress. Science is the standard we set for medical research. Why should we accept quackery for education?
—Caroline Hoxby (2005b, 3)

To really understand what is going on here you'd be well advised to spend as much time delving into the political theory literature around power as the literature around public schools and charter schools.
—Eduwonk blog, August 21, 2006

The idea that wise governance should be guided by science has deep roots. Some would trace them to the founding of the nation. Thomas Jefferson, Benjamin Franklin, and others who set the country on its course were, by almost all accounts, wise statesmen who framed their deliberations about governing in terms of the best available knowledge of the physical and social worlds. One assessment goes so far as to characterize President Jefferson's funding of the 1804 Lewis and Clark expedition to explore the northwest areas of the nation as perhaps "the first major federally supported social research" (Lynn 1978, 12). Confidence in this vision of a harmonious relationship between governance and scientific expertise ebbs and flows, but has peaked at various points in American history: the Progressive Era during the early twentieth century, the New Deal under President Franklin Roosevelt, the War on Poverty under Presidents Kennedy and Johnson.

In education policy, this ideal of an informed democracy has undergone similar cycles, alternately celebrated and bemoaned as being hopelessly out of reach. One traditional argument for why education should be considered a "public good" and especially worthy of public attention and resources is that it creates a citizenry smart enough to digest available evidence and use it to make the best decisions in the voting booth. The turn-of-the-century Progressives, who argued in favor of a knowledge-based approach to governance across a range of policy arenas, arguably had their greatest impact in restructuring school governance precisely because schooling was seen as too important to be left to politicians. However, though the arguments in favor of research-based policy may be particularly compelling in education, the weight of contemporary judgment is that education research is unusually poor in quality, shaped by ideology more than evidence, and thus politically ineffectual.

Both the residual hope and the contemporary disappointment are echoed in the federal government's emphasis on establishing a scientific basis for its efforts to reform the nation's schools. The Institute of Education Sciences, formed within the United States Department of Education in 2002, describes its goal as "the transformation of education into an evidence-based field in which decision makers routinely seek out the best available research and data before adopting programs or practices that will affect significant numbers of students."[1] The massive No Child Left Behind (NCLB) legislation makes more than 100 references to the importance of basing educational policy decisions on scientifically based evidence (Cradler and Cradler 2002).

When political advocates feel a powerful need to counter a study such as the AFT's charter school report, when they mobilize immediately even in the lazy days of August, when they dig deep in their pockets to purchase full-page advertisements in major newspapers, and when they frame their ad as a tutorial in research methodology and enlist prominent scholars to sign their names and print these in large font instead of the microscopic size more common in such public petitions— when things like this happen, it is tempting to conclude that policy research has finally come of age. At least on the surface, one might expect these behaviors in a society in which research and knowledge are taken seriously and in which citizens are seen as intellectually engaged, well schooled in the language and standards for good research, and likely to form and re-form their policy preferences based on new information.

Was the back and forth over the charter school study and its aftermath, then, an indication that an increasingly educated public has been integrated into a mode of collective deliberation once seen as limited to a small cognoscenti? A sincere effort to elevate democratic discourse to a level aspired to but not yet realized? Or, despite its seeming affirmation of the authoritativeness of science and methodology, was the advertisement criticizing the AFT report better understood as a tactic to neutralize embarrassing and possibly damaging evidence? Caroline

Hoxby, whose question about quackery leads this chapter, is one of the sharpest tongued participants in the charter school debate. Her confidence and consistency in asserting unambiguous evidence in favor of markets and her tendency to favorably cite only a handful of studies that support her position and ignore or dismiss those who assert alternative claims lead some to see her as a warrior-researcher who adds fuel to the bitterness that characterizes public discourse on the issue. When she claims the high ground of science, is that because she is rightly exposing the ideological biases and fuzzy-headedness of those who reflexively resist charter schools, or a prime example of "science abuse" (Mooney 2005)?

When those on both sides of the charter school debate cite studies to defend their positions, does it reflect serious efforts to interpret conflicting evidence or just a cynical effort to fight fire with fire? The answers to some extent may depend on the details of the case, the particular volatility of the school choice debate, or the idiosyncrasies of the cast of characters. I argue in this chapter, however, that the flap over the AFT study exemplifies broader forces in American political discourse and process, and that through it we can gain some leverage on challenging questions about the kind of society we'd like to be and can realistically hope to become.

The chapter sets the stage for the analysis of the AFT case by presenting four competing visions of the relationship between science and research, on the one hand, and governance and politics on the other. I begin with the vision—crafted around the turn of the twentieth century by the Progressives and echoed by more contemporary proponents of what has been called the policy sciences—that arguably has dominated thinking about how research and governance ought to align. This perspective sees science as handmaiden to good governance, with researchers ideally "speaking truth to power" (Wildavsky 1987). Politics, in this model, operates in a separate dimension. Politics affects who leaders are and what they try to accomplish; research affects how effectively and efficiently they go about it.

When the political process is fair and democratic, research is seen, then, as complementary to democracy, generally the case for much of American history. During the 1960s and 1970s, however, a sharply different understanding began to take root, leading to two alternatives to the Progressives' vision. Rather than as a window on truth and a facilitator of good governance, social science research came to be thought of as a political weapon serving special interests and ideological ends. This perspective came in two flavors. One view, favored by some on the political left, characterized research as serving conservative economic and political elites. The other, favored by those on the right, saw research as serving pro-government liberals and a socially liberal elite.

These views share a belief in a fundamental disconnect between social science and democracy, as if they are fish swimming in different streams. To the Progressives, politics presented a messy world in which appeals to folk wisdom and symbol swayed politicians and voters; if rationality and science were to be heard, politics had to be barred at the door. The research-as-weapon perspective, whether the more liberal or more conservative version, rejects the possibility of an apolitical, neutral expertise. It considers appeals to such as little more than an ideological justification to allow reigning elites to disguise their interests with the garb of science.

There is a fourth possibility, one that holds open the notion that research can work through pluralistic and democratic politics. It is this vision, I suggest, that has the potential to marry the hopeful aspects of the Progressives' dream to a more realistic understanding of the limits of science and the realities of power. It requires understanding science as open-ended and contingent and therefore not directly linked to any one agenda. It also requires confidence in the ability of citizens to recognize and critically digest evidence claims rather than to either defer to them or treat them as irrelevant. In that sense, it requires recognizing that the contribution research can play must come through its place within politics, not its rivalry with politics. Later in this chapter, I sketch an outline of this perspective and point out how it relates to the others in terms of expectations the motivation, behavior, and ability of researchers, funders, the media, and the public. One of the goals of this book is to probe—by looking intensely at a case where politics and research seem to clash—whether the elevated confidence needed to support a vision of informed policy through informed democracy is well placed or delusional.

Speaking Truth to Power: Policy Sciences for Rational Analysis

It is no slap at our Founding Fathers to admit that it was easier to be a polymath in those simpler days. Experts estimate that the average human brain may be able to hold about 200 megabytes of information. If every man, woman, and child in the world memorized different things, the total human memory capacity would be about 1,200 petabytes (a petabyte is 1 billion megabytes). This is less than half the estimate of the total information in the world in the year 2000 (Lesk 1997).

By the early twentieth century, the institutionalized explosions of science and industry were already requiring specialization of knowledge and role. Even true generalists—those who could effectively and with authority draw on knowledge from various spheres of physics, biology, psychology, economics, philosophy, and the arts—depended more and more on those with deeper and more technical understanding of complicated methodologies and sector-specific terminology for their intellectual fuel. It is against this backdrop that the Progressive movement laid the groundwork for its vision of the relationship between policy makers and policy sciences as one in which social scientists and professional experts would counsel public officials about the best way to maximize democratically defined goals.

Progressive Era and the Elevation of Scientific Expertise

The turn of the twentieth century was a period of social, intellectual, and political dynamism when science came into its own as a paradigmatic model for a nation moving into the modern age. In the corporate world, American business muscled to new levels, led in part by Frederick Winslow Taylor. In 1910, Taylor's *Principles of Scientific Management* became the rage; the notion that industries could be reorganized to function in the "one best way" gradually came to be applied beyond the factory walls, as a prescription also for how government could be made more efficient and effective (Kanigel 1997).

The Progressive movement sought to bring to the task of governance the attention to evidence, objectivity, and systematic analysis that were believed to be propelling these new achievements in business and science. Governance up to that point, the Progressives believed, had tended to be driven instead by tradition, power, and prejudice. It was late in the 1800s that university chairs in social science first began to appear and "by 1920 all self respecting universities had social science departments" (Banfield 1980, 3).

> By then it was widely believed that government no less than business should—and therefore could—be expertly run. . . . Naturally the social scientists in the universities were looked to as a principal source of expertise for the organization and management of government, and thus of society generally. (Banfield 1980, 3-4)

It was around this time, too, that the nation's first think tanks emerged, funded by the new corporate elite and the industrial era and the foundations they established. Andrew Rich identifies the Russell Sage Foundation and the Bureau of Municipal Research, both launched in 1907, as the first designed to straddle the gap between basic research and practical applications to make government work better. Both "reflected the broader Progressive movement ideology of depoliticizing public decision making" by placing "a premium on the promise of objective social science and the contributions of experts in devising solutions to public problems" (Rich 2004, 35).

Central to the Progressive vision was the distinction between politics and administration. Politics was an arena through which the disparate interests of individuals could be weighed and aggregated into a democratically defined public agenda. Administration focused on how decisions, based on expertise, were made about how best to actualize that agenda. Politics was a realm in which beliefs, opinion, and values inevitably would play important roles. Once policy priorities were established, however, reason and science should take full rein. Decisions about program details and implementation were properly the realm of experts who would be buffered from political interference.

George Washington Plunkett, the colorful Tammany Hall machine politician, famously derided the Progressives as "mornin' glories" who looked good at first but faded quickly because they lacked the political savvy and organization to institutionalize and effectively manage power. Locally elected Progressive reform regimes were often short-lived, but their impact on the basic mechanics of government was substantial and long lasting. Victories were marked at the national level by such things as the Pendleton Act of 1881, establishing the federal civil service system, and the Budget and Accounting Act of 1921, which sought to rationalize the federal budgetary process and established the General Accounting Office (GAO) as an independent body charged with investigating how funds are spent. At the local level, Progressive reforms helped to launch much larger, better-paid, more professionalized bureaucracies charged with running police, fire, sanitation, and other services in ways aligned with the best available knowledge as objectively interpreted and without consideration of partisan politics or personal preferences. Municipal research bureaus were established in many cities: forerunners of contemporary policy evaluation units and think tanks. Within education specifically, the Progressives won battles to buffer policy making and implementation even more emphatically from the vicissitudes of political interference. Rather than be a part of the general purpose government responsible to mayors and councils, schools would be run by boards either appointed or elected separately in nonpartisan elections often held apart from the general election. These boards would select, based on expertise, superintendents who would run the system on a day-to-day basis (Howell 2005; Tyack 1974).

The Idea of the Policy Sciences: Enlisting Research and Researchers to Solve National Social Problems

The Progressive Era institutionalized the notion that good government should be informed by science and expertise, but it took some time before the idea of the policy sciences that could dissolve tough national social problems came into flower. It took even longer before education policy research peeked out from behind the shadow of more prestigious areas of social research. In the 1920s and 1930s, most of the responsibility for social problems was concentrated at the local level, and the local agenda as the Progressives conceived it consisted mostly of technical challenges—building bridges and roads, providing basic services like sanitation and clean water—not the more politically combustible issues relating to matters like poverty and race. "The questions in a city are not political questions," declared Andrew Dickson White, the first president of Cornell University and a leading Progressive of the time. "The work of a city being the creation and control of the city property, it should logically be managed as a piece of property." (1890, 213). A catchphrase of the time put it in slightly different terms: "There is no Republican way or Democrat way to clean a street."

Education research picked up steam at the national level later than other forms of economic and social research did. Simple bungling may have played a role in this. The United States Department of Education was created and charged with collecting and disseminating data shortly after the Civil War. Maris Vinovskis suggests, however, that the poor management and political skills of Henry Barnard, the nation's first education commissioner, led to its rapid eclipse (2002).[2] Education research as a profession had begun to take shape during the Progressive Era, but focused primarily on psychology and testing. Its methodologies and research were often quite strong, but subtle and not-so-subtle biases against a profession that at the time was dominated by women and considered intellectually soft meant that education psychologists earned more status by emphasizing basic research or applications in the business world than by wrestling with what happened inside schools and classrooms (Lagemann 2000).

By the mid-1960s, two cataclysmic events—the Great Depression and World War II—and two social upheavals—the war on poverty and the civil rights movement—had helped shift responsibility for many social problems to the national government and had regularized the expectation that leading social scientists might shuffle in and out of the District of Columbia as part-time advisers. Increasingly, social scientists—usually in universities or in think tanks such as RAND and Brookings—played key roles in shaping the national policy response to regulating the economy, designing social security, expanding the social welfare net, and guiding national security efforts.

In this new environment, as during the Progressive Era, education policy research trailed the policy sciences movement more generally. Government and research were striking new partnerships in pursuit of a Great Society, but it was research on the economy, on science and health, on social welfare, on housing, on national security that stirred hearts and minds in Washington, D.C. The high hope that research could lead to more rational policy carried education in its wake. During the mid-1960s, for example, Congress established nine large university-based research and development centers with the mission of stimulating and coordinating research on specific aspects of the education process. It followed that with what were called educational laboratories, which were intended to help translate research into usable products (Vinovskis 2002).

Although much of the growth of governmental investment in research was associated with Democrats and the Great Society, a generally upbeat assessment of the marriage of research and governance carried over into the Nixon administration. The early 1970s saw Congress institute major policy experiments to assess the possible consequences of income maintenance programs and subsidized housing (Greenberg, Linksz, and Mandell 2003). The National Assessment of Educational Progress (NAEP), which had percolated during the Johnson years, was launched in 1969 to monitor educational outcomes across the nation. The National Institute of Education, modeled in part on the National Science Foundation and National Institutes of Health, was initiated in 1972.

Education research, however, was far from a leader. As Ellen Lagemann notes, compared with other fields, investments in the new National Institute of Education "were paltry" (2000, 208). David Greenberg and his colleagues identify seventy-three social experiments conducted between 1962 and 1982. Of these, twenty-three (31.5 percent) had some education and training focus,[3] but by far the bulk related to vocational education; only four (5.5 percent) dealt with basic K-12 education, including GED and education subsidies (Greenberg, Linksz, and Mandell 2003, table 2.2).

A few possible explanations come to mind that may help account for the relative impenetrability of the education arena to the rising spirit of systematic research. They are far from exhaustive. One relates to capacity and inclination. The policy sciences notion was closely associated with more quantitative approaches to research. Within education schools and departments, psychologists in the field excepted, these were in limited supply and, indeed, often regarded with skepticism or hostility. Then, as now, social scientists trained in the disciplines and housed outside of education schools also conducted research on education policy issues. For example, perhaps the best known school study was the 1966 *Equality of Educational Report*, written by sociologist James Coleman. Ironically, for many readers the take-home message was that schools did not matter.[4] Partly in response to the Coleman report and partly in response to the fact that judicial efforts to undo school desegregation dominated the agenda during that era, much of the attention of serious researchers with an interest in education became focused on issues relating to student and community characteristics rather than the nitty-gritty of what was happening within schools and classrooms, further limiting the impact of the policy sciences movement on education research per se. Furthermore, those pushing hardest at the national level for stronger and more systematic education research tended to be interested in research as a way to better monitor local education providers and hold them more accountable for their performance and uses of federal funds (Lagemann 2000, 200–23). Thus, perhaps more than in other areas of social policy, research came to be seen by many within the education community as something used against them by others rather than as a tool they could employ to improve their practice.

The Backlash Against Expertise: Research as Political Tool

The notion that research and policy should be conjoined was never unanimous. Some critics have been fueled by mistrust of universities and self-proclaimed elites of expertise. Others have had a greater allegiance to other guidance: to tradition, to faith, to good old common sense. There is no ready metric by which to weigh the history of public sentiment or find a precise point at which faith in science peaked or wariness and cynicism toward it began to build. Yet, if the heady days of the Great Society marked a high point in enthusiasm for a new era of the policy sciences, the later 1970s and 1980s saw the intellectual and political coalescence of two distinct challenges, one from the left and one from the right.

Both—what I refer to broadly as the backlash against the idealized vision of research leading toward more rational and effective policies— grew out of a sense that the War on Poverty and Great Society programs had failed to meet the high aspirations that the partnership of policy makers and social scientists had articulated. Both reject the notion that research is or can be apolitical. Both contain a populist strain—in rhetoric at least, if not necessarily in its enlisted cast of characters—that portrays researchers as the saps or hired guns of a dominant elite, out of step and essentially at odds with ordinary Americans and their concerns.

Backlash from the Progressive Left

The backlash from the left emerged somewhat earlier than that from the Right. It was fueled in part by the apparent link between the new policy technocrats and the unpopular war in Vietnam. As Lyndon Johnson's secretary of defense, Robert McNamara was known for hiring so-called whiz-kids who applied cost-benefit analysis to the task of taming the bureaucracy and evaluating weapon systems. As dissatisfaction with the war swelled, so too, in some circles, did a view of policy research as elitist, cold, and insensitive to basic human values.

Although the progressive left was on the whole much more supportive of the domestic policy initiatives of the Great Society, its more radical leaders resisted somewhat. They argued that the university–government axis was generating a top-down approach to social policy that reinforced passivity among the disenfranchised and stifled more egalitarian, grassroots democracy. Much of the early criticism was targeted at economists and particularly policy analysts, whose a cost-benefit framework implicitly elevated individual preferences over collective needs and, though framed as if value neutral, tended in practice to favor preferences aligned with the interests of elites and the status quo (Kelman 1981; Rhoads 1985). Some critics raised the broader question of whether the so-called policy sciences—and not simply the brand practiced by economists—might be complicit in a broader antidemocratic agenda. Mainstream policy analysis can undermine democracy, this line of argument goes, to the extent that it: preempts political debate with dubious value judgments, such as economic efficiency; treats ends simply, as capable of being fixed apart from the specific problem being addressed; conceives of politics in terms of technological manipulation of causal systems by an elite composed of, or advised by, analysis; reinforces hierarchical and bureaucratic notions of the control of human beings; and posits an unproblematic consensus on values, and so slides too easily into some ideological status quo (Dryzek 1989). The concern on the part of the left was less that policy analysis was self-consciously a handmaiden to the exercise of elite power, and more that the enterprise of systematic policy analysis served the interests of the status quo regardless of the researchers' intent.

> The main political function of the cumulative weight of technically sophisticated policy analysis may be to promote the idea that public policy is properly the prerogative of experts. Policy analysis that emphasizes causality may even help to reify the idea that social processes proceed through a law-like logic beyond the control of ordinary people, who can therefore only resign themselves to the inevitable. (Dryzek 1989, 103)

For many on the left, a particular danger of policy analysis was its pretense that science could and should be value-free. Research in general—and policy research in particular—could not help but be value-laden, and the operant values would tend to be either those of the researchers (themselves members of a privileged class) or the governmental agencies and private foundations that funded their research. That the embedded values were unacknowledged and even denied only made matters worse. "The great danger here is that analysts' criteria of justice will masquerade behind a façade of objectivity and thus be opaque to decision makers, the public, and even analysts themselves" (Jenkins-Smith 1990, 60).

Arguably, this backlash from the left turned out to be less potent than that from the right, if for no other reason than that the right proved to be political ascendant at the time. If its direct impact was somewhat attenuated, however, it nonetheless affected the debate about the proper relationship between policy and research in at least two ways. First, it opened a wedge within the constituency that generally supported strong and active government, dividing those who favored using research and systematic analysis to make government work better from those who were skeptical of that enterprise. Some, like Christopher Jencks, dedicated themselves to articulating a vision of how federal programs—including progressively structured school vouchers—could leverage more redistributory consequences at the local level (1966). Others, for instance those influenced by Saul Alinsky's characterization of all War on Poverty programs as political pornography or Ivan Illich's suggestion that "only by channeling dollars away from the institutions which now treat health, education, and welfare can the further impoverishment resulting from their disabling side effects be stopped" (1971, 6) argued that top-down governmental interventions were predestined to induce dependency and acquiescence. Some favored grassroots organizing over research, some favored more qualitative and normative analysis, but the result was a splintering of the left that left it weaker. Second, this attack on policy research from the left established populist themes that those on the right later expropriated.

Skepticism from the Right

It is easy to see why conservatives, sitting in the mid-1970s, might see policy research as implicated in the growth of government. Just as some on the left had come to see scientific policy analysis as inherently political because it unavoidably favored the reigning elites, some on the right argued that policy analysis was inherently tilted in favor of a pro-government and aggressively antitraditionalist agenda. Others argued that the liberal tilt was time-bound, and that astute conservatives could turn it into a political weapon of their own. The former were more prominent during the 1960s and 1970s, when many conservatives felt marginalized in national politics; when they thought about research serving insider interests, they thought about it as outsiders themselves. As conservatives became more strategic about how they could gain political dominance, and as they came to realize that systematic research could be used to discredit the Great Society programs that seemed so well entrenched, the latter group became more influential.

Those on the right feared that emphasizing the importance of policy research inevitably would lead to emphasizing the importance of policy researchers. Those on the left feared that increasing the influence of researchers would come at the expense of the masses, who would be cowed into submission or marginalized as too uninformed to warrant serious attention. Some of the most articulate criticisms from the right suggested that it would come at the expense of elected representatives in their role not as direct delegates of the masses but as statesmen better equipped than the public to understand evidence, but better equipped than the researchers to make judgments when evidence is limited, uncertain, or not all that needs to be taken into account.

Edward Banfield was an especially influential voice for what some in the 1970s referred to as the neoconservative perspective on the limits and possibilities of government. His influence came not least from his willingness to use vivid language in place of the dry and pared-down terminology more usual among academics. In an essay titled "Policy Science as Metaphysical Madness," he took on directly the seemingly straightforward premise that "our society improves by becoming more knowledgeable."

> One may well reach a contrary judgment: that professionals, because of their commitment to the ideal of rationality, are chronically given to finding fault with institutions...and, by virtue of their mastery of techniques of analysis, to discovering the almost infinite complexity and ambiguity of any problem. Like the social researchers of a generation or two ago, the policy scientist contributes problems, not solutions. (Banfield 1980, 18)

Seen this way, policy research is inherently anticonservative in several ways. First, it treats traditional beliefs and norms as inherently suspect—presumed guilty in the court of social science unless they can muster empirical evidence in their support. Second, in multiplying perceived problems, it provides fuel to those who would use the shortcomings of existing institutions and practices as a base for mobilizing constituencies for radical reform. Third, because framing a condition as a problem implies that a solution exists, it implicitly supports the notion of a bigger and more activist government to tackle these problems, with social scientists in the lead.

The most important social problems, Banfield argued, are not technical matters that could be solved by smarter government. "Social problems are at bottom political; they arise from differences of opinion and interest and, except in trivial instances, are difficulties to be coped with (ignored, got around, put up with, exorcised by the art of rhetoric, and so on) rather than puzzles to be solved" (1980, 18). The kind of knowledge and skills needed are those of the wise statesman—not those of the policy scientist, who is likely to exhibit a "trained incapacity" for doing what is necessary. Overinclined to think about the good that can be achieved by the well-meaning and well-informed, the policy scientist fails to appreciate the need to "find the terms on which ambitious, vindictive, and rapacious men will restrain one another, and, beyond that, to foster a public opinion that is reasonable about what can and cannot be done to make society better" (18).

Others on the right, however, believed that the marriage between social science and the growth of government was an historical fact but not a necessity. They concluded that conservatives had ceded the field to those with more liberal inclinations, but that this could and should be reversed. Stuart Butler, a vice president of the Heritage Foundation, was labeled by the *National Journal* "one of 150 individuals outside government who have the greatest influence on decision-making in Washington." In the mid-1980s, he drafted a detailed plan for how conservatives could perform political jujitsu: turn the techniques that liberals had used to build the welfare state into a privatization strategy to shrink government. Bureaucrats, Butler argued, historically had used government contracts and research grants to "produce data that tend to favor the expansion of programs" and to identify potential program beneficiaries who could be mobilized for political support (1985, 21). Capturing the White House in 1980 had not been enough to reverse this, he explained, because career bureaucrats could still steer contracts to organizations and individuals with a pro-spending bias, but this too could and should be reversed. Conservatives should use the leverage they were gaining within government to turn policy research to its advantage. In awarding research grants "the administration should adopt a conscious policy of bypassing the cozy research network that has developed around current federal programs" and in its place "develop that research base for privatization coalitions while denying it to the public spending coalitions" (Butler 1985, 113). Policy research, in this view, was less about studying social conditions to make government more effective than about studying the distributional consequences of policy options to help partisan operatives more effectively find and mobilize their political base.

Competing Interpretations of the Charter School Case

The vision of research embedded in the vision of the policy sciences and the Progressives' ideal of rational governance is one of cool objectivity, high quality data, sophisticated analytic techniques, and judicious weighing of evidence, conducted for the most part outside the hot glare of public attention. Considered through this lens, the AFT charter schools report and the responses it engendered are signs of egregious failure—examples of the bad things that can happen when amateurs meddle in complex undertakings or when experimental products from the laboratories are prematurely released.

Modern-day counterparts of the Progressive idealists can be found among some contemporary proponents of scientific based research. For them, the case reveals how partisan and interest group politics corrupts informed governance. The corruption, from this perspective, involves both the who and the what of the AFT report. The AFT is an advocacy group, not an independent research organization. The report it issued was technically unsophisticated. It compared average test score performance between charter and noncharter public schools with only rudimentary controls for possible differences in the populations served. The report did not—could not, because the AFT did not have access to the requisite data—base its analysis on individual students, controlling for their personal characteristics, past performance, and aspects of the districts that might be relevant.

That the AFT report was honest and up front about these limitations is relevant. Even from the standpoint of the more idealized vision, the problem is not that the AFT acted inappropriately; it did not mask its sponsorship of the report, distort or mischaracterize the data, or draw dramatic policy conclusions that could not be supported. Indeed, as we shall see, when subsequent and more sophisticated analyses of the NAEP were released, it became apparent that the initial presentation was pretty much on the mark. What is meaningful and troubling is that major media, interest groups, politicians and others allowed this report to eclipse other research, and that long-standing indifference toward research quality and lack of investment in the basic infrastructure of research had created a societal vulnerability: the kitchen cupboard of charter school research lacked studies with real nutritional value, leaving a hungry audience ready to pounce on whatever snack food was put on the table.

For adherents of the view of research as a political weapon, on the other hand, the story is less a morality tale than a case study proving a general point. Research has no independent base from which to wield influence; it is useful to the extent that it serves the purposes of battling partisans, and it serves those interests by delivering not compelling knowledge about societal problems but instead nuggets of information that can confer tactical advantage and a language, style, and symbolism that softens the hard angles of ideology and political self-interest. For those on the right, the key story is one of implicit cooperation between the education establishment, represented by the AFT, the liberal media, represented by the *New York Times*, and partisan Democrats looking for any opening through which to weaken the Bush administration and its conservative base. For those on the left, it is a story of the AFT liberating data from a politically motivated administration. Charter supporters had used their access to the administrations to push for collecting the NAEP charter school data in the first place, expecting that the results would redound to their benefit. When they began to realize that a simple comparison of test scores would reveal that charter schools did not have a magic key for creating test score masters out of low-income and minority students from disadvantaged neighborhoods, they shifted strategies. Rather than pushing for the release of the data, they worked to slow the process down, called for more complicated and multivariate analyses they had initially opposed, and—when it became apparent that those too would not come out they way they hoped—challenged the fundamental legitimacy of the NAEP data as an analytical tool.

Both the left and right versions of the research-as-weaponry perspective wrap their position in the mantle of science, even as they charge that the evidence claims made by the other side are disingenuous, based on shoddy research, or completely fraudulent. The average citizen, considering this spectacle, can be easily drawn to issue a pox on both houses. The AFT's claim that charter schools do no better than conventional public schools, the Center for Education Reform's advertisements reciting higher standards of scientific evidence and authority, these, seen through this lens, are predictable efforts to look right, not to be right.

But are we limited to a choice between naïve faith in apolitical science and dispiriting cynicism?

Pipedreams or Possibilities? Prospects for a More Informed Democracy

Neither the idealized vision of the policy sciences nor the critical views of research as political weaponry hold much hope that research will lead to better policies by creating a more informed and efficacious electorate. Both take a rather dim view of the public's interest in and ability to grasp what social scientists might have to say. The rationalist ideal depends on policy makers opening their ears and minds to science and using that knowledge to better meet the public's needs; the challenge—sufficient in itself to be intimidating—is to get policy makers to understand and have the courage to act on the advice they are given, because the course directed by knowledge and evidence is one that impetuous publics are likely to find either too radical or too timid. The research-as-politics model sees the masses as subject to a battle for their hearts, not their minds; the left and right differ simply in their premises about whose hearts are in the right place.

It has never been easy to explain how a system that puts a premium on broad participation by an often-inattentive public can handle complex and technical issues. Since the invention of modern survey techniques, researchers have been taking readings of Americans' political knowledge and beliefs, and their diagnoses have been rather dismal (Berelson, Lazarsfeld, and McPhee 1954; Campbell et al. 1960). Voters, they concluded, had little information about candidates, inherited their party identifications from their parents without reflection or understanding, and expressed inconsistent attitudes that fluctuated erratically. In an oft-cited article, Phillip Converse concluded that Americans' political beliefs appear to be "meaningless opinions that vary randomly in direction" and might just as well have been generated by "flipping a coin" (1964, 244). This dim view of the public's potential is widely shared. A more recent survey of national policy-makers found that fewer than one in three members of Congress and fewer than one in seven presidential appointees and senior civil servants think Americans "know enough about issues to form wise opinions about what should be done" (Pew Research Center for the People and the Press 1998). When the capacity of the public to grapple with complicated evidence and ideas is doubtful, the risks are more palpable that policy experts will be used to manipulate opinion and win political games rather than to lead us closer to collective enlightenment.

Yet, when it comes to how research and knowledge are used in democratic decision making, the choice is not as stark as either naïve idealism or sharp-edged cynicism. Political scientists and democratic theorists offer two concepts—deliberative democracy and macro (collective) rationality—that can be fused to suggest a realistic and yet optimistic vision: one that recognizes the overall value of research, the importance of good versus bad research, and at the same time both accepts and welcomes the fact that politics is as unavoidable a force in collective decision making as gravity is in the movement of mass.

Among contemporary political scientists, the dominant view is that politics involves negotiation and conflict among sharply etched interests. Competing groups make trade-offs, seek victories, or accept defeat. Research is just another weapon in the arsenal, a way to confuse the enemy, obscure one's true interests, seduce less attentive actors to ally with one's cause. The concept of deliberative democracy suggests that interests are more malleable. What initially appear to be fundamentally competing interests may rest on inadequate information, misunderstanding, failure to consider longer-term consequences, and lack of reflection. Accordingly, thoughtful and mutually respectful discussion among citizens under specified conditions can lead to more rational and broadly accepted policies.[5]

The concept of macro- (or collective) rationality also challenges the reigning understanding of democracy. Common sense seems to suggest that rational democratic policy making depends on a base of highly informed and rational voters who weigh the issues in light of their own goals and preferences, evaluate parties and candidates, and vote in and out of office those whose performance shows that they are both inclined and able to enact policies that work on their behalf. From this perspective the evidence of mass inattentiveness is disheartening. Macro-rationality, however, argues that democratic societies can produce thoughtful, sensitive, and informed policies even if many of the individuals who make up the society are not thoughtful, sensitive, or informed (Erikson, MacKuen, and Stimson 2002; Jacobs and Shapiro 2000; Page and Shapiro 1992). This can happen if voters take cues from more informed actors, if those who are more informed are more active and influential, and if institutional parameters—including those that support and protect the research enterprise—make it selectively harder for bad ideas to get enacted, implemented, and sustained over time.

Taken together, theories of deliberative democracy and collective rationality suggest that it is desirable and possible to expect citizens to become more informed consumers of policy-relevant research and that one does not need to make all citizens into sophisticated researchers for their interaction within democratic processes to generate better policies. But is this vision any better grounded in the realities of research and politics? Does it fail to grasp the corrupting power of politics? Does it overestimate the potential for discerning consumption by attentive citizens? Is it, in other words, its own version of naïveté lite?

A Challenge

The idealized vision of research and democracy sets a powerful normative vision that is undermined by its empirical naïveté. As a guide to shaping our understanding of the potential role of research to contribute to better social policies, it comes up short in two ways. First, its overenthusiastic claims about the potential of good research to provide clear and certain policy guidance trip over the observed phenomenon of studies that offer complex and contingent findings with implications for policy that are indirect, inferential, and open to debate. Second, its overly naïve understanding of politics as something that can and needs to be restricted to the agenda-setting function both underestimates the potential of politics to infuse research and fails to appreciate the fact that politics can sometimes be a tool of good governance as well as a corrupter. Despite these empirical shortcomings, the idealized vision also has served a positive role, helping to construct and defend normative and institutional bulwarks against gross politicization. As the idealized vision is brought down to earth and refurbished, we need to make sure that key aspects of this positive role are kept alive

Whether mass democracy and science can be complementary is partly a question of aspiration, but also open to empirical analysis. Is science corrupted or is it up to the challenge of providing insights? If science can produce the goods, are the institutions of transferring knowledge to the public up to the challenge of conveying it accurately? Is the public up to the challenge of putting it to good use?

I argue in this book that we can do better, and I base that argument not just on wishful thinking but also on a close analysis of what politics and research really entail. The next chapter, which shows the extent of public polarization involving research into school choice and charter schools, makes clear the extent of the gap between where we are and where we might be. The challenges are serious. Some are specific to the charter school debate. Some emerge from structural changes in the key institutions responsible for generating, disseminating, interpreting, and legitimizing research across social policy issues. Yet, I will suggest, the core research enterprise is healthy, the threats can be countered, and the potential for more informed discourse has not yet been tested.

Chapter 3

How Cool Research Gets in Hot Waters: Privatization, School Choice, and Charter Schools

Charter schools are a high stakes political and policy issue right now. . . . That's the crux issue here: Charter schools displace existing power arrangements, people naturally get bent out of shape about that. To be sure there is an empirical component to this debate, but it's more where the battle is being fought out than its true cause.[1]

—Eduwonk blog, August 21, 2006

Those who labor in the fields of social science and education research are accustomed to laboring in obscurity. The 2006 Annual Meeting of the American Educational Research Association, held in San Francisco between April 7 and April 11, included 1,946 substantive panels, at which 8,361 scholars presented papers and 12,444 researchers—including coauthors—presented their findings.[2] One would think that such a volume of work would attract at least some attention in the national media. A search on Lexis/Nexis, however, returned only seven articles related to research presented at that meeting. Three were published in the same issue of the *Chronicle of Higher Education*. Two were written by Greg Toppo of *USA Today*, one of the only education journalists from a major newspaper who consistently covers this event. One was in a Bangor, Maine, newspaper, reporting on a local researcher who presented a paper at the conference. One—by far the longest—was a biting satire by Rick Hess and Laura LoGerfo of the American Enterprise Institute, in which they characterized the five major fields of educational inquiry as "imperialism; ghetto culture; hegemonic oppression and right-thinking multiculturalism: cyber-jargon; and the utterly incomprehensible" (Hess and LoGerfo 2006).

Why do some issues command attention? Why, of those that do garner attention, is research and evidence only sometimes a central part of the debate? What accounts for the fact that in some areas of public policy concern the lines between research and politics seem especially flimsy or obscure?

Almost all of the researchers interviewed for this book thought that charter school research was highly politicized—which is to say that they believed that issues relating to partisan tactics, ideology, and political interest had a strong role in the way research is attended to and used. Asked how politicized they felt education policy research is in the United States today, using a scale from 1, "almost completely evidence based," to 5, "almost completely driven by political and ideological factors," the average score was 3.9; not one of the twenty researchers I interviewed gave a score of less than 3. This chapter wrestles with the question of why the pressures of politicization have been especially (though not uniquely) evident in the debate over school choice and charter schools.

Part of the answer lies in how the charter school debate quickly became aligned with much broader arguments about the proper role of government versus markets. Whereas topical issues come and go, competing visions of the proper role of government versus markets continue to be the driving force of the deep-plate tectonics of partisan and ideological maneuvering.

When issues cut across the conventional market versus government divide, lines of political conflict get muddied. This in turn creates pressures that keep political extremes in check. It is one thing to engage in harsh attacks on those with whom one expects to be consistently at war, but quite another to risk alienating and undermining the credibility of those one hopes to enlist as an ally in future battles.

Some issues, though, come to be understood in terms that neatly and precisely overlay the standard ideological alignment. When that happens, they can readily become proxies for the big war between right and left. This was the case with school vouchers, which from the beginning—when the conservative economist Milton Friedman proposed them—have been inextricably linked with broader arguments about the limitations of government and the virtues of markets. As a result, key interest groups have been unwilling or unable to find common ground; any movement toward a position of compromise is resisted as symbolic defeat, a first step down a slippery path toward either a Leviathan government or a Wild West scenario in which corporations run amok and the only consumers who count are those with cash in their pockets (Henig 2005). This chapter discusses this history of thinking and political maneuvering around issues of schools to clarify how and why charter schools, which could have been treated like an interesting but incremental and uncontroversial reform in service delivery, instead came to occupy a pivotal position in an ideologically polarized strategic debate.

That political forces drew the charter school issue into a broader maelstrom is partly a story of this being the right (or, depending on your perspective, wrong) issue at the right (or wrong) time. What makes the charter school case more significant and potentially disturbing, however, is the extent to it reflects broader forces in contemporary American politics.

Charter Schools as a Pragmatic Public Sector Reform

Like the Greek hero Theseus, who slew the Minotaur, the charter school movement had two fathers. One of Theseus's fathers was mortal (Aegeus, king of Athens), the other, a god (Poseidon). The charter school movement was ultimately elevated on the national stage because of its ties to the high ideas of systemic privatization, but its more earthbound roots lay in pragmatic notions about how public school systems might be incrementally reformed to make them less uniform and rigid.

Charter schools as a pragmatic public sector reform choice grew out of a history including alternative schools, magnet schools, and various visions of a more decentralized form of public education. Whereas the dominant norm in American public education has been to assign children to schools based on where they live, experiments with alternative schools that offer different programs targeted to different audiences go back to early in the last century. Walnut Hills High School, in Cincinnati, was created in 1918 for academically gifted, college-bound students. Programs such as the Bronx High School of Science in New York City, Lowell in San Francisco, Lane Tech in Chicago, and Boston's Latin School existed long before the term *school choice* came into public parlance (Smith, Barr, and Burke 1976). The more famous examples have focused on children with special abilities or on progressive curricula outside the mainstream, but there have also been, for many years, special schools or programs intended for troubled students or providing technical skills for those thought unlikely to go to college.

The first real explosion of public school choice came in the 1970s and into the 1980s, when many districts adopted some form of magnet schools. In 1972, magnet schools were virtually unheard of. In 1982, the count was more than 1,000. Magnet schools offered special teaching approaches, curricula, or other unusual elements to attract students from outside the immediate neighborhood. What gave them impetus initially was their appeal to parents to voluntarily transfer their children among schools in a direction that would improve racial balance (Henig 1994). In some cases, magnets were part of court-ordered remedies; in others, districts turned to magnets to forestall judicial intervention. Over time, magnets developed a constituency based less on their use as a tool for integration and more as a vehicle for introducing variety and options into relatively bland local districts.

The third strain of public sector reform was the impetus to decentralize the locus of decision making. Through most of the twentieth century, a combination of population increase and consolidation of school districts led to larger and larger districts, even as organizational change and educator professionalism led to more hierarchical and insular bureaucracies. By the 1960s, an emergent backlash was evident in a call for decentralizing authority from central offices to schools and neighborhoods. This ideal has come in different flavors.

One, associated with advocacy organization, calls for minority empowerment, tended to emerge from outside the education community and to envision a substantial transfer of power and authority from the bureaucracy to communities. The historical apotheosis was the late 1960s New York City experiment with community control (Gittell 1971). The most contemporary—albeit only slightly more durable—version was Chicago's mid-1990s initiation of local school councils (Bryk et al. 1998).

A second grew in part out of changing corporate notions about the advantages of devolving responsibility. Business leaders interested in school reform translated these into notions of school-based decision, less as a reallocation of political power away from education systems than as reallocation of responsibility within education systems so as to increase innovation and efficiency.

The third, and the one with the most direct tie to the birth of charter schools, came from within the education community It is most associated with the thinking of Albert Shanker, the highly visible and influential president of the AFT from 1974 to 1997.[3] His concept of professionalism was less tied to a shared orthodoxy of pedagogical thought and more accommodating to the notion that teachers should be innovators, experimenters, and shapers of a school-based learning communities. Although committed to union democracy and collective bargaining, Shanker was distressed when those processes sometimes seemed to stomp down potentially valuable but somewhat iconoclastic views enthusiastically held by a minority of the union's members. He laid out some of his ideas about how teachers, unencumbered by bureaucracy, might bring about meaningful change in a March 1988 speech at the National Press Club in Washington. This speech, and related columns that he wrote on the topic, came to the attention of reform-minded folks in Minnesota. They invited Shanker to Minneapolis to discuss these ideas, and some date the coalescence of the charter school to that very meeting.

These notions of reform had little or nothing to do with theories about markets, competition, and inherent limits of government. All envisioned change as exercised through democracy expressed in and implemented by public institutions. Had charter schools stayed framed in these terms, it is quite possible that they might have evolved as a far less controversial, incrementally absorbed policy innovation. Had that occurred, the process of empirically studying charter schools and their consequences might have been more subdued. But other winds were rising.

The Politics of Privatization

The national debate over government versus markets was somewhat muted from the 1940s through the 1960s, for a variety of reasons. The perceived political and economic success of the New Deal put traditional laissez faire conservatism on the defensive. Postwar prosperity contributed to an American optimism that most social problems could be solved by concentrated effort. Wariness of politicians, suspicions about faceless Washington bureaucrats, and resentments over high taxes and constraints on personal freedoms never sank far below the surface of the nation's political consciousness, but the momentum was behind the growing role of government as a source for the collective good. This included the idea that the national government would play a leading role in orchestrating a federal system in which the parochialism of states and localities could be kept within bounds.[4]

There was another, more ignoble, reason that the government versus market cleavage was less pronounced during those years. Across a range of issues, and especially in education, race often overshadowed economics as the defining issue in political conflict. The 1964 presidential election offered an unusually clear choice to American voters between Democrat Lyndon Johnson, who represented a commitment to using national government to carry through a civil rights and war on poverty agenda, and Barry Goldwater, whose suspicion of big government made him a more purely conservative candidate than the Republicans had nominated in quite some time. Johnson's political thrashing of Goldwater—in which the Democrat received more than 60 percent of the popular vote and more than 90 percent of the electoral vote—seemed to many to mark the end of any conservative dream of rolling back government to pre-New Deal levels.

By 1980, though, the political winds had begun to shift. Partly by chance and partly by design, conservative advocates developed a new way to package their antigovernment arguments. Americans seemed to want many of the things that liberal Democrats had championed—financial protection in old age, equal opportunity for racial minorities, programs to provide job skills to the healthy poor, and support to poor children and the frail poor. Shifting from government to markets did not have to mean giving up on these attractive goals, the new conservative privatization proponents argued, it simply meant obtaining them more efficiently and effectively through other means. Hardcore arguments for the benefits of markets and the dangers of government monopolies—ideas that Milton Friedman and others had been talking about for years, but ideas generally associated with a harsher world of competition and inequality—were now being offered in a sweetened version, and accordingly began to move from the margins to the mainstream of political debate. Conservative think tanks, such as the Heritage Foundation and the Cato Foundation, were honing these ideas into strategy not just for how to govern but also, and more immediately, for how to permanently reverse the political dynamics that had been supporting the growth of an American welfare state. Still, it took a while for education politics to get drawn in.

Ronald Reagan generally ran against big government, but his 1980 campaign and first term emphasized traditional themes of federalism, states rights, and individualism more than market theory per se. Shifting federal support from categorical to block grants as a way to liberate states to innovate and reflect local values were key themes, both generally and in education. Reagan proposed consolidating more than forty grants programs into two block grants that would give states considerable discretion in how they set about helping students with special needs and leveraging improvements in school performance. The 1980 Republican platform portrayed teachers in a positive light, suggesting that federal education policy created the greatest barrier to teachers' freedom in the classroom and thus the greatest barrier to enabling students to meet high standards. Accordingly, the Republican platform argued to deregulate and eliminate the Department of Education as a way to place teaching and learning decisions in the hands of the students, parents, and local education personnel. Other themes included voluntary prayer in schools, tuition tax credits, and eliminating busing because it "blighted whole communities across the land with its divisive impact," failed to provide achievement results, and diverted funding better used for other programs.[5]

Reagan scored major legislative victories during his first term, most notably related to tax cuts and combining categorical grants into broader (but typically less well-funded) block grants. His education agenda, however, was pursued half-heartedly and with little success. More significantly, by his second term, some conservatives were becoming alarmed that even the early victories were being offset. Stuart Butler, director of domestic policy studies at the Heritage Institute, saw it this way: "After some initial success in 1981, the White House seemed completely to lose control of the budget. To say that the administration missed its target would be a colossal understatement. . . . Ronald Reagan is now on record as the big spender to end all big spenders—an irony indeed for such a conservative politician" (1985, 6).

In the mind of Butler, an influential strategist within the political right, the problem was not one of will but of understanding and strategy. It was not enough to articulate a goal of smaller government—that was something Reagan did masterfully. What was needed, instead, was to better understand the political dynamics that accounted for the growth of government and then to offer a plan to turn those dynamics around.

Butler argued that the cause of governmental growth was the array of interest groups that benefited from public spending. Because the benefits were relatively concentrated, those on the receiving end had a powerful motivation to ensure that the spigot stayed open. Because the costs of the programs were spread widely and were not clearly itemized, taxpayers had less motivation to insist on fiscal restraint. Over time, moreover, pro-spending interest groups solidified their standing by linking arms with politicians and bureaucrats who also stood to gain from the growth of the programs they championed and administered.

The privatization strategy Butler laid out was strategically designed to replace "this set of dynamics with another that discourages citizens from demanding public-sector services and encourages them instead to seek similar services from the private sector" (1985, 43). Key components of the strategy would be to

- Emphasize that government can be a guarantor of services without necessarily providing them itself. Butler argued that conservatives fall into a trap when they argue against any governmental role in delivering popular programs. Instead, they should propose ways that government could ensure that the same goods and services are delivered through the market.

- Use policy tools such as users fees, tax incentives, and vouchers to encourage citizens to rely on the private sector to meet their demands. Butler labeled this the "heart of privatization," suggesting that it combined "political expediency" with the goal of shrinking government by allowing conservative politicians to "gain points with constituencies by promising more, not less, and by giving people the freedom to choose the service provider most attractive to them" while simultaneously reducing opposition to budget cuts (1985, 45).

- Detach elements of the pro-spending coalition. Butler cited here what looked at the time to be a compelling example from Great Britain. The Thatcher government had offered discounts to public housing residents to purchase their units, and initial reports suggested that the newly invested property owners were showing weakened allegiance to the opposition Labor Party.

- Create "mirror image" private sector coalitions that would counterbalance the pro-spending groups. Privatization would involve the "conscious creation" and nurturing of antispending coalitions around targeted tax incentives or regulatory relief. Once in place, these coalitions would battle the pro-spending groups and "take on a momentum of their own" (47)

- Resist the temptation to engage in out and out battles for radical change in favor of an incrementalist approach that would more slowly but more surely lead toward fundamental and sustainable change. Although it is sometimes possible to bring about sharp policy changes, pro-government forces more typically gained by "creating small, inoffensive programs" that then became seedbeds for further expansion. Going for big victories means risking big and visible defeats. Learning from their counterparts, "the privatizer should attempt to get a foot in the door" with a small tax or regulatory change and then use that as a platform for expanding the pro-market coalition (61).

This game plan would later play out very neatly in the education arena. Initially, however, conservatives put their primary efforts elsewhere. Americans' attachments to public education—both the broad ideals and the local manifestations—made this a politically risky area for conservatives to feature.

The Privatization Debate Gets Around to Education Policy

For years, the public's general affection for the image of common schools and especially their local community schools—what Terry Moe somewhat dismissively refers to as the "public school ideology" (2001)—inoculated education from the kinds of privatization efforts that took hold in other policy areas. Even in 1983, when asked shortly after *A Nation at Risk* drew widespread attention for its scathing critique of America's schools, citizens were 50 percent more likely to give public schools a grade of A or B than D or F (Rose and Gallup 2003). Making this latent mass support for the existing system of public education even more significant was the fact that it was topped off by well-organized and powerful teachers' unions. At the time, too, conservative strategists were primarily focusing on the battle over federal policy; changing education seemed to require fighting many battles in fifty state legislatures and 15,000 school districts.

Butler devoted entire sections of his 1985 book on *Privatizing Federal Spending* to possibilities to privatize the United States Postal Service, Amtrak, air traffic control, weapons procurement, and commercial possibilities in space. He even offered a full chapter on Social Security. The word *schools* does not appear at all in his index, however. The word *education* appears only in reference to the unfulfilled Reagan proposal to abolish the Department of Education. Last, only two or three references are made to school vouchers, each submerged in a broader discussion of vouchers in other policy contexts.

This was not because the theoretical rationalization for privatizing education had not yet been developed; it most certainly had. Milton Friedman had laid out the basic economic argument for school vouchers as early as 1955, and it received a full and widely read treatment in his important book on *Capitalism and Freedom,* published in 1962. He argued that traditional public schools were lazy monopolies, with no incentive to provide quality or responsive service because parents were forced by law to pay taxes to support the system and limited by policy to sending their child to whatever school the local district assigned. Friedman proposed converting the funds raised to support the public system to families and letting them select the school of their choice, whether it be publicly run or run by private for-profits, nonprofits, or religious organizations. Government's regulatory role should "be limited to insuring that the schools met certain minimum standards, such as the inclusion of a minimum common content in their programs, much as it now inspects restaurants to insure that they maintain minimum sanitary standards" (Friedman 1962, 89).

Try as they might to make the case that the existing system was inefficient, inept, and even corrupt, voucher proponents could not bring enough wind under the sails of Friedman's voucher idea to bring it into political reality. Reagan had made an effort. In 1983, 1985, and 1986, he submitted voucher proposals to Congress, but all of them came up short (Viteritti 2005). Other Republicans lacked Reagan's personal popularity and vaunted Teflon status. When they too aggressively aligned themselves with vouchers and school choice, they were nailed with the label of being antischools or in favor of an elitist and hierarchical education system in which middle- and upper-income white children attended one set of schools and poor and minority children another. They were punished accordingly at the polls. Despite the fact that George H.W. Bush tried to fashion himself as an education president with a vision that emphasized high standards and accountability,

education voters (those who indicated education was the issue mattering most to their vote) supported Clinton over Bush by a more than two-to-one margin (55% to 27% for whites, and 90% to 7% for blacks). Clinton did equally well on the education issue among the general electorate, with polls showing that voters thought Clinton better able than Bush to improve public education—by almost a two to one margin, 47% to 24%. (McGuinn 2006)

The tide began to turn in the 1990s as a somewhat reformulated school choice argument was shaped, one that sanded down some of the rough edges that had made the Friedman-esque pure market version politically unpalatable. Friedman's vision was of a universal and substantially deregulated voucher system. In it, all families with school age children would receive vouchers, traditional public schools supported directly by tax revenues would cease to exist, and regulations would be kept to the minimum needed to protect health, safety, and core elements of nondiscrimination. In keeping with Butler's privatization strategy, proponents of market solutions for education adopted a more incrementalist approach. It took advantage of available political openings instead of taking on well-defended positions, and portrayed school choice as complementary, rather than a threat, to the existing public school system and Americans' abstract commitment to the idea of schooling as a vehicle for social harmony and class mobility. More due to accident than design, to opportunistic politics than grand strategy, charter schools emerged as the surrogate to vouchers as the battleground on which the market versus government conflict would be staged.

Charter Schools as Surrogate Battlefield

If time were a racetrack, the early 1990s would be an incredible horse race in which an unknown steed of uncertain heritage came out of nowhere to pass the front-runner. The unknown was charter schools. The front-runner was voucher schools.

Vouchers Fail to Sweep the Nation

In 1990, the Wisconsin legislature did what no state legislature previously had been willing to do: enact a voucher program that would let students attend private K-12 schools at public expense. The program was limited. It applied only to Milwaukee families, the number who could get the vouchers was capped, and eligibility was restricted to low-income families. To voucher proponents, however, the Milwaukee voucher program appeared to represent a critical beachhead. Although its origins owed something to idiosyncratic elements of Milwaukee politics,[6] the simple fact of its passage redeemed the notion that vouchers could be politically viable. And for some very conservative proponents of privatization, the Milwaukee voucher program was seen as a critical breakthrough.

The Lynde and Harry Bradley Foundation, based in Milwaukee and established in 1985,[7] played a key role in setting the stage for the voucher program, in helping it to take root, and in funding and disseminating research that proclaimed its virtues. Harry Bradley was a wealthy industrialist who had been a member and major contributor to the John Birch Society (Micklethwhaite and Wooldridge 2004). In 1987, the Bradley Foundation helped launch the Wisconsin Policy Research Institute, which "issued report and after report criticizing the public school system" (Anrig 2007, 162). It played the major role in funding Partners Advancing Values in Education (PAVE), which began offering private scholarships that could be used at religious or secular private schools. Labeled as scholarships to avoid too-direct an association with the controversial notion of vouchers, these private grants were a way to keep the momentum going while the publicly funded Milwaukee program built its base and was institutionalized.[8] Bradley contributed about half a million dollars per year to PAVE during its first three years in operation, and more than $2.7 million between 1986 and 1995 (Hess 2002, 105). From 1985 through 2003, the foundation gave almost $7 million to the Wisconsin Policy Research Institute and more than $17 million to PAVE.[9] Once in place, believers were confident the program would build a constituency of parents who saw a new opportunity, schools that could count on a new supply of students and revenue, and—most important—a broad audience both locally and nationally that would be convinced by the success of the program in raising academic performance.

The Milwaukee program, once in place, developed local roots and expanded, just as its proponents had hoped. Initially the growth was low. In the fifth year of the program (AY 94-5), fewer than 800 students used the vouchers; this was still below the program cap, which at that time was set at 1 percent of the Milwaukee public school district's enrollment. Demand rose incrementally at first, but then shot up dramatically after the cap on the number of schools was raised. In 1998, it shot up again after the state supreme court approved an expansion of the program to include religious schools. According to Greg Anrig's account "the Bradley Foundation was intimately involved in those battles. It reimbursed the state of Wisconsin $350,000 for legal services to argue in favor of religious choice" (Anrig 2007, 166). The expansion and institutionalization led to a dramatic increase in enrollments; in the fall of 1998 5,740 students participated, compared to 1,501 the year before. By the fall of 2005, the number rose to 14,517.[10]

The institutionalization of the voucher program within Milwaukee did not, however, have quite the contagious national impact that

Table 3.1   Votes on Major Voucher Referenda

State	Year	Vote Against	Vote For
MI	1970	43%	57%
MD	1972	55	45
MI	1978	74	26
DC	1981	74	26
OR	1990	67	33
CO	1992	67	33
CA	1993	70	30
WA	1996	64	36
MI	2000	69	31
CA	2000	71	29
Average		65	35

Sources: People for the American Way, "History of Failed Vouchers and Tax Credits" accessed at http://www.pfaw.org/pfaw/general/default.aspx?oid=2969; National School Board Association, "Keep Public Education Public: Why Vouchers Are a Bad Idea," Appendix, accessed at http://www.nsba.org/site/pdf.asp?TP=/site/docs/33800/33743.pdf.

proponents had anticipated, despite plenty of attention from policy entrepreneurs, especially in its early years. Like fancy Parisian fashions on show in a middle-class shopping mall, there were many lookers and almost no one ready to buy. The Ohio legislature passed a voucher program—limited to low-income Cleveland families—in 1995. Florida enacted a program in 1999, but the state supreme court ruled it unconstitutional in January 2006. This was hardly a groundswell. Most important from a political perspective, whenever voters were given a direct opportunity to express themselves, vouchers went down to dramatic public defeats. Voucher or tuition tax credit proposals[11] went to public referenda at least ten times (in six states and the District of Columbia) between 1970 and 2000; all but one failed on average by about a 2 to 1 margin (see table 3.1). As one voucher proponent reluctantly concluded, "school choice was not a viable national issue, and the market concept remained a cute metaphor in the minds of most citizens" (Viteritti 2005, 141).

Charter Schools Catch On

Charter schools emerged against this backdrop of a stalling voucher movement. They were quickly drawn into the ideological and political currents of the privatization debates. To many contemporary observers, the charter school movement seemed to have sprung from the politics of vouchers much as Athena is said to have sprung fully formed from the head of Zeus. That was not the case, however. The initial conception of charter schools had less to do with ideas about markets as alternatives to government and more with a vision of choice as integral to a strategy for public sector and civic reform.

Charter school legislation has been supported by coalitions of diverse interests. Laissez-faire proponents of pure-market solutions, minority rights advocates, disgruntled parents, education entrepreneurs, progressive educators, and even teachers' unions at times have advocated for increased school-level control and have contributed to the political momentum that led, by 2005, to the enactment of charter school legislation in forty states and the District of Columbia. Though united in their rejection of what they consider to be a stifling bureaucratic system of public education embracing conformity over innovation, these interests have competing visions of what the alternative ought to be.

The first charter school law was passed in Minnesota in 1991. Despite the fact that that the nation's first real voucher system was percolating across the state line in Wisconsin, Minnesota's enactment of charters was little influenced by Freidman-esque visions of market-based reform. Instead, it was propelled by a local brand of decentralization coupled with Albert Shanker's notions about a more open and flexible form of education professionalism.

The ground for charters was softened by two decades of experimentation with public school choice in Minneapolis, St. Paul, and later the state. These experiments grew out of grassroots efforts to add variety to the offerings within the public school districts. The point was to provide options for parents whose children had special needs or interests, and for teachers who wanted to try innovative pedagogical techniques. As in many other cities drawn to public school choice during the 1970s and early 1980s, there was also a belief that such mechanisms could provide a way to integrate schools naturally and with public support. By the mid-1980s, the notion that families could select schools outside a rigidly defined attendance zone was a familiar one.

Joe Nathan, one of the recognized founders of Minnesota's charter school movement, identifies 1988 as the year that the charter school idea was conceived. The Minneapolis Foundation organized a conference attended by a number of local school activists and addressed by Shanker and Seymour Fliegel. Fliegel was a New York City educator who had been influential in building a public choice element within that city's East Harlem Community District 4 (Fliegel 1993; Schneider, Teske, and Marschall 2000). Shanker introduced the term *charter*, suggesting that this was a vehicle by which local districts might grant groups of teachers the authority to run schools that differed from the cookie-cutter models too often promoted by centralized bureaucracies. Sparked by those presentations, a small group of the Minnesota activists sat down that evening "and wrote their ideas down on a napkin"

(Nathan 2002, 20). One key element was the notion that there would have to be chartering authorities in addition to the local districts, lest the bureaucratic and self-protective forces within the local districts snuff out truly innovative alternatives just as they did so internally. Another key idea, attributed to Ted Kolderie, was to make an explicit trade-off: in return for greater autonomy, charter schools would accept the responsibility to produce better outcomes or risk losing their right to operate.

The market rationale for vouchers was linked to a vision of educators as part of a so-called lazy monopoly, motivated by self-interest to protect prerogatives even at the cost of student welfare. The original Minnesota-brewed vision of charter schools, however, was "the ultimate form of teacher empowerment" (Nathan 2002, 30). The key to school reform, from this perspective, was giving teachers the space and resources to use their full range of skills and imagination to educate. The kernel of this philosophy was grounded in the concept of the agricultural cooperative (Rofes 2000). Teachers would be given an incentive to contribute to the greater well being of the school by becoming stakeholders, part-owners rather than employees. "One of the central objectives of the charter school movement," Nathan explained, "is to empower classroom teachers, administrators, and parents, giving them the opportunity to create the schools they believe will help youngsters" (Nathan 1999, 8). A second strain of this communal perspective puts less emphasis on educational professionalism and more on a set of animating values that create a bond between teachers and families. These values may be pedagogical—for example, when families and teachers together subscribe to a common vision of progressive education or a back-to-the-basics approach—but they may also have their roots in racial, ethnic, or religious identity. The key is the shared nature of the commitment, cultural affirmation, and the social capital that this can engender (Henig et al. 2005; Coleman and Hoffer 1987; Bryk, Lee, and Holland 1993).

Everyone Likes a Winner

Whereas vouchers were the fashionable idea that few were willing to try, charter schools took off like the iPod would. Friedman had first broached the idea of vouchers in the 1950s. A federal government effort in the mid-1970s fizzled (Cohen and Farrar 1977; Henig 1994). Not until 1990 was a voucher program on the books, and only in one city, for a limited number of families, and far more targeted than the universal program Friedman envisioned. In contrast, the ink had barely dried on the Minnesota charter school law before other states were discussing—and enacting—charter school programs of their own.

In 1992, only one charter school in the nation had opened its doors, and only two states—Minnesota and California—had charter school laws on the books. Six more states passed legislation in 1993, three in 1994, and eight in 1995. By 1996, more than half the states and the District of Columbia had laws on the books. By 2006, the number of states was up to forty, the number of schools to just under 4,000, and the number of students to somewhere around 1.1 million (Center for Education Reform 2006).

Part of the explanation for the broad and rapid spread of the concept was that some conservatives recognized supporting charters could serve several tactical ends. First, charter schools were proving popular. Perhaps because they were formally public schools, they did not seem radical or threatening; they were similar to vouchers but presented a friendlier face.[12] Charter schools could provide conservatives a campaign platform issue in line with market ideas but more likely to gain than to lose votes. Second, by pushing charter schools, conservatives might sow seeds of discord within the core Democratic constituency. Conservative strategists anticipated that teachers' unions would resist charters and that their power within the Democratic Party would lead most of the party's national leaders to do the same. Charter schools, though, would appeal at the grassroots level to community-based organizations, parents frustrated with their local school bureaucracies, and minorities who felt trapped in their assigned public schools. Third, charter schools, once in place, could become a staging ground for further privatization-oriented policies. Charter school providers include a growing array of for-profit companies that would partner with the schools. These providers and charter school parents could become a loyal source of support and a political lobby. Lobbying would be a multifront effort: to fight for expanding the number of charter schools; to make sure that states reduced the regulatory burden on them; to increase the per pupil funding; to initiate capital funding to help charter schools buy or rent buildings; and perhaps eventually to revive the push for vouchers as a simpler and more compelling alternative.

As the seeds of this strategy were taking root, a few conservative foundations took on the responsibility of bankrolling the charter school movement and helping sustain it until it matured. Several of these had supported vouchers from the start. The Walton Family Foundation, for example, has been a major funder of charter schools and charter advocacy organizations, as well as charter school research, as discussed in chapter 6.

The history of the Charter School Coalition in the District of Columbia illustrates how organizations committed to vouchers switched gears to support charters when it became clear that that strategy was more politically viable. The Coalition was launched, staffed, and funded by Friends of Choice in Urban Schools (FOCUS), initially established as a pro-voucher organization. FOCUS had ties to conservative foundations and to conservative Republicans in Congress. The advantages these provided were counterbalanced by the fact that overt association with conservative Republicans ensures political isolation in the heavily Democratic District of Columbia. Accordingly, FOCUS made a series of tactical decisions to deemphasize vouchers and market language, to form a coalition of charter providers that for the most part consisted of liberal and community-based leaders with little sympathy for national Republicans, and to work through the coalition to establish a local constituency (Henig et al. 2003).

Although conservative support was important, it is unlikely charter schools would have spread so quickly had Democrats unified in opposition to what they might have characterized as a voucher in sheep's clothing. Partly because they saw the momentum behind charter schools, and partly because they were genuinely intrigued with the potential for charter schools to leverage progressive change, a number of Democratic governors and so-called New Democrats at the national level decided to jump on the charter school bandwagon rather than make a futile attempt to stand in its way. As president, Bill Clinton simultaneously opposed vouchers—as a potential drain on revenues needed by the public system—and aggressively supported charter schools. In July of 2000, the White House Web site boasted of the administration's efforts in this regard.

> The Clinton-Gore administration has worked to expand public school choice and support the growth of public charter schools, which have increased from one public charter school in the nation in 1992 to more than 1,700 today. More than 250,000 students nationwide are now enrolled in charter schools in 30 states and the District of Columbia. The President won $145 million in FY 2000—and has proposed $175 million in his FY01 budget—to continue working toward his goal of establishing 3,000 quality charter schools by 2002. (Accessed at http://clinton4.nara.gov/WH/Accomplishments/additional.html)

Clinton took pains to distinguish between good charter schools and bad ones, and between good charter school laws and bad ones, arguing that success depended on careful oversight. That said, his message was one of support. Speaking in Minnesota in the spring of 2000, he praised that state's leadership on the charter school front: "We now have enough evidence that the charter school movement works, if it's done right. . . . Very often we see charter schools provide an even greater atmosphere of competition that induces kids to work harder and harder to learn" (Goodnough 2000, A24).

Even the national teachers' unions found it prudent not to fight charters, at least not head on. Of the two major teachers' unions, the AFT has been the more supportive of charter schools. As noted, many credit its former president Albert Shanker as being among the intellectual founders of the concept. Some advocates believe the AFT is disingenuous in proclaiming its support for charter schools. Responding to the *New York Times* coverage of the AFT report, they take offense at the portrayal of the union as open-minded on the issue. Their claim is that both the AFT and NEA pose as friends of charters simply to then suffocate them in their embrace. While proclaiming their support, this argument goes, the unions lay out a vision of charter schools as highly regulated and with unionized teachers in control. These critics of the teachers' unions are almost certainly right that national leadership is wary of the charter school movement and especially wary of charters when they are defined primarily in the language of markets. Those who were close to Shanker, however, insist that his promotion of charters was not a case of jumping on a rolling bandwagon. Shanker, they explain, saw the original concept as consonant with his vision of professionalism, which included allowing minorities of teachers to experiment with alternative approaches, even if this did not conform with either the conventional wisdom among educators or the preferences of the majority of union members. This is not to say that everyone in the AFT leadership shared his vision. Some were skeptical, especially when they saw the way conservative groups were uniting behind—they would say co-opting and perverting—the charter school movement. Even Shanker reversed course somewhat, writing several critical columns when he saw the way that some conservatives were reformulating charters as a pro-market and anti-union privatization plan. The NEA, the largest national teachers' union, was probably even more wary. Its pattern, more than the AFT's, might be characterized as a Johnny come lately. It too, however, found it wise to fight over the meaning of charter schools rather than the schools directly. By the mid-1990s, NEA was praising some local affiliates that had started their own charter schools. "NEA is interested in learning firsthand what it takes to make a successful charter school. What better way to lead in one of the hottest areas of school reform?" it proclaimed in its newsletter. "As for the law: NEA supports charter school legislation that's consistent with this country's commitment to free, universal public schools. The Association opposes charter school laws that promote the privatization of education" (National Education Association 1998, 1).

Although political maneuvering had a lot to do with the dynamics of charter school politics at the national level, there were several more pragmatic reasons why the policy proved so attractive to governors and state legislators. Since the 1980s, a new crop of governors had been playing leading roles in the national debate about education reform, prompted largely by their perception that better schools could be critical for economic development in their states. States in general were also taking on more and more of the burden of funding public education, partly in response to state court decisions that had forced school finance reform based on grounds of equity and adequacy. State officials were thus eager to find a policy that might help them appear responsive, possibly really help, and do so without putting a significant dent in the state treasury. Charter schools looked like a low-cost solution, given that the state might be simply redirecting its funding to follow the students into charter schools. The appeal was especially strong in states with growing school age populations, which were under pressure to help districts meet the demand for new schools. Charter schools might absorb some of that pressure, and because most state laws did not provide capital budget funding for charter schools, it would be up to the charter schools to find their own buildings at their own expense. Even some of the teacher union support is probably best understood as a pragmatic effort to avoid internal friction rather than a tactical maneuver to mask a plan to defend the status quo. In both the NEA and AFT, some of the pressure to be supportive came internally, from local affiliates and teachers—especially in large city systems and among black and Hispanic members—who had concluded that charter schools, as they were emerging in their communities, were an experiment to nurture, not to snuff out.

The precise causal role to be allocated to these various tactical and pragmatic factors is unclear, but two things about the charter school expansion can be said with confidence. First, one of the key political issues was over how charter schools would be understood in the public's mind. Second, what was driving the expansion of charter schools, at least initially, was not any systematic empirical evidence that they could deliver on their promise to improve student learning.

The Politics of Policy Framing: What Do Charter Schools Stand For?

Sgt. Joe Friday, the fictional police detective in the 1950s television show *Dragnet*, was famous for asking for "just the facts, Ma'am."[13] To those with an idealized view of the policy sciences, this guideline should be applied to evaluating charter schools as well. Social scientists, though, have increasingly found that objective evidence is at best only part of the process that drives policy change. How issues are framed—the concepts with which they are linked and the images and symbols to which they are attached—has much to do with how groups of citizens come to understand policies, formulate their positions on them, and decide whether to mobilize politically to support or oppose policy change (Baumgartner and Jones 1993; Kahneman and Tversky 2000; Kuklinski and Hurley 1994; Jones 1995; Rochefort and Cobb 1994).

Charter schools began to spread, unusually rapidly for a new policy idea with more or less built-in opposition from several powerful interests and no evidence yet to back it up. The primary impetus, it seems, was a sense in many state legislatures that this was a relatively low-cost way to give a jolt to the school reform crusade. State-level entrepreneurs played a role (Mintrom 2000b), as did the federal government, albeit to a relatively small but symbolically important extent. Although the state charter laws shared important core characteristics, they differed in many respects as well. In some states, such as Arizona, the legislation set up a relatively unencumbered market-like system in which new schools could open easily and with relatively little regulatory oversight (Maranto and Gresham 1999). Other measures set high hurdles by placing caps on the number that might be established, prohibiting the conversion of existing public or private schools, restricting how the approved schools operate (limiting the use of uncertified teachers), or establishing strict oversight regimes (requiring considerable documentation from charters, instituting regular site visits, or limiting the length of time for which a charter is granted).

Whereas the phenomenon unfolded at the state level primarily in response to localized political configurations and conditions, nationally conservatives, liberals, Republicans, and Democrats all scrambled to hitch their favored definitions onto the fast moving train. For conservatives and Republicans, the challenge was to sell the image of charter schools as friendlier and less threatening than vouchers while arguing that charters were very much in keeping with the market-based concepts vouchers embodied. Liberals and Democrats were hesitant and divided about how to portray charters, some wanting to attack them as pseudo-vouchers and others to embrace them as representations of progressive ideals.

For proponents, a critical selling point was the fact that charters, unlike voucher programs, were still public schools in at least three senses. First, they are public in funding. Charter school funding comes primarily from government; indeed in almost every case charter schools are prohibited by law from charging parents tuition above and beyond the federal, state, or local support that follows the student into the school.[14] Second, access to charter schools is public. All students are eligible to attend charter schools. When schools are oversubscribed, state laws typically require them to use lotteries to allocate scarce seats. In almost every case, charter schools are barred from applying special admissions criteria that might screen out some students. Third, charter schools are approved and overseen by public agencies, which have the authority to close them down if they are found to be engaging in improper behavior or simply failing to achieve the educational goals set by the state or stipulated in their charter application. There are ways, too, in which charter schools are not public, or at least not public in ways the term is often used. Charter schools, like private schools, have their own boards that directly oversee the school and are responsible to it and not the broader public. Charter school teachers and administrators may not be treated as public employees and the buildings they operate in are typically not public property. Charter schools are exempted from many of the governmental regulations that apply to conventional public schools. Although the applicability of the market metaphor to charter schools depends on the fact that they are analogous to private schools in many ways, that they have public qualities is what makes them seem less radical, less threatening, and less unpredictable to citizens and politicians. Tactically, it made sense for supporters to emphasize these factors when addressing broad audience, even if it was charters' market-like properties that explained why they were on board.

Democrats, as mentioned, were divided. Two cleavages are worth noting. At the national level, the main split was between the so-called old-line Democrats and the so-called New Democrats. The former were understandably wary about charter schools as a possible threat to traditional public schools, a precursor to vouchers, or an element in a strategy to weaken teachers' unions generally by creating a mirror system in which contracts and collective bargaining did not apply. The latter believed charter schools were consistent with their vision of a more flexible, pragmatic, decentralized public sector. New Democrats were also proponents of standards and accountability, and believed they could make more progress on those fronts if they avoided getting overly tangled in the volatile issues of school choice. The second divide was between groups operating within the venue of national politics and those operating on the local and community level. At the national level, partisanship and ideology were powerful forces. At the state and local level, issue framing was less potent because citizens, parents, and others were taking their positions primarily based on their trust (or lack of trust) in the reigning public school leadership and charter school founders. The founders were often individuals, social service organizations, teachers, or community-based organizations with deep roots in the community, seen not as crusaders for privatization but as respected and accomplished do-gooders. It was misguided and counterproductive for liberal Democrats to rally against charters, one national supporter noted, because in doing so they were shooting at their own kind.

> And the things with charters I think . . . it is not about right wing conspiracy, but it is about left wing conspiracy. Most of these schools—and

there are of course exceptions, there are conservatives—but most of the schools are started by liberals. A lot of them are refugees from the alternative school movement; they are progressive. [A3]

The political viability and vitality of the charter school movement at the local and state level probably had more to do with its ties to civil society than to its ties to market ideals, although one cannot discount the role played by conservative funders enticed more by the latter. Indecision and division on the left, however, meant that this alternative vision of charter schools was overshadowed in national debates by the market versus public bureaucracy framing that conservative groups preferred.

Once set in such terms, the charter school debate was drawn into a whirlpool of political contentiousness. Prospects quickly faded that research could easily and simply unfold, methodically and systematically driven by internal logic and cumulating based on evidence, analysis, replication, critique, reformulation, and further study. The point is not that researchers eagerly enlisted in one camp or the other and then set out to provide the ammunition the generals requested for the front. Some of that no doubt occurred, but—as I later explain—it seems that the core enterprise of knowledge building did maintain its bearings despite the noise outside. Framing charter schools in terms of markets versus government, however, raised the stakes, the visibility, and the prospects that findings would be put to political ends whether with the active cooperation of the researchers, their complicit assent, or to their frustration or dismay.

High-Stakes Politics and Fear of Giving Ground

Charter schools became a high stakes issue in national politics because the issue has been defined as one that pits markets against government. Certainly, there are other issues that distinguish liberals from conservatives, Democrats from Republicans. These can involve deep and long-standing questions about authority versus freedom, individualism versus community, responsibility versus rights. They can also involve specific issues—such as abortion, the death penalty, or intervention in the Middle East. Decade in and decade out, however, some of the sharpest and most consistent national partisan conflicts have pitted those who hold that private property and private markets are the nation's source of creativity, economic well-being, and social progress—and therefore ought to be taxed, regulated, and otherwise constrained only when necessary and in the least intrusive ways—against those who argue that unconstrained markets are a threat, that properly constituted government is more reflective of the public will and more suited to drawing out the nation's "best angels" of cooperation and shared progress, and that market forces must therefore be firmly held within bounds by democratic and authoritative government.

Many issues cut across this grain at oblique angles. That can create crosscutting pressures that mute polarization and hold politicization in check. When your opponents on some aspects of an issue are your potential allies on another, it makes sense to soften your attacks lest you permanently alienate those you might wish to enlist in a later battle. This is why social scientists who study conflict find that prospects for cooperation can be greater in iterated than one-time games (Axelrod 1984).

Take an issue like federal regulation of broadcasting. Conservatives would be expected to, and often do, take a position against it. In some instances, however, they advocate more aggressive regulation and enforcement. The American Decency Association, for example, a fundamentalist conservative group whose mission is "to educate its members and the general public on matters of decency; to initiate, promote, encourage and coordinate activity designed to safeguard and advance public morality consistent with biblical Christianity," devotes an entire section of its Web site to complaints about the failure of the Federal Communications Commission to more aggressively sanction radio and TV personality Howard Stern.[15] In education, to take another example, the accountability issue often cuts across the standard ideological grain in much the same way. Traditional conservative beliefs about limited government lose some of their traction when they come into conflict with other conservative notions about maintaining high standards, getting tough with teacher unions, and ensuring that future workers have a core set of skills and future citizens a core of knowledge and values.

That charter schools would be drawn into the debate over the role of governments and markets was not preordained. Whether a specific policy debate comes to be understood in this framework is only partially determined by the objective characteristics of the issue at hand. The context that key interest groups bring to bear can be just as important. Early proponents did not present charter schools as market-based innovations but as a vehicle for decentralization within the public sector and a way to better mobilize the energies and ideas of parents and teachers at the community level. For tactical reasons relating to national partisan politics, however, some interests on the right found it advantageous to promote charters as a test case for markets. Charter schools need not have taken on this framing if the original concept had prevailed. Some moderate Democrats, including President Clinton, self-consciously attempted to create such a counter-frame—arguing that charter schools should be understood as examples of the so-called new public administration, a more flexible and responsive approach for government but certainly not an alternative to government. Others within the traditional left continued to regard charters as a stalking horse for vouchers and for privatization more broadly. Once this became the dominant frame, the stakes were grossly inflated.

Opponents of systemic privatization believe that conservative ideologues seek nothing short of a wholly dismantled welfare state and a return to a form of social Darwinism in which the rich—particularly those whose wagons are hitched to the wagon of global capitalism—get richer as the rest are forced further down the side streets of dependence and subsistence living. Proponents see every assertion about the limits of markets and the legitimate role of government in protecting social values as an effort by those who benefit from the government to mask their privilege. Because the two major political parties have aligned themselves at different points along the market-government continuum, partisan stakes are huge as well. Republicans present themselves as the party of the future and Democrats as defenders of an obsolete set of institutions and practices.

Citizens and more pragmatic politicians might wish that charter schools could be debated in less ideological terms, but for activists in both parties the current framing is useful. Many liberal Democrats think they win when Republicans can be portrayed as opposed to public education. Many conservative Republicans think they win when Democrats are portrayed as in the pocket of the unions. For neither group, then, is there an incentive to pull the fuse off the charter school issue.

The high-stakes, winner-take-all character of these politics accounts for much of the skittishness and hyperreactivity of school choice debaters, who have come to regard the arguments about school choice as freighted with connotations that go well beyond the particulars of the subject at hand. In this milieu, there is little room for research that admits to ambiguity, uncertainty, complexity, and mixed public-private solutions. These are weaknesses sure to be exploited by the other side.

What, though, of the possibility that research—carefully conceptualized, well-designed, objectively implemented, thoughtfully interpreted—might ratchet the debate out of the quicksand of ideological warfare? Is there an audience for good research that is sufficiently open to evidence to reconsider its interests and preconceptions in the light of what social science brings to bear? Is this audience powerful enough to have an impact on the political processes of decision making? The next chapter reviews the way charter school research, and school choice research more generally, has in fact been used in broad public discourse. This will not be the final word, but the story is discouraging. If research is seen as petty and partisan and a tactical weapon in political battles, its capacity to convince the convincible may be tragically undermined.

Chapter 4

Research in the Public Eye: Personalization, Polarization, and Politicization

Everybody is waiting for Godot. They are waiting for the final word that will then tell them whether vouchers and things like this are good. And that is never going to happen because the ideological filters are more powerful than any data results . . .

[R1]

We're talking about such a polarized field here, that there's nothing the AFT is going to put out that's not going to generate a response from certain groups. . . . I think that it's just a very politicized debate. People are assuming that research is coming from a particularly ideological perspective.

[R19]

Once somebody else brings a knife to the fight, you have to bring a knife to the fight, too.

[R5]

In 1991, when Minnesota put into place the nation's first charter school law, charter schooling was a little more than a notion. The notion was that schools would perform better if held accountable for results than constrained by bureaucratic regulations about process. This simple notion quickly became attached to more a general theory, one with broader application and more politically potent ramifications. The theory was that markets, and specifically competitive pressure to win and hold consumers, would generate efficiencies, stimulate innovation, better engage families, and weed out nonperformers. It was the link between charter schools and the general theory of markets, we have seen, that accounts for why this area of research has become a surrogate political battleground. In 1991, however, the first charter school had yet to

56

open. With no empirical evidence of their effects to battle over, debate was limited to clashing ideas, loosely aligned analogies, and symbolic and rhetorical appeals.

Since then, much has changed. Choice programs have moved from idea to reality. School vouchers—potentially the purest of market approaches to education reform—have titillated conservatives since Milton Friedman first proposed them in the mid-twentieth century, but remain limited in scope. Despite the 2002 United States Supreme Court ruling that voucher programs that include religious schools do not necessarily violate constitutional limits on church-state entanglements, voucher champions continue to be stymied by political resistance and legal obstacles at the state level. With the rapid spread of charter schools, however, market-oriented approaches to education are no longer simply a theoretically informed notion; they have become a significant element in the American education landscape. For choice proponents, this presents the opportunity to show that market processes could perform better than public monopolies. For skeptics, this provides the opportunity to show that their concerns about re-segregation, inequality, underfunding, and the loss of democratic control were not exaggerated. For those who believe in the ideal of informed democratic discourse, it means the opportunity for social scientists to inject conceptual clarity and a bracing dose of evidence into a debate too long driven by ideology and partisan maneuvering.

The expectation that research can help us learn from experience is the one we address here and in chapter 5. Has school choice research delivered the goods? A close and careful look at the research and its trajectory, I will argue in the next chapter, supports the encouraging conclusion that we can and are learning from the charter school experience, not only about charter schools themselves, but also about broader issues relating to government, markets, community, inequality, and race. This chapter focuses on the public face of research and highlights both a problem and reasons for alarm. For those who believe in the potential for social science research to fuel a more reasoned and informed democracy, the track record in the area of school choice and charter schools is—at least at first glance—hugely disillusioning. Based on what they read in the newspapers or hear from competing political candidates on Sunday morning news shows, informed citizens attempting to make sense of the school choice research can be forgiven if they are tempted to throw up their hands and say "it's all politics."

"In a perfect world, policy makers more interested in fashioning effective programs than in scoring partisan points could turn to academics to help cut through the rhetorical brawling," writes University of Nebraska political scientist Kevin Smith. "Unfortunately, it has not turned out that way" (2005, 285). Rather than cooling the histrionics, research—at least as it has stepped onto the public stage—has seemed to replicate or even amplify the strident and destructive forms of ideological trench warfare.

That the AFT report, a straightforward presentation of results downloaded from a Department of Education Web site, made it onto the front page of the *New York Times* might seem to show that the age of reasoned and scientifically informed discourse had arrived. Here, after all, is indirect evidence that the public wants and will receive the latest empirical information on an issue of national, state, and local concern. Even its prompt rebuttal in an advertisement endorsed by prominent researchers and highlighting proper standards for evidence and inference could be taken as a positive sign that debate would hinge on the quality of evidence instead of captivating anecdotes, ideological preconceptions, uninformed biases, and political muscle. This optimistic assessment, though, is thrown into question by the subsequent chain of events. The AFT report sparked not the first step in a public weighing of evidence but instead a quick descent into name-calling and caricature that could only reconfirm to many the suspicion that social science is little more than an additional arrow in the quiver of partisan advocates on either side of the great political debates.

The brouhaha over the study is not an aberration. It occurred against a backdrop of very public and personalized disputes that seem to belie the preferred self-image of research as cool, calm, collected, and collective. What's notable is not so much that there is disagreement and debate. Only the most unsophisticated adherents to the notion of the policy sciences imagine that research proceeds in a steady parade of scientific consensus, like a marching band in step and in tune. Tales about the intrigue and competition that marked the pursuit of major scientific undertakings like the discovery of DNA's double helix (Watson 1968) or the sequencing of the human genome (Shreeve 2004) make it clear that the pursuit of knowledge is messier and more contentious than that. Good research often challenges existing presumptions, and good researchers often show jealousy and zealotry in the pursuit of their vision of what is true.

There are risks, however, if the expected pull and tug of scientific pluralism turns into a barroom brawl. Let's you and I agree, at least for the moment, that social science research has something of potential value to contribute to a healthy democracy. I believe this, and I will present evidence later about how this is the case even in a seemingly polarized area like charter school research. Some, however, simply do not believe that science offers enough new knowledge or certainty to add much beyond what can be brought to bear based on faith, tradition, or common sense. Some think the ability to "lie with statistics" makes research more dangerous as a tool of manipulation than it is valuable as a tool of enlightenment. There are some signs of encroachments on the role of science in shaping public policy when the views of science do not align with partisan goals: an effort by political leaders to limit the independence of scientific advisers, for example, and to ensure that their views do not reach the public's ear until they have been made to conform to a set party line.[1] If the face of research on school choice and charter schools is personalization, polarization, and partisanship, the loss of authority and fueling of skepticism toward social science research may be further fed and its potential contribution to democratic discourse diminished as a direct result. As one advocate I spoke with put it, summarizing what the public may conclude if researchers on opposing side simply seem to cancel one another out: "Oh my God, these researchers, these social scientists, you know, piddling and piddling and one day it is this and one day it is that: a pox on all your houses" [A4].

What the Public Sees: Research as Tag Team Wrestling

The average citizen—and, for that matter, the average politician—is exposed to social science research, if at all, in small doses and indirectly. The scholarly journals that for many researchers are the favored path for disseminating their work have small circulations and are written for niche audiences with intense and specialized interests and a background familiarity with the jargon and previous studies. Other than the journals that come free to members of certain professional societies, the circulations are tiny. Even studies considered important and influential usually can count their citations in the hundreds, not thousands. Parents, voters, and public policy makers who want to know "what the research tells us," typically depend on other media to sort through the forests of research to identify studies worth talking about and to distill their findings into simpler terms.

The major media, however, do not devote a lot of time or prominent space to dissecting education research. As I discuss in chapter 7, even when newspapers write about education issues, the focus is more likely to be on matters such as hot debates at school board meetings than a detailed exegesis of the latest empirical study. Indeed, that the *New York Times* so infrequently devoted prominent coverage to charter school studies was one of the reasons charter school proponents reacted so vociferously when the AFT report erupted on the front page.

However, when school choice research has garnered attention, the picture often has not been pretty. The *Wall Street Journal*, for example, in 1996 and again in 2005 took the time to publish long articles beginning on the front page and delve deeply into some complicated methodological issues. These articles are both important and atypical because they represent the ascension of social science research to a much more prominent position than it typically enjoys. It was extraordinary for the paper to give a featured place and large amount of space to a detailed discussion of such things as randomized experiments versus statistical controls, and the proper and improper use of instrumental variables. "I thought that the [2005] piece was brilliant and I admired it greatly," said one education journalist at another major paper.

> I think I probably could have written that . . . but I couldn't have gotten that at such length in the metro section or the A section. It would not have been a front-page story probably. I probably could have written it for a magazine . . . if I had really juiced it up. But it takes a certain kind of a newspaper that is willing to sort of do this little fine grain thing and make it large. [J3]

The structure and content of the articles, though, reinforced the image of research as politicized, personalized, and petty, with findings as polarized as the partisan battles and neatly canceling out one another. This pattern, as we shall see, is repeated in the AFT report and response as well. Rather than displaying research as an arena distinguished by adherence to agreed-upon rules of science and to evidence as the final arbiter of disagreement, when research on school choice and charter schools climbs onto the public stage, the players at times have been presented as if they were wearing silly hats and hitting one another with water-filled balloons.

The Witte-Peterson Dispute

The 1996 article focused on research into the effectiveness of the Milwaukee voucher program, the nation's first real experiment with school vouchers, the ins and outs of which, accordingly, have been the focus of much attention (Davis 1996). It pitted John Witte, a University of Wisconsin political scientist, against Paul Peterson, a political scientist from Harvard. The State of Wisconsin had asked Witte to evaluate the Milwaukee program, and he had been issuing annual reports on its progress since 1991. Peterson was a scholar of substantial standing in the field, based on his earlier works on such issues as urban politics, federalism, and the political history of Chicago schools. Beginning in the 1990s, he began to be more and more identified by his work on school choice, work that was sharply critical of traditional public education systems and consistently supportive of moving toward vouchers.

"Education scholars were hoping the Milwaukee experiment would finally settle the question," wrote Bob Davis, the article's author. "Fat chance." Instead of converging on a cooler and clearer understanding of how the abstract market-based theories behind vouchers translated into real world consequences, he wrote, the research appeared to have done little more than add a new kind of fuel to the fires of ideological debate. "The Milwaukee voucher plan has become entangled in a brawl between two leading political scientists with clashing egos, ambitions and analyses. They look at the same student data and reach opposite conclusions. No matter."

In some senses, Witte's yearly reports on the Milwaukee program appeared to be the realization of the compelling notion of the policy sciences as elaborated on in chapter 2. Public officials often are wary about systematically studying something they have supported politically, sometimes because they are so unabashedly convinced it will work that they see further research as a waste of funds, sometimes because they are afraid of being embarrassed if research shows the program has not delivered as promised. In this case, though, the Wisconsin Department of Public Instruction asked Witte to evaluate the voucher program at the onset. He did so for five years, issuing annual reports that monitored implementation and outcomes, making the reports quickly available on the Internet for interested parties to download (a common practice now, but relatively unusual in the early 1990s). The reports were evenhanded in tone, longer on data than on interpretation or spin, and took care to remind readers that this was a policy in progress.

The structure of the early voucher program, too, conformed in some ways to the model proposed by advocates of what they called an experimenting society.[2] Donald Campbell, an influential psychologist, proposed that the nation should become an experimenting society that tries out new programs using controlled designs and systematically analyzes outcomes before adopting them on a wider scale. Rather than make vouchers universally available from the outset, the Wisconsin legislature had limited them to low-income families and imposed a cap on how many vouchers could be used in a given year, which made it possible, at least in theory, to delay decisions about how large a commitment to make until preliminary evidence began to accumulate. The findings, as they unfolded, were illuminating. Some seemingly confirmed hopes of voucher proponents (parent satisfaction; low income minority parents will take advantage); some failed to confirm these hopes (test scores); some confirmed fears of opponents (even with a strict income cap, there was evidence that the better educated households were more likely to exercise choice), and some suggested those fears were overdrawn.

Witte characterizes himself as a positivist—a firm believer in the importance of relying on evidence rather than ideology—and, if anything, someone who leans toward a favorable view of choice (2000). Peterson and other voucher proponents, however, argued that Witte's stance of open-mindedness was a guise. As the *Wall Street Journal* article related, Peterson had charged in a critique circulated to the Wisconsin legislature that "the real Mr. Witte, 'the unabashed critic' of vouchers, hides behind the facades of an objective social scientist and a friend of voucher schools" (Davis 1996). Peterson ultimately got access to the data that Witte had used for his analysis. Using a different type of analysis,[3] Peterson concluded not only that vouchers were having a positive effect on test scores, but also that the effect was sizable enough that, if extrapolated to all white and minority students in the United States, it would have the potential to eliminate most of the achievement gap in reading and all of it in math.

Looked at one way, the Witte-Peterson exchange exhibited attributes of the scientific enterprise as it ought to unfold. Here were two established and respected social scientists focusing on an issue of immediate policy relevance, and demonstrating, through the application of different techniques, how methodological choices can affect findings. Peterson's argument that experimental controls can be superior to statistical ones was legitimate and important, and foreshadowed the heavy emphasis on randomized field trials that the United States Department of Education would adopt some five years later. His recognition that a lottery structure like that associated with the Milwaukee voucher program provided an opportunity to compare outcomes of students in choice programs to those of students whose families also tried to get them into such programs, and therefore were likely similar in important respects, would become a favored method for evaluating charter schools.

Peterson's aggressive and complete dismissal of Witte's findings was misleading at best, however. Many charter and choice supporters then and since continue to rely on nonexperimental findings when they conform to their preferred outcomes (Carnoy et al. 2005; Hess 2006). Peterson's own subsequent work, which included lottery-based experimental analyses of private voucher programs in New York City, Dayton, and Washington, D.C., revealed that applying a randomized design does not in and of itself free researchers from having to make design, measurement, and interpretive choices open to subsequent challenge. Nor, because the experimental sites have idiosyncrasies, does it permit definitive, universally framed conclusions such as those Peterson offered at the time. The exchange might have unfolded as an illustration of collective learning in which researchers push one another toward sharper thinking and stronger evidentiary claims. The Milwaukee program, however, was invested with too much symbolic pressure as being *the* national experiment with choice, and the highly charged partisan conflict over markets and privatization generated too much actual pressure to draw any clear and decisive lesson. An in-depth feature article such as that offered by the *Wall Street Journal* might have been an opportunity to highlight both how research could help illuminate the issues and how much still remained to be learned.

Although the article delved into some of the methodological issues that may have accounted for the differences in findings, readers could not be blamed for concluding that research was less illumination and more a schoolboy spat. "The two men have come to despise each other, with Mr. Witte at the Milwaukee university calling his foe a 'snake' and Mr. Peterson shooting back that Mr. Witte's work is 'lousy.'"[4] Davis concludes his *Wall Street Journal* article pessimistically: "So after four years of charge and countercharge, the results of the Milwaukee experiment remain ambiguous. Mr. Witte doesn't plan to lead a new voucher-research project. 'The payoffs are too low, and the dangers too high,' he says." Rather than whetting political leaders' appetite for more research, the high-profile, acrimonious debate was enough to convince Wisconsin leaders that research was more trouble than it was worth. The acrimony over the voucher fight grew so intense that the Wisconsin legislature called off new evaluations until 2000. Subsequently, the Wisconsin legislature for a time gave up on evaluation altogether, ironically doing so at the very time that the program was beginning to get larger and potentially more consequential.[5]

Round 2: Rothstein Versus Hoxby

Nine years after the Witte-Peterson altercation, readers of the *Wall Street Journal* were treated to another front-page story on school choice; one with almost eerie parallels. Like its predecessor, it gave an impressive prominence and space to arcane matters of measurement and research design. It too featured drawings of the principal opponents (economists this time), lacing the description of social science methodology with comments about their personalities and backgrounds. Once again, charges of bias and a tone of vitriol and charges were prominent.

Like Paul Peterson, Caroline Hoxby was a Harvard professor who had been highly vocal and highly cited in support of school choice, vouchers, and charter schools. As mentioned earlier, it was Hoxby who rushed after the AFT report to release a preliminary version of a study claiming that charter schools significantly improved student achievement. But the focus in the *Wall Street Journal* article was an earlier study she had conducted that had become a standard citation in the school choice field. "Does Competition Among Public Schools Benefit Students and Taxpayers?" did not look directly at vouchers or charter schools. Instead, it attempted to indirectly assess the impacts of markets and competition by comparing what happens in metropolitan areas in which there is a lot of competition among school districts to those in which there is only a little. The logic of her analysis was compelling. In metropolitan areas where there are many districts, families will have numerous options about where to live. School districts, in turn, presumably have to compete to attract families. If competition provides the necessary spark for innovation and efficiency—as the market theories behind school choice proposals contend—those high-competition metropolitan areas should be the places in which schools are doing the best job.

What made Hoxby's article first famous[6]—and later infamous—was the way she solved a particular methodological challenge. Conceivably, the number of school districts in a metropolitan area could be the consequence, rather than the cause, of school quality. This could happen, for example, if citizens seeking to escape poor schools successfully pressured state legislatures to create and protect small, buffered school districts. Economists, facing this kind of methodological challenge, often rely on a statistical technique using what are known as instrumental variables—those correlated with the independent variable of interest (in this case, the number of districts in the region) but not likely to have a causal impact on the dependent variable (in this case, school quality). Hoxby chose to use counts of the number of large and small streams running through the region as her instrumental variable, reasoning that waterways as natural barriers historically have played a role in determining where jurisdictional boundaries lie and how many there will be (a place with numerous rivers being more likely, then, to have developed multiple jurisdictions) but that rivers and streams could not conceivably make children do better or worse on standardized exams. With this at the root of her analysis, she found a clear relationship between competition and school outcomes. Increased choice among districts led not only to substantially higher levels of student achievement, but also to lower levels of per pupil costs (Hoxby 2000).

The cleverness and decisiveness of her presentation helped make the article highly cited. Google Scholar, for example, indicated on December 11, 2006, that it had been cited at least 309 times. Five years after its publication, however, Hoxby's analysis was sharply criticized by Jesse Rothstein, a Princeton economist, who raised questions about the accuracy of her data and the substance of her claims (2005).

Jon Hilsenrath, the 2005 *Wall Street Journal* reporter, described the resulting attention as "a bitter dispute . . . that is riveting social scientists across the country." Rothstein released his analysis as a working paper on the National Bureau of Education Research (NBER) Web site. The NBER is a private, nonprofit, nonpartisan research organization "committed to undertaking and disseminating unbiased economic research among public policymakers, business professionals, and the academic community."[7] Its working paper series has become a favored vehicle for economics researchers to get their work out and widely read more quickly than through the traditional journal route.[8] After attempting to replicate Hoxby's analysis, Rothstein concluded that "Hoxby's positive estimated effect of interdistrict competition on student achievement is not robust, and that a fair reading of the evidence does not support claims of a large or significant effect" (2005, 2).

Replication is, in principle, a cornerstone in the foundation of the scientific method. Collective learning is expected to accumulate through cross-checking and the aggregation of evidence—not, with rare exceptions, through paradigm-busting findings from a single study that resolves past uncertainties and generates a new consensus from which to proceed. It is because cross-checking through replication is important that good scientific technique requires researchers to clearly spell out the steps of their designs. These include the details about instruments, measures, and conditions that others would need to understand to see whether a particular study's findings are robust enough to stand up to alternative specifications in process and context. Various factors make replication efforts less common in policy research than one would like. Probably the most important are the incentives to researchers to do something new and different. Simple replications, especially if they confirm what others had previously found, might be valuable for societal learning, but add little to personal scholarly reputation. They also risk being rejected for publication by reviewers or editors who see them as predictable and stale. Here, in Jesse Rothstein's paper, was a classic effort at replication of a study that many had cited but few had closely probed. For researchers who share a view of the enterprise as collective and cumulative, having one's study subjected to such reanalysis might be a welcome, even flattering, invitation for a productive exchange. In the high stakes spotlight of the school choice debate, however, that was not how the story unfolded.

Hoxby replied, but only partly in kind. In a paper also posted on the NBER site, she presented a similarly detailed rebuttal, but where Rothstein had framed his points drily and buried any direct criticism in references to glitches and anomalies, Hoxby was much more biting. Stating that she had reviewed every claim "of any importance" that Rothstein had made, she concluded that every claim was "wrong." She charged Rothstein with being confused, relying on innuendo, presenting her work as his own, making bad decisions "repeatedly" and worse. "It should surprise no one," Hoxby wrote, "that if a person makes a determination to change data and specifications until a result disappears, he will eventually succeed" (2005a, 30). Hilsenrath reported on the subsequent exchange in which Rothstein complained of Hoxby's "name-calling" and "ad hominem attacks" and she accused him of "ideological bias." Even John Witte, a veteran of the politicized squabbling over school choice research, was taken aback. "They're fighting over streams," he told Hilsenrath, "It's almost to the point where you can't really determine what's going on." An economics blog, Hilsenrath concluded, "sums up the squabble as a 'nerdy Celebrity Death Match'" (2005, A1).

The AFT Report and Response Reflected in the Public Arena

Both charter school proponents and critics at times have, for varying tactical reasons, taken the stance that the AFT report was not a "real study" at all. For critics, this fueled their indignation that the *New York Times* had given the report so much publicity and credibility at the same time that other and better studies were being ignored. For defenders of the report and of the *Times'* decision to write about it, this provides the explanation for why the data should be considered credible and authoritative despite the fact that the organization bringing it to light was a teachers' union with a presumed stake in defending the traditional public school system. The AFT Web site, for example, characterizes the argument that the NAEP results are tainted because they come from the AFT as "false claim #2" in a strong counterattack to criticisms they attribute to their opponents. "The recently released scores are not AFT data," reads their rebuttal. "They're a presentation by the AFT of the NAEP data" (AFT 2004).

The AFT is not at its core a research organization. It is a union and proud of it. Established in 1916, it defines its mission in part as to "represent the economic, social and professional interests of classroom teachers."[9] With about 3,000 local affiliates and claiming more than 1.3 million members, it is a substantial component of the broader national labor movement, an affiliate of the AFL-CIO. The AFT is smaller, and some would say feistier, than the National Education Association (NEA), the larger of the two major teacher unions in the United States.

The AFT does have a research operation of its own, but as a proportion of the overall organization it is a minor actor, and only rarely does it undertake original research projects. Compared to the NEA, it was late to develop its own research operation, and its commitment to research has never quite been as strong as that of its sister union (Vinovskis 2000). According to Howard Nelson of the AFT, the role of research is "evolving," broadening from an instrumental focus on bread-and-butter issues to encompass broader issues where research is needed to arm the organization in political battles. Partly, this is a defensive reaction to the fact that other organizations—especially more conservative think tanks—have greatly expanded their use of research.

"If other people are throwing studies out there," Nelson observes, "you need to be able to respond" (personal interview).

Research is meant to serve the interests of the organization, but those at the top often need to be convinced that it is worthwhile. That is partly because research is costly, and the national organization needs to be able to demonstrate that it is using its money in ways that affiliates and members see as serving their interests. It is also because, strategically, the AFT recognizes that research it conducts will not have the same credibility as studies done by others in universities or independent think tanks. "Because, as an example, if [prominent economist] does a study it gets enormous credibility and it could be exactly the same study that we might do," Nelson explains. "So we talk about this, and we are completely comfortable going 'oh we don't need to do work in this area' because so and so is already . . . doing the research that we would like to do if nobody else is doing it" (personal interview). But independent researchers cannot always be counted on to come up with results that neatly align with the union's mission and message. Even when they might, they often move at their own pace and are unlikely to frame their findings in quite the way the organization would wish.

Bella Rosenberg, in her own words, is "no highfalutin researcher," but she is the impetus behind the original AFT charter school report. Rosenberg came to the AFT in the early 1980s, in the first half of the Albert Shanker regime, and remained there until she left the organization in late 2005. Shanker often drew on published research to account for positions he took in his speeches and the columns he placed as paid advertisements in major newspapers. One of Rosenberg's responsibilities was to keep him abreast of the research literature. Shanker, besides being one of the intellectual founders of the original charter school idea, was also a major voice in support of national standards and national data systems to assess outcomes. Rosenberg had thus also followed the NAEP closely. It was through monitoring the meetings the National Assessment Governing Board (NAGB), which Congress created in 1988 to oversee and set policy for NAEP, that she became aware of available but not publicized data on charter school performance. She recalls reading an article about an NAGB meeting, sometime in the spring of 2004, that briefly mentioned about a delay in the release of charter school data. "And I looked at it, and the back of my neck started to go up" (personal interview). It reminded her of an earlier meeting when she had heard about charter schools being included in the NAEP data. At the time, the allusion had slipped past her, but now she began to look deeper into the matter.

From Rosenberg's and Nelson's perspective, they were not so much conducting a study as they were trying to bring to light data that they were convinced—and remain convinced—the Department of Education was deliberately keeping under wraps. Certainly interest in finding out what the NAEP data would show about charter schools was widespread. Indeed, in 2002, NAGB had decided to expand data collection on charter schools to ensure a nationally representative sample and thus meaningful inferences about how the sector was performing. Some of those who had pushed for this effort did so because they expected that the results would be favorable to charters.

When the regularly scheduled report was released in November 2003, it included no discussion of the charter school results. National Center for Education Statistics (NCES) officials announced at the time that the special report on charter schools scheduled for January 2004 would be delayed until June. In March 2004, according to the AFT, NAGB members were given a summary of the results in a closed-door meeting but still expected the report in June. Then, in May 2004, NAGB was told that there would be another delay—until December—and a change in the report's planned format.

The Bush administration and the Department of Education aggressively promoted charter schools. If the data on charter school performance existed but was not being publicly discussed, Rosenberg and Nelson concluded that something in the data reflected poorly on charter schools. Using the data tool that the Department of Education Web site makes available for extracting information online, they were able to generate a comparison between charter and noncharter public schools. Doing this, they say, was challenging: the system made it hard to find what they needed.

This is one of several points on which various principals disagree. Charter school proponents and the Department of Education maintain that the information was public rather than hidden: after all, it was available on the Web site for anyone to find and download. The Department of Education "just didn't put blinking arrows" leading to it [R6]. The AFT argues that this is disingenuous; if it were easy to find these data, they reason, others would have already done so.

> NCES never announced publicly that the NAEP scores were available on the NAEP Data Tool—an unprecedented and unwise handling of data that were supposedly made public. Independent researchers could learn of the data's existence on the Data Tool only by reading the minutes of NAGB board meetings. But, until AFT's researchers uncovered the charter school scores, no outsider seemed to know the data could be accessed. (AFT 2004)

The AFT argues that the administration was deliberately delaying a promised report on the results, hoping to hold this off to a less sensitive time, presumably after the upcoming election. NCES answers that delays were necessary to ensure that the analysis was accurate.

The AFT also was concerned that NCES was proposing to have the December 2004 report present a sophisticated multilevel (HLM) quantitative analysis rather than the more basic descriptive reports that were the norm for the agency's NAEP reports. NCES claimed that this more sophisticated analysis was necessary to take into account the fact that charter schools and traditional public schools are serving different populations. The AFT argued that this was both a violation of NAGB's norms and of specific policy. Out of concern that statistical adjustments of NAEP data would be "subject to serious methodological and political challenges,"[10] NAGB had decided in 1989 that only the straight descriptive results would be reported. This position had been reconfirmed after further discussion in 1994. At that meeting, according to the AFT report, then NAGB member Chester Finn was recorded as saying that "while it was proper for researchers to prepare adjusted scores, it would be wrong for them to [sic] part of a government report, such as NAEP. He said such scores would damage the credibility of program [sic]" (Nelson, Rosenberg, and Van Meter 2004, 2).

The union argued it was not conducting original research product as much as liberating data that were being held hostage. It also insisted it needed to do this lest the Bush administration bury the results until the multilevel analysis was complete.

As discussed earlier, what the AFT investigators found was that students attending charter schools by and large were doing no better, and arguably somewhat worse, than students attending traditional public schools. The data allowed them to look at both math and reading scores for both fourth and eighth graders and they could measure achievement by average test scores, by the percentages reaching the Basic and the Proficiency levels. Table 4.1 summarizes the overall pattern, showing where average scale scores differed by statistically significant de-

Table 4.1   Charter School Achievement on 2003 NAEP AFT Report

Average Scale Score	All Students	Eligible Free Lunch	Central City	Minority
Grade 4 math	Advantage noncharter	Advantage noncharter	Advantage noncharter	—
Grade 4 reading	Advantage noncharter	Advantage noncharter	—	—
Grade 8 math	—	Advantage noncharter		
Grade 8 reading	—	—		

Source: Author's compilation; Nelson, Rosenberg, and Van Meter 2004.
Note: Statistically significant results reported. Sample sizes did not allow for comparisons based on city location or racial status in grade 8.

grees. Overall, traditional public school students did better than charter schools students, with the differences meeting tests of statistical significance (meaning there was a less than 5 percent likelihood that they were due to chance) in fourth grade math and reading. Because it was possible that the two types of schools were serving different kinds of students, the AFT report offered several rather basic tests to determine whether score differences were due to poverty (measured by eligibility for free lunch programs), race, or location in central city. Traditional public schools outscored charters in all but one of these comparisons,[11] with the difference meeting tests of significance for low-income children in fourth grade math and reading and eighth grade reading, and for central city children in fourth grade math.

From the AFT to the New York Times

It took only about a week for Nelson, Rosenberg, and Nancy Van Meter to produce a first draft. Once they saw the results, they knew the information could be provocative. Before they could go public, however, they needed to get clearance within the organization. It took only about a week to draft, but circulating it within the organization and getting approval to go public took nearly a month. Even after approval to go public was secured, more questions arose about how to get the information out.

Concern is justified when the lines between scholars and advocates get blurred. Scholars, by and large, have a powerful motivation and incentives to get findings disseminated to interested audiences regardless of their substance; advocates can have very good reason to keep some findings to themselves. In criticizing the administration for delaying its report, the AFT stands proudly on the side of public information for an informed democracy. Even when the shape of the findings were apparent, however, it was by no means certain that the union leadership was going to approve the release of a report bearing the organization's name.

Charter school proponents present the AFT as an unambiguous and powerful opponent of charter schools. As noted, some of them scoff at the union's frequent claim that Albert Shanker was a founding father of the charter school notion. Shanker, they imply, was talking about a highly regulated, teacher-dominated concept unlike the market-based, consumer-driven vision many contemporary advocates favor. To its critics, the union's claim that it only wants to make sure that charter schools are good schools is disingenuous, little more than a pretense for regulating charter schools so heavily that they mimic all that is bad about the traditional system. Based on their portrayal, the union was salivating at the chance to discredit charters and would do anything in its power to play the findings to bring this about.

It is true that the AFT's professed support for charters is partly tactical, designed to allow them to look responsive to reform pressure while fighting off more extreme market-based proposals like universal voucher programs. It is an oversimplification, though, to assume that the AFT organization is unified in its opposition to charters and always eager to take a public role in the debate. As Bella Rosenberg put it, "we had a lot of internal wrestling about this" (personal interview).

Although many in the union's national leadership are wary of charters because they see them as a stalking horse for more radical reforms, local affiliates and their members are more divided. Some are excited about charter schools as a vehicle for freeing them from what they consider stultifying local district bureaucracies. Significantly, the lines of support and wariness toward charters run somewhat along sensitive racial and ethnic lines, with some minority teachers quicker to see charters as a potentially empowering reform. Added to the risk of creating internal dissension was the risk of alienating groups that they might want help or support from on non–choice-related issues. These included New Democrats, who had adopted strong pro-charter positions but were natural union allies on some other issues, and the administration, an unlikely ally on any front, but a powerful force with which it made sense to pick battles carefully. At the time, the union leadership was more concerned with blocking the administration's effort to institute a voucher program in the District of Columbia and "there was some thinking that to be effective in the voucher fight it was a good idea to be neutral and passive in the charter school fight because charter schools are public schools" [A4]. All things being equal, the AFT wanted the information in the report to get out, but that did not necessarily mean that it wanted to be the one getting it out.

Union leadership's approval to release the report eventually was granted, but the ambivalence may have played a role also in the decision about how to do so. The standard option would have been to prepare a big press release, possibly hold a press conference. For some issues that makes the most sense for at least two reasons. First, it has a chance to make the information and the organization visible to many more people, creating a stir and generating coverage across the different types of media and in many geographic markets. Second, it has the potential to excite and rally the membership, to remind them why they are paying union dues. These arguments seemed less compelling in this case. The newsworthiness of the report might be weakened by its obvious association with the AFT; some might see the portrayal of disappointing charter school performance as a predictable and therefore uninteresting claim by a partisan interest group. In addition, there were enough currents of disagreement about charter schools within the broader union membership that this was not the most promising issue around which to attempt to rally the troops. They took another tack instead. "We decided that rather than have a big deal press release and invite everybody, that we would be more passive and therefore appear more scholarly, or more neutral" [A4].

The decision was made to offer the story as an exclusive to a reporter at a major newspaper. That, presumably, would increase the likelihood that the paper would use the use the report as a news peg for a longer and more prominently featured article. Furthermore, though it would still be clear that the extraction of the data was done by the AFT, the article might put more emphasis on the fact that it relied on well-established, trustworthy data collected by a government agency.

The first place they went was not the *New York Times*. A reporter at another prominent paper was interested but "the editor said that, well, we are not surprised that charter schools would do worse because they have kids that are harder to educate so there is no news here" [A4]. The *Times*, and Diana Schemo, was the second stop.

Schemo was a seasoned reporter who had been covering education for the *Times* for about three and a half years. Some critics of the *Times* article have publicly claimed that Schemo was not familiar with education, having previously covered primarily Latin America, but that is not really the case. During the 1980s, she reported on poverty and social services at the (now defunct) *Baltimore Evening Sun*, and then served as the *Baltimore Sun* bureau chief in Paris and Berlin. She moved to the *New York Times* in the early 1990s, serving as bureau chief in Rio de Janeiro from 1995 to 1999, where she covered Brazil, Venezuela, Colombia, Ecuador, and Paraguay. She also covered metro news, religion ,and culture for the *Times* and had been doing education out of the Washington bureau since September 2000. A search on ProQuest shows that she had published 878 articles since coming to the *Times*, with more than 200 of them on education issues. Many of her previous articles had dealt with issues relating to test scores or other measures of student outcomes,[12] and she had also written generally about national education politics[13] and school choice.[14]

Rosenberg was the person who brought the story to Schemo, who'd had at least some contact with the AFT before.[15] Until she had interviewed Rosenberg for a different article around June 2004, however, they'd had little or no contact. According to Bella Rosenberg, "I didn't know her from a hole in the wall" (personal interview).

How The Times *Handled and Presented the AFT Report*

Schemo had written stories about NAEP test results before. She knew that many considered NAEP the gold standard for gauging academic competence. As a reporter at a newspaper with a national audience, she also was attracted by the fact that this would provide a chance to examine national data of charter school performance. "Until then, all the reports had involved charters in a specific state, not across the country." That she was familiar with the data made it easier for her to understand the report and to check its overall accuracy. "I've written many times before about NAEP," she notes, "so I was not totally at a loss upon seeing the NAEP results. I checked the figures against what was buried in the NAEP Web site" (email correspondence).

Schemo knew that the AFT was not a disinterested collection of scholars. These meant she had to exercise caution, but it did not in her mind necessarily discredit the data in the report or undermine its significance.

> Of course, the teachers' union would have its spin on data, and the Center for Education Reform (or the Department of Education itself) would have another spin. But part of covering this story was evaluating the data independently, by sending it around, getting feedback and thinking it over myself. That's why this story didn't run 24 hours after the AFT gave me the report, but took a full week to report out and write. (email correspondence)

Having the opportunity to treat this as an exclusive meant that Schemo did not have to rush a story out to beat the competition. She spent a week sending the charts to a number of experts, some but not all of whom ultimately were quoted in the article. These included Amy Stuart Wells (Teachers College, Columbia), who was considered a skeptic on the school choice and charter school issue; Chester Finn (Fordham Foundation), considered a generally strong proponent of charters and choice; and James Cibulka (dean, University of Kentucky College of Education), Tom Loveless (Brookings), and Ron Zimmerman (RAND), who were not firmly identified in either camp. Schemo also interviewed Jeanne Allen from the Center for Education Reform, not for a researcher's expert reaction but to get commentary from a clear pro-choice advocate. "In each case," says Schemo, "I just sent the data, not the accompanying report, because I wanted each source to evaluate and respond to the test scores, not to a side issue, like who came up with them" (personal interview). Some later criticized Schemo for this, arguing that the fact that the data came from the AFT was important to the context. Finn was quoted in the article as saying: "The scores are low, dismayingly low" and "A little more tough love is needed for these schools. . . . Somebody needs to be watching over their shoulders" (Schemo 2004a, A1). That a known proponent of charters and choice appeared to accept the core finding added credibility to the study and to the article, but when Finn later found out about the AFT's involvement he felt sandbagged. As he remembers it, Schemo

> inveigled me into commenting on tables that she didn't tell me where they had come from. She had faxed me some tables from a forthcoming study without any attribution as to their source. And I looked at them fairly casually and mouthed off a few sentences of comment the gist of which I didn't think was a satisfactory performance from what I was seeing by charter schools and thought that was the end of it. Little did I know at the time either that the study was the AFT's nor that I would be the chief vindicator of the AFT in paragraph 2 or 3 or 4, whatever it was of her article a day or two later. . . . So I felt ill-used actually by the *New York Times*. (personal interview)

Critical to Schemo's thinking was her belief that the story had to do with the data and not who happened to download that data and bring it to her attention: "As far as I was concerned, these were U.S. government figures, not AFT figures. The AFT just happened to dig them up" (personal interview).

Schemo's insistence on getting expert and advocate responses to the basic data made the union nervous. This was not because they thought that experts would discredit their basic finding—they had been careful and were confident this would hold up to scrutiny—but because they feared that pro-choice groups would get wind of the forthcoming article and have more of an opportunity to mobilize their counterattack. One of the conditions the union had agreed to with Schemo, was that they would not leak the results to their own affiliates before the article appeared. "Well, that was an agony for us," Bella Rosenberg recalls.

> Because here we were, by the terms of this we couldn't send it out to our people...and we really struggled with that. Because we figured that some of those people would be our enemies. . . . And they would get the word out, and they would be all prepared. . . . And we couldn't even send it to our own people. (personal interview)

Deconstructing the Article

The *Wall Street Journal* did not give the AFT charter school study the same kind of prominent attention that it offered the tag-team match-up between Witte and Rothstein versus Peterson and Hoxby. The *New York Times*, which did give it prominent first-page status, did not present researchers and research as ideologically infused in the same way that the *Wall Street Journal* seemed to: it did not present the issue either with the same degree of personalization nor the same close reading and methodological scrutiny.

Taken on its own terms, the article provided a more positive image of research and the role it might play in leading toward a more informed policy. One way it did this was by minimizing the focus on the AFT as an advocacy group. To many observers, the union is a far cry from a reliable research organization. Choice proponents in particular see it as an advocacy group that professes to be open-minded about charters but works behind the scene to weaken charter laws and undermine the charter movement. As one researcher who is generally seen as being in the pro-choice camp explains,

> I think it is always surprising when anyone takes an AFT study or a union study at face value because they are an interest group. They are not a research group that is interested in the truth and that suffers like all of us academics suffer, when we [researchers] are wrong. You know, we have a stake in being correct because if we are not, then our reputation suffers. They are an interest group and so they do have an axe to grind and you know what they are going to come up with. I mean they are opposed to charter schools and they are going to come up with something negative. [R8]

The *Times* item did not mention the AFT until almost one-third of the way through the article[16] and then characterized it as an organization that "has historically supported charter schools but has produced research in recent years raising doubts about the expansion of charter schools" (Schemo 2004a, A1). This was seen by charter advocates, and some others besides, as misleading precisely because it seemed willfully ignorant of the fact that the union might have produced the report and then selectively released it to the *Times* for tactical reasons having more to do with political objectives than the enrichment of public knowledge. Although that description of the AFT's formal stance is basically accurate, critics contend with some justification that it downplays the union's general orientation against market-oriented choice policies in favor of its tactically designed position of supporting regulated charters as a way to better enable them to block vouchers and more unrestrained charter school policies.

A second way that the article presented research in a more positive light was by quoting and citing sources in a way that reflected their differences in interpretation and emphasis, rather than pitting them head-to-head with each criticizing the fundamental integrity of the other. Instead of discounting the findings entirely, those generally more sympathetic to charters emphasized the incompleteness of the findings, in particular the need to better take into account the characteristics of the students and whether charter school performance might be improving over time. Jeanne Allen, according to the *Times* article, indicated that the results "reflect only 'a point in time,'" and said nothing about the progress of students in charter schools." But Allen also found something positive in the data to interpret as supportive of the charter school movement, "suggesting that charters take on children who were already performing below average. 'We're doing so much to help kids that are so much farther behind, and who typically weren't even continuing in school'." Schemo devoted a paragraph to Tom Loveless's "two-year study of 569 charter schools in 10 states [which] found that while charter school students typically score lower on state tests, over time they progress at faster rates than students in traditional public schools." And the article ended by quoting Robert Lerner, then the federal commissioner for education statistics, who did not challenge the data—which, after all, had been produced by his agency—but simply emphasized the need for additional and more sophisticated analysis.

> But Mr. Lerner said he thought such an analysis was necessary to put the charter school test scores in context. He called the raw comparison of test scores "the beginning of something important," and said, "What one has to do is adjust for many different variables to get a sense of what the effects of charter schools are." (Schemo 2004a, A1)

The *Times* coverage, compared to the two front-page *Wall Street Journal* articles discussed earlier, deemphasized how politics can infuse research, but it had quite a lot to say about how politics can influence whether research reaches the public. Although the headline and first paragraph focused on the substantive findings, the second sentence located the debate in the broader national political context, in which the Bush administration was seen as supportive of charter schools and complicit in a process of keeping potentially embarrassingly evidence hidden: "The findings, buried in mountains of data the Education Department released without public announcement, dealt a blow to supporters of the charter school movement, including the Bush administration" (Schemo 2004a, A1). In a very real sense the article had two stories embedded: the one about charter school performance and the one about the Administration's reluctance to have that first story come to light.[17] Indeed, a number of those interviewed for this book speculated that it was this second story line that may have accounted for the *Times'* decision to give the story such prominent placement.

The New York Times *Ad: Scientific Rigor—or Politicization—Affirmed?*

The *Times* article presented researchers as engaged in civil discourse, calmly discussing ways in which further research could be improved, with the backdrop issue of bad-guy politicians attempting to keep important information from coming to light. In doing so, it both reflected and reproduced the historical view of policy sciences as an ideal, a way to bring more knowledge and expertise to the task of governance if only partisan politicians could be held at bay. Yet those paying reasonably close attention—those who followed subsequent developments, including the advertisement taken out by charter proponents and what was written in other media and education blogs—might have also noted a different tale, much like the one communicated in the 1996 and 2005 *Journal* articles pitting Peterson against Witte and Hoxby against Rothstein. That is, researchers are entrenched in firm and opposing camps, each side is equally armed with studies supporting its claims, and policy research is less a form of collective learning than a form of political warfare.

A day or two before the AFT story broke in the *Times*, Jeanne Allen received a call. Allen is the founder and president of the Center for Education Reform (CER), a Washington, D.C.-based advocacy group that has been a major voice in support of vouchers, charters, and school choice more generally. Before launching CER in 1993, Allen was a staffer at the conservative Heritage Foundation. CER received its early funding support from sharply conservative foundations with a free-market agenda, including Olin, Scaife, and Bradley. Nonetheless, CER has tried to position itself as a less openly ideological voice than Heritage. Allen suggests that it was in part a desire to escape the rigidity of ideology that led her in this direction.

> I felt like there was too much polarization ideologically and I felt like just because you are at a conservative think tank, people assume then that everything you are saying is conservative. No. Just because you are at a liberal place everybody thinks what you are saying is liberal. . . . So the idea was to actually create a mainstream group, regardless of what anybody's attachment had been before. And to try to reach out to people on the issues as opposed to the ideologies. (personal interview)

CER strategically has used original data collection as a way to position itself as a source of expertise about charter schools. Combining the collection of basic information on the number and type of charter schools with information about state laws and a process of scoring the extent to which the laws met CER's standards, the group's data is frequently cited by others—including journalists and social scientists—as the most up-to-date account of what is happening in the various states.

Allen recalls speaking with Diana Jean Schemo about the article while boarding a plane. Although she was somewhat relieved to hear that Schemo "actually did have a little teeny bit of balance," she characterized herself as outraged when she subsequently saw the published version, which in her judgment failed to adequately portray the points she had made to Schemo. But "the front page thing was what really took us by surprise" (personal interview).

Even before she knew the details of what the article would say and where it would appear, however, Allen was concerned.

> I was thinking we can't afford to let people wake up in the morning un-aware that this was coming. Legislators are coming back in September and here's another damning article about charter schools. So [I said to my staff] "what we are doing this week and next week is we are trying to grab people's attention so that we can positively influence their thoughts." The AFT was doing the same thing. So they needed to have some counter balance. What are parents going to think? What are policy makers going to think? What is every other member of the media going to say when they see that? Is it going to reach a level so the only sound bite people hear as they are driving to work or getting out of the shower is that charter schools are bad? (personal interview)

Left unchallenged, Allen feared the AFT study would do both im-mediate and sustained damage. The last time something somewhat like this had happened, she recalled, "there was a shelf life of twelve months." The likelihood of long-lasting damage, she felt, was greater now—in the age of the Internet—than it had been even five years be-fore. In the new era of Web-based research, one negative story, even if subsequently rebutted, could linger in cyberspace and continue to creep into the research of journalists, researchers, and others for years to come.

It's said that the best way to fight fire is with fire. Similarly, CER de-cided the best way to fight a claim about evidence in the *New York Times* was with another claim about evidence in the *New York Times*. It strate-gized about the pros and cons of various formats: "Is it a letter to the ed-itor, is it an op-ed, would they publish that? Could we get somebody else at the *New York Times* to write a piece? Do you go to the *New York Post*? It became very clear that if we wanted just as big a response it has to be a paid ad." The advertisement would cost $116,000. "And that is not something I take lightly," Allen notes. "But to be able to hit poten-tially thirty million people over time with an advertising drop that changes the dynamics of the debate, it would have cost us in human and other terms, probably half a million dollars to fight it over the next year" (personal interview).

The first step, even before the article came out, was to more or less in-oculate supporters at the grassroots level by making sure they knew what was coming and giving them enough information that they would know how to respond. This was an all-out effort. Allen said, "I mean it was absolutely directed, not accidental, because we felt like we had to have the same kind of war room as they did." According to Allen, there was "probably a larger flurry of activity across the country, coming through this office than we had ever seen on any issue" (personal interview).

The second step involved taking on the AFT and the *Times* head to head in a forum that would reach the same audience as the offending article did. As they sought input from specialists with whom the organization had good ties, CER discovered considerable indignation about the story within the research community and—significantly—that this indignation extended beyond the tight core of researchers who were already closely identified with the pro-charter school position.

Based on what it was hearing, CER decided that it might be possible to get a relatively broad assortment of researchers to allow their names to be used in an advertisement that would challenge the legitimacy of the report and the *Times'* coverage.

Allen, along with some of the strongly pro-choice researchers, began making calls. They deliberately reached beyond what might be referred to as the usual cast of characters, Paul Peterson, Caroline Hoxby, Jay Greene, and others who had prominently and consistently supported market approaches to educational reform.

They also called others who were seen as moderate voices who sometimes had produced research critical of some of the choice claims. Some of these less predictable folks agreed to sign on; others did not. John Witte was among those who did not. He strongly felt that the story was misleading, respected some of the people who ultimately did sign, and agreed with the thrust of the ad's argument when it appeared, but his relationship with Jeanne Allen had been contentious and he ultimately was not able to separate the ad from his mistrust of its sponsor. Gary Miron was another moderate researcher who refused to sign, largely because of his rocky relationship with Allen. "We lock horns, as you can imagine . . . she loves our findings one day and hates them the next" (personal interview). Allen called Miron herself, twice, and reminded him that he had always talked about the importance of using sound research designs and noting uncertainties and study limitations, suggesting that these were the very standards the proposed advertisement would underscore. She also worked hard to play down the CER connection. "She knew she was tailoring the message for me, so she said this is not CER. This is led by researchers, [they're] just asking me to help" (personal interview). But Miron was skeptical of this argument and leery about publicly criticizing Howard Nelson and the AFT for failing to meet elevated standards that very few studies—including those by other signatories—had managed to attain.

Other moderates, like the University of Florida economist David Figlio, did sign. Figlio had published some studies that were seen as broadly supportive of school choice. At the same time, he had also spoken openly about his unhappiness with researchers who are too quick to call a press conference, too willing to overinflate the implications of their findings. He believed that the *Times* had done a disservice to serious researchers who were more careful and attentive to methodology and the need for careful review.

> I was sufficiently outraged by the *Times* coverage of this that I was very happy to sign. In fact, even knowing how the ad could be used in some circles, I don't regret signing on to that ad because it was a statement of disgust with un-vetted research being given the type of prominence that it is. (personal interview)

The text of the ad (reproduced as Appendix 3) criticized the "prominent, largely uncritical coverage" that the *Times* had given to a study that "does not meet current professional research standards." It identified as the study's primary flaws, poor data quality, the lack of adequate background data on students and their families, and the fact that the test scores came from a single point in time. Because of these flaws, the study "tells us nothing about whether charter schools are succeeding." The ad suggests that journalists need to be especially critical of research sponsored by "interest groups engaged in policy debates" and suggests "such studies need to be vetted by independent scholars, as is commonly done in coverage of research on the biological and physical sciences." There was, according to the ad, one thing that the NAEP data did reveal: that charter schools tend to educate students who are relatively disadvantaged.

Most of the researchers signing off on the CER advertisement did so out of a belief that they were trying to elevate the level of public discourse and help articulate and lend authority to a vision of collective learning in which good social science would trump sham social science and evidence would trump ideology and partisan spin. My interviews make it apparent to me that many of the researchers active in this arena are personally wrestling with the tension between wanting to be relevant and helpful in meeting social needs, on the one hand, and being wary, on the other hand, of the distortions, simplifications, and misuses of evidence that seem at times to be endemic to interactions in the political sphere.

Regardless of the motivations of the signers versus those of the sponsor, any chance that the advertisement would mark an important first step in the direction of more reasoned debate and more sophisticated utilization of social science quickly evaporated.

That the ad was paid for by an advocacy group that was at least as firmly anchored in interest group politics as the AFT made it unlikely, in any event, that it would somehow elevate discourse above the historic political infighting. But this fate was ensured when one of the signers immediately released a study that fell far short of the standards the advertisement had proffered. Despite this new study's weaknesses, some of the other signers of the CER ad were soon rushing to trumpet its findings as important and unambiguous evidence for the superiority of charter schools.

Battling Studies: The Hoxby Study on Charter School Achievement

Caroline Hoxby does not mince her words. Her "initial response to the AFT study was that it was such a lousy study that it did not deserve a response. It did not deserve to be considered for even a few minutes" (Hoxby 2005b).

> Several people have asked me to debate another scholar about the AFT study. I've replied each time by saying that, if they could find me a scholar who will support the study, I'd be glad to debate him or her. Despite scouring the scholarly world, they've not been able to come up with a single serious researcher who will defend the AFT report.

Hoxby juxtaposed her vision of how social science should be used to inform debate with the standard met by the AFT study, and found the latter to be sadly lacking. "In America, we need to have education reform based on science if we're going to make progress," she declared. "Science is the standard we set for medical research. Why should we accept quackery for education?" Concerned about the attention being paid to the AFT study "probably owing to the *New York Times'* irresponsible coverage," Hoxby told an audience at the Manhattan Institute, a conservative think tank, this "eventually convinced me that it would be a good idea for someone to produce evidence that addressed the AFT study's most egregious failings" (Hoxby 2005b).

Within weeks of the *Times* article featuring the AFT report, Hoxby began disseminating a paper claiming to offer a methodologically and much more positive study of academic achievement in charter schools.[18] In that paper, Hoxby criticized the AFT study on several grounds, including its "crude" controls for student characteristics and that the NAEP data are based on only a sample of charter schools. Her study, she suggested, offered a better means of ensuring that apples were compared to apples. She would compare charter school students to students in the nearest public school and the nearest public school with a similar racial composition, under the assumption that these students would be drawn from the same neighborhood. Also, rather than a sample, she would include 99 percent of all fourth grade charter students in the country.[19] Hoxby's results indicated that, in most states and in the nation overall, charter schools were outperforming the comparison schools in both reading and math. Nationwide, charter school students were almost 5 percent more likely to be proficient in reading and about 2.5 percent more likely and math than students in the nearest traditional public school with a similar racial composition. In some states, the differences were huge. In the District of Columbia, which had by far the highest concentration of charter schools, her data suggested that charter school students were more than 36 percent more likely to be proficient in reading and more than 41 percent more likely to be proficient in math.

Charter school advocates were quick to promote Hoxby's study as a complete refutation of the AFT results. In mid-September, Chester Finn's electronic newsletter, *Education Gadfly*, announced that "Harvard economist Caroline M. Hoxby has just issued the most effective rejoinder to the misleading AFT 'study' of charter school achievement that's been much in the news of late: she's done a far better study, and it yields far different result" (Education Gadfly 2004). CER, on its Web site, judged that "Hoxby's study goes a long way in providing quantifiable proof of widespread charter success" (Center for Education Reform 2004).

Critics were almost as quick to attack Hoxby's study as charter advocates were to ballyhoo it. There were three lines of attack. First, some researchers challenged Hoxby's claims that hers was a superior design. Joydeep Roy and Lawrence Mishel, for example, questioned her assertion that her method of identifying comparison schools provided an adequate set of controls for student background characteristics known to be associated with test scores. When looking at the schools she claimed had "similar racial composition," they found that "the charter schools have a disproportionately higher black population (34% vs. 28%) and higher white population (43% vs. 36%), while the share of Hispanics is lower (18% vs. 30%)." They also found that her sample of racially similar charter schools had fewer low-income students than the public school comparison group (49 percent to 60 percent). When they statistically controlled for the racial differences, they concluded that Hoxby's claimed charter school advantage "vanishes" (Roy and Mishel 2005, 2-3).

Second, critics pointed to what they characterized as sheer hypocrisy. Hoxby was a signer of the CER advertisement, but her study violated several of the standards the ad had highlighted in critiquing the AFT study. Edward Fiske, a prominent journalist and former education writer for the *New York Times*, in an October 6 letter to the editor of *Education Week* wrote:

In fact, Ms. Hoxby's study can be faulted on the very same grounds that she and her colleagues quite appropriately critique the AFT report. Like the AFT comparisons, hers are based on student performance at only one point in time. But in contrast to the AFT report, which is based on data for individual students, she uses school averages. That means she uses no family-background data on students. Instead, she must take it as a matter of faith that students in charter schools have similar background charac- teristics as those in the "nearest" public school. Yet she accuses the AFT study of being "unsophisticated.". . . It appears that Ms. Hoxby's concept of "professional standards" rose dramatically between Sept. 8, 2004, and Sept. 15, 2004. Or perhaps her standards vary depending on the conclu- sions of the study in question. (Fiske 2004, 33)

Third, and even more telling, critics revealed that Hoxby's early Sep- tember 2004 version of this paper included serious errors. The most bla- tant of these involved Washington, D.C., where her report had claimed to find the sharpest advantages for charter schools. There are two pub- lic bodies with authority to charter schools in that city, but Hoxby in- cluded only schools chartered by the Public Charter School Board, an entity created by Congress and generally considered to be the more careful and professional of the two. As a result, her study failed to in- clude almost half of the charter schools for which test score data existed at the time. In addition, and even more consequential, Hoxby made a major error in the test scores she used to assess performance. For char- ter schools, she used figures used by the District to assess NCLB profi- ciency standards (set at the +fortieth percentile on SAT-9 in 2003). For her traditional public school comparison groups, she used data based on the much tougher definition of proficiency set by the company that designed the test. Finally, her identification of the nearest traditional public schools was suspect. When researchers at the AFT looked more closely, using driving distance as determined by MapQuest, they found a different set of comparison schools in almost every case. When cor- recting for these, the AFT found that the huge charter school advantage Hoxby reported actually turned into a small deficit (Nelson and Miller 2004).

What is significant here is not that Caroline Hoxby made a mistake. Even the most careful researcher makes mistakes. This is one reason why researchers who want to be accurate and who care about their pro- fessional reputations usually prefer to let their work percolate a while—ask colleagues to look it over, present it at conferences, go through the slow and sometimes tedious scholarly journal process of peer review before going fully public with a big bang. Hoxby, in Octo- ber, posted her paper to the Web site of the National Bureau of Eco- nomic Research. Economists frequently take this approach—both as a way to get their findings out more quickly to interested colleagues and as an opportunity to invite scrutiny that might uncover errors or suggest alternative interpretations. Moreover, Hoxby was quicker and more forthcoming than most researchers in making available to others the original data she used in the paper, including those, like the AFT, who were able to use that data to identify its flaws. Here, then, too, are hints of the kind of open exchange and reliability testing that proponents of social science see as one of its greatest advantages: the built-in process of self-correction.

Charter school proponents, however, did not simply sit back to wait until her paper had been tested in this way. Indeed, Hoxby herself sought out public venues in which to promote her findings as superior to those of the AFT. On September 14, for example, she appeared on the *Market Watch* program and told listeners that her study was superior because the union study depended on a tiny sample. Her study, she said, revealed that charter schools students are doing better. She went so far as to offer explanations of why that was the case:

> I think it's mainly better school management. It's principals and teachers making better decisions about how to manage classrooms. It's also principals making better decisions about how to hire teachers. They're more likely to pay teachers a bonus if a teacher is a high-performing teacher. Or if a teacher teaches in a subject where they have vacancies, like math and science. Some of it is better teachers. And a lot of it is better school management.[20]

Two weeks later, in an opinion piece in the *Wall Street Journal*, she advised readers to "Forget about studies that compare apples to oranges, based on tiny samples." She repeated her claim about charter school superiority, asserting "In fact, the more similar the schools are, the more positive the differences," and her claim that DC's charter school students were "about 36% more proficient in reading and math." Taking direct aim at the AFT, she added, "Disadvantaged children in the U.S. do not have a special interest group to get their version of things on front pages—but they deserve good education" (Hoxby 2004).

To many of the researchers who work in this area, not just those who are critical of school choice, the rush to promote the Hoxby study as an antidote to the AFT report was an example of the very politicization of evidence that the *Times* advertisement had decried. According to one researcher who has reported results both favorable to and critical of charter schools, the inconsistency between the high ground staked out by the advertisement and the heavy promotion of the Hoxby report was "so stupid." Didn't the signers know, he wondered "that Caroline Hoxby was going to release her study two days later? Caroline Hoxby signed this. . . . Look at her response. It was even as weak and limited and even more ridiculous in terms of violating all the things that were spelled out in that letter" [R17]. This researcher was getting calls asking for comment even before the reporters or the researcher had seen a full copy of the study.

> I was getting some things from some journalist who asked me to comment and I said, "Well, send me what you got from her so I can see." And they sent me these 3-to-5 page summaries of her report. And I told them, until you see the technical report, you shouldn't publish this. This is just research by press release. This isn't a technical report. [R17]

Moreover, this researcher emphasized that some of the errors Hoxby made were sufficiently obvious that they could have been caught and corrected easily had she allowed her draft to circulate quietly for more time. "And I was shocked to see these results, like D.C. doing 25% better than comparable groups. And these are just phenomenal differences that I just couldn't imagine that they could be so great."

In December 2004, Hoxby released a revised version of the paper that cleaned up many of the problems for which the earlier draft had been criticized. Consequently, her results for the District of Columbia changed. In the September paper, she had claimed that the nearest public schools in the District with similar racial composition had 36.6 percent lower proficiency rates in reading and 41.5 percent in math compared to charter schools. In the December paper, the comparable figures were 12.3 and 13.0. Despite this, based on other changes in the analyses and data, her bottom-line estimate of the national charter school advantage was even higher than in the earlier version.

As already noted, the fact that Caroline Hoxby made a mistake is not what is significant. What is significant is that the high-speed, high-stakes political debate over charter schools drew research into its vortex based more on whether the findings fit partisan arguments than on whether they were solid, reliable, and right.

More Sophisticated Analysis, Same Results: NCES-Sponsored Studies of Public, Private, and Charter Schools

In the CER-sponsored advertisement criticizing the *New York Times* coverage of the original AFT report, two of the major points highlighted were limited background information and unsophisticated analysis. The AFT presentation of the data was able to introduce some rough controls for student background—primarily race and eligibility for free-lunch. However, the researchers signing the advertisement noted that the analysis "did not take into account such key characteristics of students . . . as parental education, household income, and the quality of learning resources in the home." Even where the AFT tried to control for family background, its unsophisticated analysis "considers differences in only one family background characteristic at a time. To obtain accurate estimates, all available background characteristics must be considered simultaneously."

In December 2004, the National Center for Education Statistics did finally release its analysis of the 2003 NAEP data on which the AFT report had been based.[21] This was the long-promised report that the AFT had suspected the administration of hiding. This study was largely descriptive and not much more sophisticated than the AFT's, but because it came from a putatively objective government agency rather than a deeply invested interest group, its findings had a sheen of legitimacy that the union's had not. That said, the findings were broadly similar: at best charter schools students were holding their own. In the press conference at which the study was released, Eugene Hickcok, the outgoing deputy secretary of education, put to rest any naïve speculation that the administration was ready to let even its own evidence trump its established policy positions. "In case there's any doubt, we are big supporters of charter schools," Hickcok asserted. "So as I read these studies on charter schools, I read them through that lens." Hickcok emphasized the limits of the data and the fact that charter schools tended to enroll more black students, and were disproportionately located in cities, where the challenges of education were more intense. "Given those differences, he said, the scores were 'not a bad sign'" (Schemo 2004b).

Still to come, however, were two studies that—because they used sophisticated statistical techniques to control much more precisely for differences in the backgrounds of students and characteristics of the schools and districts they attended—addressed some of the core criticisms that school choice proponents had leveled at the AFT report and the December 2004 descriptive analysis by NCES. They were released in July and August of 2006. Like the AFT report of two years earlier, these studies challenged the notion—promoted by early school choice proponents—that market-based competition would lead to quick and dramatic increases in student outcomes. Like the AFT report, they sparked a quick and public response.

The July 2006 study compared the performance of public schools to private religious and nonreligious schools and its August counterpart compared charter and traditional public schools (Braun, Jenkins, and Grigg 2006a, 2006b). Both were undertaken by same team of researchers from the Educational Testing Service. Both analyzed 2003 student-level NAEP results using hierarchical linear modeling (HLM), a sophisticated technique for taking into account variation at multiple levels of analysis. Both took into account student background character-istics such as gender, race and ethnicity, disabilities, English learner sta-tus, eligibility for free or reduced-price school lunch, and indicators of at-home support for learning (such as the presence of a computer and the number of books in the home). As the CER ad suggested, the analy-ses isolated the relative role of school sector (public, private, charter) and took student background and school characteristics into account.

The two studies were extremely modest in their claims and cautious in their implications, but for the most part were welcomed by support-ers of traditional public schools and treated skeptically by proponents of choice. For years, the conventional reading of the education policy literature had held that private schools—especially Catholic ones—out-stripped public schools even when differences in the family back-grounds of the students were taken into account (Bryk, Lee, and Hol-land 1993; Chubb and Moe 1990; Coleman and Hoffer 1987). The July study found that private school students tested higher on average when unadjusted test scores were compared. However, once student and district background factors were taken into account, public school students performed better in fourth-grade mathematics and as well as private school students in fourth-grade reading and eighth-grade math. Private schools beat public schools only in eighth-grade read-ing.[22] The August study in large measure confirmed the results that the earlier AFT report had highlighted. After adjusting for student charac-teristics "charter school mean scores in reading and mathematics were lower, on average, than those for public noncharter schools" (Braun, Jenkins, and Grigg 2006b, vi).

As things developed, it was the study on private schools, the earlier of the two, that stirred the speedier and more dramatic response. The results were reported on the front page of the *New York Times* the next day, and battles over the interpretation came fast and furious.[23] The president of the National Education Association, the AFTs larger sister union, complained that the Bush administration, to promote its goals of vouchers and charter schools, "has been giving public schools a beating since the beginning," and argued this new study proved public schools were "doing an outstanding job" (Schemo 2006).

Despite the fact that the study employed methods similar to, if tech-nically more sophisticated than, the classic studies school choice advo-cates had cited for years to support the claim that private schools gen-erated superior schooling outcomes, advocates of vouchers and other market-oriented approaches took the position that the findings were ei-ther insignificant or wrong. The Bush administration seemed at pains to distance itself from the report. As the *Times* reported, Chad Colby, a spokesman for the Education Department, "offered no praise for public schools and said he did not expect the findings to influence policy. Mr.

Colby emphasized the caveat, 'An overall comparison of the two types of schools is of modest utility'" (Schemo 2006).

That weekend, *Times* columnist John Tierney argued that the study said less about realities of school performance than it did about the clever ability of teachers' unions to exploit ambiguous data. "Thanks to a new federal report comparing public and private schools, there's no doubt that public schools have one huge advantage," he wrote, "the leaders of their unions are unrivaled masters of spin." The unions "spun so well that the report was treated as a public-school triumph that "casts doubt on the value of voucher programs." According to Tierney, the report should have been read to support "just the opposite. It concluded, after compensating for socioeconomic differences and other factors, that public-school students score slightly better on tests in fourth grade, while private-school students score slightly better in eighth grade. Given a choice, would you rather be ahead in the fourth inning or later in the game?" (Tierney 2006, A21).

Within just two weeks of the July release of the public versus private school study, supporters of market-oriented school reforms had a new study to use to blunt its impact. Paul Peterson, once again, was in the forefront. With Elena Llaudet, he released a rebuttal that not only critiqued the methodology of the original report, but offered a reanalysis of the same data using different indicators and models and came up with dramatically different results (Peterson and Llaudet 2006). They argued that reliance on NAEP data, as both the private school and charter school studies had done, was "an anachronism." Even using the same NAEP data as Henry Braun and his colleagues, Peterson and Llaudet argued that their statistical models—using what they argued were more appropriate independent variables[24]—resulted in the opposite conclusion. Private schools, especially Catholic and Lutheran schools, they concluded, seemed to outperform their public counterparts.

Again, as in the head-to-head battles between Peterson and Witte and again between Rothstein and Hoxby, the rapid-fire response by Peterson and Llaudet stimulated at least some observers to simply throw up their hands. The *New York Sun*, a newspaper generally supportive of charter schools and school choice, concluded in an editorial that: "Though Mr. Peterson's analysis is more credible than the research he rebuts, the real lesson from this duel is that policy wonks will never be able to tell with certainty whether schools are offering a good education" (2006).

Two years after the initial AFT report, more and better studies had been done, but the public face of research remained as polarized as ever. Even using the same data, researchers were reporting diametrically different findings about whether school sector—traditional public, charter, and private schools—made a difference. Studies were accumulating, but at least on the face of it they were not aggregating in any meaningful way.

"There are three types of lies," a saying variously attributed to Mark Twain, Benjamin Disraeli, and others puts it: "lies, damn lies, and statistics." The charges, countercharges, and counter-countercharges could only serve to reinforce the popular impression that policy research is an extension of partisan debate and not a cooler and more objective alternative to it. Outside of the glare of public controversy, however, other research on charter schools was operating in a much different—and ultimately much more useful—mode.

Chapter 5

Research Outside the Spotlight: Accumulation, Convergence, Contingency

Question: Does it feel like to you that the research community has converged a little bit on this issue [the consequences of charter schools] over time?

Answer: Oh yeah, definitely. And the other thing is policy can't fight the research too much or policy loses; and even ideology can't fight the research or it will lose. . . . As the facts come out and become more believable no matter what your ideology, you have to change at some point.

[R4]

Question: Do you see an arc in the literature that's leading towards more of a consensus, or do you see—?

Answer: Sure, I do. But unfortunately it's not a consensus that either political side would want to hear.

[R20]

The public face of charter school research is not a pretty one. Advocates at each extreme wave studies to support their position and claim that their opponents are willfully perverting the canons of social science methodology to mislead the public and gain higher political ground. Researchers have been swept into the currents, or perhaps dived in headfirst. Those hoping for a more deliberate and thoughtful merger of science and democracy are faced with tough questions. Is their vision naïve at its core? Can there be a zone of objective investigation and technical expertise that is both protected from and able to exert an influence upon the hot realm of politics? Would better research—more rigorous, more scientific, more authoritative—solve the problem? Would a better-educated public, better political institutions, a more informed and responsible press? The outlook is dim if researchers themselves cannot even begin to circle in on common ground.

This chapter offers a different—less cynical, more encouraging—perspective on charter school research, however. Despite the perception that charter school research is plagued by ideology and partisanship—a perception subscribed to not only by a marginally attentive public but also by most of the researchers—a serious review of the evolving literature makes it clear that research can bring increased focus and sophisticated understanding, and perhaps even shift the terms of public discourse in ways more conducive to reasoned and effective policy. Even as they fret about the polarizing and politicizing forces they see around them, many school choice researchers are converging on a set of findings that suggest collective learning is going on. These findings do not provide the universal, certain, unambiguous maps for policy makers that the more naïve proponents of the policy sciences envisioned. They are tentative, conditional, and contingent. In many ways, they complicate things more than they simplify. However, though they hold little prospect for erasing the sharp disagreements that divide the committed and reflexive liberal from the reflexive and committed conservative, these emerging findings suggest that research is doing what it is supposed to do. It is narrowing points of disagreement, discrediting clear falsities, and bringing us at least a little closer to an understanding of the world in its messy complexities.

Two distinctions merit attention. The first is that between research as research and research as it is employed in public debate. At the same time that public uses of research have been polarized and politicized, incremental clarification and learning has been taking place within the research community, if below the radar. The second distinction is between realistic expectations for what social science research can contribute to collective learning and democratic policy making and idealized expectations. Those who portray the promise of policy research as leading to definitive solutions that displace political conflict have laid the foundation for disillusionment.

The line between good research and clever politics is drawn with a smudgy pencil, not etched with acid on a metallic plate. The notion of research as a pure and independent source of knowledge—unfiltered, unadulterated, and unspun—is idealized and probably unrealizable. Research does not have to be pure to be valuable, however. It does not have to be unambiguous to be enlightening. Just below and outside of the hot glare of public controversy, a different dynamic of research is unfolding. This subcurrent is more slow-moving than the breakneck pace of political maneuvering and media ambulance-chasing, but it is perhaps steadier and more true to course. At this level, social science policy research looks different and ultimately more encouraging.

Although research on charters and school choice has not tied up tough arguments into a neat package of conclusions and policy advice, it has been gradually accumulating information and building a shared understanding about what matters and how things work. Despite the very public evidence to the contrary, we do know quite a bit more than we did two decades ago. Despite the image of a highly polarized research community, researchers identified as firmly entrenched in one camp or the other reveal, in interviews, considerable convergence in their emerging understanding of what is and is not known.

How to Draw Meaning Out of Provisional, Partial, and Evolving Evidence

Since choice programs have moved from idea into working models, numerous reviews and studies have focused on the unfolding phenomenon—some rigorous and revealing, some flabby and misleading, none definitive. This chapter will sift through the evidence with an eye toward distinguishing strong findings from weak ones, suggestive evidence from mere speculation.

My goal here is not to be exhaustive. Research on charter schools is a moving target; the number of studies is multiplying quickly and for the most part their quality is increasing as well. Moreover, as I will discuss, the very phenomenon of charter schools is changing. The early schools are maturing. For some that may mean honing their mission and building capacity, for others calcification or the dissipation of enthusiasm. New types of providers are entering the field, bringing new ideas, and targeting different kinds of students. Charter laws are changing, in some cases to add muscle to standards and oversight, in others to relax restrictions that seemed prudent when charters were a great unknown but may seem less necessary now. States and charter authorizers are becoming more informed and strategic. Even the best of the studies completed to date will leave unanswered some important questions about charter schooling as it might yet evolve.

I focus in this chapter more on broad patterns across studies than on technical aspects of any particular study. The particulars of research design and modes of analysis are important to attend to, and I will discuss how and why that is the case. For those interested in delving deeper into these issues, however, other sources deal with them more extensively and well (Carnoy et al. 2005; Betts and Hill 2006). I weight more heavily those studies that have stronger designs, use better data, and are more confirmed over time by comparable studies. A handful of states have invested in superior student-level, longitudinal databases and made these available to researchers; as a result, these states figure disproportionately in the evidence I cite.

The decision to focus on broad patterns evolves out of my view of the nature of science as a collective enterprise and the inherent diffi-

culty of isolating the impacts of incremental and differentially introduced policy initiatives on complex social behaviors. By referring to
science as a collective enterprise, I mean to suggest that societal learning across all areas of inquiry depends on sifting through, weighing,
and interpreting evidence produced from multiple and disparate studies and not from the unambiguous and universal findings from any single definitive investigation. Complex social behaviors, like student
learning, are the product of many factors—personal ability and motivation, family support, societal reinforcement, curriculum, teachers,
peers, and media to name several. Only some of these can be purpose-
fully manipulated by governmental policies. Even where policies do
make intended impacts, the particular contribution from any single
strand of policy is likely to be small. That the impacts might be small
overall does not make them unimportant, because everything we can
do to nudge social conditions in desirable directions is something to
celebrate. It does mean, however, that those impacts may be hard to isolate. That challenge becomes greater in a pluralistic and relatively decentralized political system like the one in the United States, that in
general shies away from sharp, large-scale interventions in favor of
more modest, negotiated changes applied in different forms across
states and communities.

Politicization of research can come in several varieties. It can constitute outright violation of the most basic norms of good research. It can
also constitute patterned selectivity in which studies to cite, which findings to acknowledge, which researchers to hold up to intense scrutiny,
and which to give generous benefits of doubt. Among the most important but least understood faces of politicization is the extent to which
the particulars of policy, type of school, context, and stage of implementation are handled appropriately in claiming broad lessons for policy from what are almost always partial and contingent results.

This chapter highlights broad findings that constitute what I, and
many of those I interviewed, take to be the emerging themes of common understanding. I don't pretend that all charter and school choice
researchers would sign on to this list. I don't pretend that there are not
many remaining differences in nuance, emphasis and degree. I also
don't pretend that our knowledge is anywhere close to final. I do make
several claims. First, regardless of where they have been identified in
the public debate, most of the researchers whom I interviewed would
accept most of these as at least broadly accurate summaries of our current state of knowledge. Second, these are not simply truisms or self-ev-
ident banalities, but represent a convergence of an understanding that
is substantially different from that which characterized predictions
about the intersection of markets, government, and schooling in the
pre-charter school era. Last, if politicians and policy makers gave these

due consideration, the framing of public discourse would change more likely for good than ill.

Charters, Choice, and the Threat of Resegregation and Social Fragmentation

One of the deepest fears about market-oriented choice systems is that they might, regardless of intention, provide a vehicle for segregation of families by race, class, special needs, and religion. Concerns about racial re-segregation carry the most bite—legally, morally, emotionally—because of the history of formal segregation in the United States and the deliberate use of "parental choice" and public tuition grant programs in some jurisdictions, in the wake of the 1954 *Brown* decision, to allow white parents to continue sending their children to all-white private schools at public expense (Henig 1994; Orfield 1969). Segregation by socioeconomic class is a concern primarily because of the demonstrated effects that peers have on student test scores. One of the few things consistently shown to improve test scores for low-income minority children is attendance in classes in which the other children have parents who are better off in terms of education and income (Kahlenberg 2001). Segregation by special need—for example, those who have physical, mental, or emotional challenges that seriously interfere with their ability to learn without tailored accommodations—raise similar but somewhat distinct issues. In battling for the landmark 1975 Education of All Handicapped Children Act, now known as the Individuals with Disabilities Education Act, proponents for those with special needs drew on the symbols, rhetoric, and tactics of the civil rights movement to strengthen their claim that children with disabilities should get the educational and social services they need, and should do so, when feasible, "mainstreamed" into the "least restrictive environment," ideally in schools and classrooms attended by children who do not have such special needs. Segregation by religious belief has not been as prominent an issue in public debate about school choice in the United States, perhaps because separation by religion in private schools has been common and accepted for many years. The prominence of religious cleavages as threats to international peace and stability, however, combined with the growing intensity of religious fundamentalism as a force in domestic politics, makes it more important, perhaps, that we pay attention to the ways schools may reinforce or moderate the disintegrative potential of religious beliefs.

Although the first-order question is whether charter schools are leading to more homogenous schools, a great deal also rides on the question of why separation occurs when it does. For many, separation is seen as a problem, especially if it is imposed. For some, only imposed separation warrants concern. For others, only separation imposed by deliberate public policy—rather than the actions of individuals, private forces, or unintentional byproducts of policy—is problematic. Because these distinctions matter, researchers are not only interested in whether charter schools lead to separation, but also whether any observed separation is attributable to family preference, screening by schools, or failure to enforce public policies requiring open admissions.

In the Aggregate, Charter Schools Are not Screening Out Racial and Ethnic Minorities   There is, of course, much we still do not know about the possible stratifying consequences of charter schools. A fair reading of the evidence, however, makes it clear that, at least in the aggregate and at least to date, charter schools have not been ignoring minority, poor, and at-risk students in favor of a predominantly white and privileged clientele.

When it comes to racial and ethnic minorities, charter schools overall have been more than willing to open their doors. According to the United States Department of Education, 51 percent of fourth-grade charter school students nationwide were black or Hispanic in 2003. This is a higher concentration than in traditional public schools nationwide, where the percentage that year was 36 percent (National Center for Education Statistics 2004).

The finding has been particularly consistent when it comes to African Americans. Almost all studies have found high—even disproportionately high—African American enrollment in charter schools. The AFT, in its original report, suggested that charter schools were "approximately twice as likely as other public schools to enroll black students" (Nelson, Rosenberg, and Van Meter 2004). Eric Hanushek and his colleagues similarly found that blacks in Texas were more than twice as likely as Hispanics and more than four times as likely as whites to attend charter schools in 2002 (2005). Robert Bifulco and Helen Ladd found that 40 percent of charter school students in North Carolina were black, compared with 31 percent in traditional public schools in the state (2005).[1] Some find Hispanic enrollment lower than in traditional public schools, but for the most part not dramatically so.[2]

It Also Does Not Appear that Charter Schools Are Steering Away from the Poor   The evolving evidence on socioeconomic status (SES) is a little shakier than that on race, at least in part because measuring SES is more difficult and open to variation. In common parlance, class is largely a matter of income and education. Researchers often have only a crude measure of class at their disposal: whether a child has been found eligible for the federal free and reduced price lunch program. At best, this is a rough measure of poverty and does not help at all in distinguishing socioeconomic differences between the working class, middle class, and wealthy. Even as a stand-in for poverty, it has important limits. Most important for the charter school debate, schools may differ in the extent to which they encourage families to enroll. If poor children in charter schools are less likely to fill out the required forms, for example, estimates about their numbers in charter schools will be systematically too low. By the same token, if smaller and more entrepreneurial charter schools are more attentive to the economic bottom line, they may have the ability and incentive to be even more aggressive than traditional public schools in reaching out to families and ensuring that those eligible fill out the necessary forms.[3] If that is the case, the school-lunch indicator could underestimate the degree of poverty in traditional public schools relative to the charter sector.

In its original report, the AFT suggested that charter schools were "a little more likely to enroll poor children"—54 percent of fourth graders versus 46 percent in traditional public schools (Nelson, Rosenberg, and Van Meter 2004, 6). Charter school proponents seized on this finding, arguing that it showed charter schools served the toughest cases and explained why the test scores in charter schools were not higher (Howell, Peterson, and West 2004).

The Department of Education's 2005 report on charter schools, however, found no statistically significant differences in the percentage of students eligible for subsidized school lunches between charter schools, 42 percent, and traditional public schools, 44 percent (National Center for Education Statistics 2004). In Florida, where the ethnic and racial composition of charter schools almost perfectly mirrors that of traditional public schools, the percent who receive subsidized school lunch is lower in charters, 36.5 percent, than traditional public schools, 44.6 percent (Sass 2006). There can be a class tilt to enrollment even when the schools are serving primarily minority and lower-income families. In North Carolina, for example, charter schools are more likely to enroll black students than traditional public schools, but at the same time the parents of charter school children are more highly educated than those in traditional public schools. Bifulco and Ladd, for example, found that 45 percent of charter school parents in North Carolina, versus 28 percent of their non-charter counterparts, had a four-year college degree (2004).

To those who think of charter schools as market-oriented, the finding that they seem in the aggregate to be serving low-income families at even close to proportional levels may be surprising. Certainly, it runs counter to the fears of those critics who envisioned charters skimming the cream of potential students by targeting an elite clientele that is easier and presumably cheaper to serve. Part of the explanation is that many charter schools are self-consciously not market-driven. Many were started by organizations with long-standing missions of helping the disadvantaged. They cannot be totally insensitive to market factors that affect their revenues and cost, but by seeking philanthropic support and hiring employees willing to work for less because they identify with the school's mission, they can push considerations of profitability toward the periphery of their decision making (Brown et al. 2005). A second reason is that market-oriented behavior does not steer charter school entrepreneurs to target white and wealthy suburbs. Parents there are generally pleased with their public schools and occasionally inhospitable toward what they see as a potential destabilizing effect. Charter schools, at least in the early years, are more likely to open in dense, central cities where per pupil revenues may be higher and where demand is perceived to be stronger.

To Say that Charter Schools Overall Are Serving High Proportions of Minority and Low-Income Students Is not the Same as Saying That They Are Creating Integrated Learning Environments   Most of the evidence offered to suggest that charter schools are not creaming is based on comparing averages across the two sectors. Averages, however, can be misleading. Charter schools on average could be serving precisely the same proportions of minority and poor students as the traditional public school districts in which they lie even if the individual charter schools were racially and economically homogenous. Imagine a hypothetical school district in which every traditional public school is 40 percent black, 40 percent Hispanic, and 20 percent white. Table 5.1 presents an imaginary array of five charter schools that, on average, serve the same populations despite being severely unbalanced internally. What this means is that serious consideration of how charter schools affect racial, ethnic, and economic integration requires looking at school-level data.

Table 5.1   Why Averages Can be Misleading

	Percentage Black	Percentage Hispanic	Percentage White
Hypothetical charter 1	85	15	0
Hypothetical charter 2	15	85	0
Hypothetical charter 3	0	0	100
Hypothetical charter 4	100	0	0
Hypothetical charter 5	0	100	0
Average for hypothetical charter schools	40	40	20

Source: Author's compilation.

Anecdotal and additional systematic evidence suggest that charter schools may be generating more homogenous learning environments, at least in some contexts. Safford is a modest size school district in Arizona, with roughly 40 percent Hispanic and 60 percent white non-Hispanic students. The district is small enough in population and geographic area that, by sending all students in a given grade to the same school, it has been able to ensure that its traditional public schools precisely reflect this breakdown. When two charter schools opened in 1996, however, they attracted very different student populations. The enrollment at Triumphant Learning Center was about 95 percent white, and at Los Milagros Academy about 75 percent Hispanic (Schnaiberg 2000). Looking at Arizona overall, Casey Cobb and Gene Glass concluded that more than half of Arizona charter schools showed evidence of "substantial ethnic separation." First, they overenrolled white students in relation to the school district population. Second, those that included a majority of ethnic minority students tended to specifically target vocational or at-risk students, further evidence of a selective sorting process that could steer minority students into a less challenging curriculum and leave them less prepared to make the move into higher education or challenging jobs (Cobb and Glass 1999).[4] In Texas, Hanushek and his colleagues found that blacks entering charter school moved into more segregated surroundings than the schools they were leaving; on average they entered schools almost 15 percentage points higher in the proportion black (2005).

Martin Carnoy and his colleagues reviewed the evidence on racial and ethnic concentration from nineteen studies focused on twelve states. Overall, the findings suggested that African Americans are overrepresented among charter school students, but were much less definitive about Hispanics and the poor. Thirteen of the studies found a higher concentration of blacks.[5] Four found evidence of a higher proportion of Hispanics.[6] Three found some indication of overrepresentation of low-income students (Carnoy et al. 2005).[7]

Some Charter Schools Consider it Their Mission to Serve Students Who Have Special Needs   Some charter schools aggressively target high-risk children: central city minorities, low-income backgrounds, run-ins with the criminal justice system, and diagnosed special needs. For example, the School for Arts in Learning (SAIL) Public Charter School in Washington, D.C., advertises itself as "a unique and dynamic nonprofit organization serving Washington DC area children and young people with special needs, special talents, and special skills."[8] Its special education enrollment in 2006 was 46 percent in its grade school and about 60 percent in its upper school (District of Columbia Public Charter School Board 2006). Dick Carpenter estimates that about one in four charter schools nationwide is targeted at students "with special needs or attributes"[9] (Carpenter 2005).

That many charter schools target high-need student populations is encouraging in that it runs counter to the fear that charters might systematically cream off the most advantaged students. It is not an unadulterated good, however. Given broader societal patterns, students with special needs often tend to be more highly concentrated among certain racial, ethnic, and economic groups. Schools that target high-need students may therefore reinforce separation along those lines. To the extent that these schools can adapt their programs to truly help high-need students, the trade-off may be worthwhile. As a nation, however, we have seesawed between the goals of targeting and mainstreaming, both as pedagogical and civic strategies. Whether charter schools are helping us to find the right balance remains to be seen.

Charter School Law, and Authorizer Policies, in Some Places Have Specifically Encouraged Charters That Target High-Need Populations   In Arkansas, for example, state law requires that the state board of education give preference to applications for charter schools in school districts where the percentage of students who qualify for free or reduced price lunches is above the state average. Connecticut requires its state board give preference to schools that will serve students from priority districts or from those in which 75 percent or more of the enrolled students are racial or ethnic minorities. In California, Colorado, Missouri, Virginia, and Wisconsin, priority must be given to schools that propose orientation to at-risk or low-achieving students or to the re-entry of dropouts into the school system. In New York and North Carolina, the law encourages or allows authorizers to favor such schools. Florida law allows a school to target students considered at risk of dropping out of school or academic failure.[10]

Research across states supports the conclusion that such differences in policies are associated with charter school enrollment patterns. Charter schools in states that provide extra funding for at-risk students predictably enroll more lower-income and minority students. So do those where state law requires that transportation costs be covered (Lacireno-Paquet 2006).

Other Charter Schools Appear to Be Underserving Some High-Cost and High-Need Groups, and Overall Charter Schools Appear Less Likely than Traditional Public Schools to Accommodate Students with Disabilities or English-Language Learning Needs   In 2003, 8 percent of charter school students nationwide had been diagnosed with disabilities, versus 11 percent in traditional public schools (National Center for Education Statistics 2004). This difference was statistically significant. Unlike most, Jack

Buckley and Mark Schneider disaggregated data to allow them to get beyond looking at averages for the two types of schools. Examining data for the District of Columbia, one of the most charterized large school districts in the country, they found that five charter schools had considerably more special education students than traditional public schools, eight had about the same proportion, and twenty-four had significantly fewer. In an earlier study of District of Columbia charters that I undertook with others, we found a similar pattern and offered evidence that market-oriented charter schools—those with entrepreneurial plans for expansion or links to for-profit companies—were least likely to have special education or English-language learning students (Lacireno-Paquet et al. 2002).

It is possible that charter schools simply underreport the number of students with disabilities they are serving. This could be the case, for example, if traditional public schools are more aggressive about labeling borderline cases of disability.[11] Gary Miron and Christopher Nelson's analysis suggests that this is not the case, at least not in Michigan. They found that, overall, the proportion of students with disabilities was more than three times higher in traditional public schools than in charter schools. Using more precise information about types and severity of disability, they also found that the differences did not depend on discretionary labeling of mild cases of disability. To the contrary, charter school students who were identified as having disabilities tended to have milder forms. Indeed, "charter schools had no children with multiple disabilities and almost none with autism, visual impairments, or hearing impairments" (2002, 87-88).

Some charter schools are quite open in suggesting that families with children who have severe disabilities might be better served in the traditional system, where the resources for supporting them are more substantial. Meeting the needs of seriously disabled children is much more difficult and expensive than attending to those with mild disabilities, so to the degree this is the case it suggests the possibility of a significant imbalance that is understated by comparisons that do not distinguish among disabilities based on their severity and type.

Some White Families in Some Locales May be Using Charter Schools to Avoid More Integrated Traditional Public Schools, but Choices Minority Parents Make Seem to Be Having at Least as Significant an Impact on Racial and Ethnic Patterns of Separation   In Texas, whites moving into charter schools moved into schools that had 10 percent fewer blacks and 2.3 percent fewer Hispanics than the schools they were leaving. This is consistent with a pattern of white flight, though the magnitude of the shift is not great. The degree of racial concentration associated with charter school selection was much greater for blacks. Blacks on average enter charter schools with 14.4 percent more blacks and 10.3 percent fewer Hispanics. In other words, blacks appear to be using charter school choice in a pattern that exacerbates already high levels of racial concentration. Hispanics were marginally more likely to move to charter schools with a higher percentage black (.9) and, unlike both whites and blacks, tended to move to those that had lower percentages of Hispanics (Hanushek et al. 2005). In California, the pattern is similar for black students, who disproportionately move into charter schools with higher concentrations of blacks, and Hispanics, who tend to choose those with lower percentages Hispanic. In California, unlike Texas, it appears that white students moving into charter schools tend to select schools that have higher percentages of nonwhites (Booker, Zimmer, and Buddin 2005). Charter school critics framed their initial concerns about re-segregation based on the expectation that the choices of white families would be the most problematic. It is not yet clear how many of those concerns will still carry bite if it is determined that minority-led self-segregation is the driving force.

Charter Schools and Achievement: What Can We Say About the So-Called Bottom Line?

The initial wave of empirical research on charter schools focused heavily on the segregation-fragmentation issue, but more recently the primary focus has been on student test scores. There are at least a couple of reasons for this shift.[12] First, it reflects a general reorientation, within the American education policy dialogue, from an emphasis on inputs and equity to one on measurable outcomes. During the 1960s and 1970s, equity, access, and integration—particularly as related to race—were the raw meat of education politics at the national and local levels. Some combination of weariness, frustration, learning, and broad partisan change within the country led to refocusing around measurable outcomes: a phenomenon evident in some states during the 1980s that crystallized at the national level with No Child Left Behind (NCLB) during the first decade of the new millennium. From this perspective, early attention to the possible resegregating aspects of charter schools might be seen as something of a holdover, a vestigial debate to be cleared before attention could be recentered around the new bottom line.

A second reason that attention to charter schools' effects on test scores was a little slower to develop in the literature involves straightforward factors of sequencing. Impacts on outcomes take time to develop and be measured; counts of who sits in the classroom, on the other hand, can be generated during the first weeks a school is open. Attention to racial, economic, and ethnic patterns of attendance has not disappeared in the face of the new focus on outcomes, but has been re-defined. Rather than being important for its own sake, the issue of racial and economic separation has been demoted to being a sidebar to the effectiveness argument, with researchers and advocates both anxious to control for student characteristics in drawing conclusions about the independent effects of charter schools on student achievement.

Some Charter Schools Have High Test Scores and Strong Reputations for Success "Smarter Charter Kids" was the headline on a July 2006 report in the *New York Post*. Citing what it called a bombshell study by the state's department of education, the article proclaimed that charter schools in the city "are vastly outperforming public schools in their neighborhoods." According to the report, eleven of sixteen fourth-grade and five of six eighth-grade city charter schools were outperforming nearby traditional public schools in English and math.

Either because they attract better students or because they provide better instruction and more appealing environments, some charter schools do indeed have higher test scores than nearby traditional public schools and are developing strong reputations for academic excellence. Nationwide, Knowledge is Power Program (KIPP) charter schools have been prominently cited in this regard. KIPP is a national network, begun in 1994, that by 2007 was operating about sixty schools in seventeen states. A search of newspapers on ProQuest Direct, a widely used database including the world's largest digital newspaper archive, uncovered 223 articles mentioning KIPP and charter schools, many with positive claims embedded in the headlines. "A Miracle in the Making? KIPP turns its efforts toward elementary schools" was the heading for one article in the April 2, 2006, *Washington Post Magazine*. Others include "Urban Success Story" in *USA Today*, "Standards are high at fledgling Harlem charter school" in *Amsterdam News*, and "Charter school's test scores outdistance gains at HISD" in the *Houston Chronicle*. *USA Today* in a 2005 editorial suggested the KIPP-sponsored programs were "probably the most successful charter schools in the U.S." (cited in Carnoy et al. 2005, 51).

KIPP charter schools are not the only ones with high test scores. In New York City's Harlem Day Charter School, every fourth-grader passed the English exam and 94 percent passed the standardized math test. At the nearby Community School District 4 in East Harlem, on the other hand, the reading and math pass rates were 52 and 76 percent, respectively. At Carl Icahn Charter School in the South Bronx, 100 percent passed the fourth-grade math exam and 86.2 percent passed the English test in contrast to 48 percent and 63 percent at Community School District 9 (Campanile 2006). High Tech High began as a single charter high school in San Diego in 2000 and six years later was operating seven schools including two middle schools and one elementary school. It has claimed great success, its African American students far outperforming others in the district and state, and all of its graduates admitted to college despite the fact that more than half are first-generation college students. SEED, a boarding school in Washington, D.C., is another that has received flattering attention. In 2005, its entire graduating class was admitted to college and it was given an Innovations in American Government Award from Harvard University's Kennedy School of Government and the Council for Excellence in Government. Numerous others could be mentioned.

Charter schools were envisioned as a way to draw in and retain innovative and energetic educators by giving them a chance to try out their ideas in an environment less structured and confining than is typical in large, bureaucratized, central city systems. That they have succeeded to some extent is undeniable. Even researchers who have been opposed to school choice concede this. One who has been vocally critical observes: "I think there are places where charter schools are quite interesting schools and . . . places where I would think about putting my son" [R2].

Some Charter Schools Have Very Low Test Scores and Exhibit Evidence of Amateurism, Disorganization, Incompetence, or Worse   Anecdotes about charter schools where test scores are dismally low are compelling. In spring 2006, New York City released the results of its new English test given to all children in grades three through eight. Overall, the city's thirty-nine charter schools and 1,063 traditional public schools performed about the same. Neither did particularly well. Among charter schools with third-graders, the average pass rate was 58.1 percent, versus 61.5 percent for other public schools. For charter schools with eighth-graders, the pass rate was 35.1 percent, versus 36.8 percent in the rest of the system. The very worst performers were disproportionately among the charter schools. Only eight charter schools, compared to 354 traditional public schools, had eighth-grade scores (2.2 percent). Two of the five schools with the lowest pass rates overall were charters (40 percent).[13] Only 4 percent of eighth graders at the Opportunity Charter School passed; none at Lindsay Charter School did.

The District of Columbia has several charter schools that have received considerable national attention. Some of this has been embarrassing, like the now-defunct Marcus Garvey Charter School, where the founder was charged with physically assaulting a newspaper reporter doing a story on the school. However, it also has some of the schools most often praised by charter proponents. One of its two chartering agencies—the Public Charter School Board (PCSB)—has been lauded for its care at the initial stage of approving charters and subsequently in providing both oversight and support. At the same time, some of the charter schools in its portfolio are struggling to demonstrate that they can produce good test scores. In 2006, only four out of thirty-one PCSB schools managed to meet NCLB standards for adequate yearly progress. These four included some with extremely poor scores. At Sasha Bruce, for instance, half of all tenth-graders were below basic level in math, and more than 6 percent were either below basic or at basic level only. Sasha Bruce was subsequently closed by the PCSB, which cited management issues as the primary reason. This fits with one of the claims made by charter school proponents, that it is easier to weed out poor charter schools than to close traditional public schools that do just as poorly. This may be true, but prospects for closing traditional public schools are changing. Under NCLB provisions, it is likely that many more traditional public schools will be closed or reconstituted than ever before.

Chartering, as one strong charter school proponent puts it, is "permission to be different," and different does not necessarily mean better:

> It is permission to be different. It is also frankly permission to screw up in a whole variety of brand new ways . . . It is also permission for often well intentioned but wholly unsuitable people to set themselves up to run schools. And occasionally not well intentioned but that is rare. And so it is not easy to generalize. Some of the most fantastic schools I have ever seen are charter schools and some of the most dismal schools I have ever seen are charter schools and the fact that they are both charter schools tells you nothing about charter schools except that they have permission to not be district operated schools. [A1]

As one researcher who signed the *New York Times* advertisement protesting the coverage of the AFT study puts it:

> The evidence suggests that there is potential for some charter schools, just like some public schools, to perform wonderfully in terms of producing high reading and math test scores. But some charter schools, just like some public schools, perform abysmally in terms of producing higher reading and math scores, and there is nothing specific about being a charter school that will guarantee that. [R13]

Overall, it Does Seem that Charter School Test Scores are Lower than Those of Traditional Public Schools   This, of course, was the controversial claim made in the AFT study. But the core finding of lower test scores—at least as measured by NAEP and at least as examined in 2003 and 2005—has held up in subsequent analyses by the United States Department of Education (Braun, Jenkins, and Grigg 2006a; National Center for Education Statistics 2004) and in several studies using high quality data sets at the state level.

Some states have much more sophisticated and detailed databases than others, and in some cases, state data are better designed to track individual student progress than national surveys like NAEP. As a result, some of the best research on outcomes has come from state-specific studies such as those for California, Florida, North Carolina, and Texas. Their real advantage is their greater ability to improve on the simple cross-sectional comparison between charter schools and noncharter schools at a single point in time. In addition, the state level data confirm, in most cases, the initial claim of the AFT study. Charter schools overall to date demonstrate test score performance roughly comparable to public schools, and, despite the high hopes and dramatic claims initially made on their behalf, they, like the traditional public schools, find it a tremendous challenge to overcome the accumulated disadvantages that some children carry with them on the day that they first enter school.

Lower Test Scores Do not Necessarily Mean that Charter Schools in General Are Failing to Perform   Similarly, the higher scores in KIPP and some of the other highly regarded charter schools do not necessarily mean that they are doing a better job. Two confounding issues relate to what researchers refer to as selection bias—in particular, the possibility that charter schools are dealing with tougher kids—and maturation effects (the possibility that new charter schools need more time in order to get their programs working to their potential).

The issue of selection bias has plagued research about school choice from the beginning. By their very nature, choice programs are voluntary. Families who opt to send their children to private schools, voucher schools, magnet schools, or charter schools are likely to be different from those who take the path of least resistance to the assigned local public school. The very ways in which they are different are in fact likely to affect how well their children perform on subsequent tests of academic achievement. For a long time, it had been assumed that selection bias worked in favor of schools of choice. This issue first emerged when statistical analyses in the 1970s and 1980s seemed to show that private school students did better on tests than public school students. Defenders of public schools argued that that was because those students had built-in advantages—more resources, families who cared more about education, more intellectually stimulating home and community environments—that had nothing to do with the relative quality of their schools. When some studies indicated that the private school edge existed even when statistical analysis controlled for observable differences, defenders of public schools argued that there might nonetheless be unobserved differences, relating to motivation and values, that gave choice families built-in advantages. Proponents of school choice typically have argued that the differences in test scores reflect real performance differences and that attempts to attribute them to speculative unobservable factors were disingenuous efforts to deny that fact. Blaming lower test scores on students' race or class or family status, some bitingly argued, is tantamount to what George W. Bush has characterized as the soft bigotry of low expectations: that all children should be able to learn, and if public schools failed to erase the achievement gap separating white from black and rich from poor, they were failing to do their job.

Somewhat surprisingly, and to some minds ironically, the selection bias debate has more recently been turned on its head. Even as they challenged the core claim of the AFT study that charter school test scores were lower, some argued that if they were lower it was because charter schools were dealing with the tougher kids. This was an argument about selection biases running the opposite direction. This argument held that charter school students, rather than being more advantaged because they had more attentive and capable parents, were possibly disadvantaged because they were likely to be the children who had been having the most problems in their previous schools.

Like selection bias, maturation effects in principle could work in ways that either mask or exaggerate the educational accomplishments of charter schools. Proponents argue, reasonably enough, that new schools need time to settle down before it is fair to expect them to generate educational gains. In the first year or two or three, a new school is often beset by distracting issues having to do with facilities, with recruiting teachers, with adapting a curriculum, with establishing working traditions and norms. Rushing to judgment, therefore, might risk prematurely finding them wanting, mistaking start-up hiccups for genuine flaws, and pulling the plug on schools that, given a little more time, would have excelled. During the early years of the movement, too, it is possible that the nation's charter school population will include a large number of ill-conceived or amateurishly run operations. The maturation of the movement—as distinct from the maturation of individual schools—could lead to a gradual weeding out of these dysfunctional programs, leading over time to better and better outcomes overall.

Like selection bias, however, maturation effects can also run both ways. New innovations often have advantages that can wear away over time. The early wave of charter school founders may include unusually innovative and well-prepared leaders. In the first blush of enthusiasm, foundations and other groups may be more willing to provide help, in the form of grants and donations, space, and participation in school events. As schools age and routinize, as founders tire or move on, as the number of schools increases, as other issues and innovations rise on the public agenda, charter schools might decline in effectiveness. Although market theory presupposes that it is the worst performers that over time will be culled from the pack, other scenarios are also conceivable. Some of the most dynamic and dramatic charter schools have been smaller schools associated with nonprofits and community-based organizations with deep roots in their community and a missionary zeal to succeed. These might be muscled aside over time by larger and better capitalized corporate charter systems, much in the way that Wal-Mart, for example, has been charged with muscling aside small business retailers. This may not be a problem if large for-profit charters displace smaller mission-driven schools based on better performance and responsiveness, but if they do so based on more aggressive marketing, under-pricing until they weed out the competition, or using political power to erect barriers to the smaller schools, the net change could be to drive down the overall performance.

Charter School Proponents are Correct When they Argue that Negative Selection Bias and School and System Maturation Effects Might Explain Why Cross-Sectional Comparisons Tend to Find Little Clear Advantage to Charter Schools. Raising These as Hypothetical Factors, However, Is not the Same as Providing Evidence that They Operate in This Way Doing a better job of taking into account differences in student background and changes over time are the likely next wave of charter school research. Some early returns are in, but they are mixed.

Researchers have used various approaches to try to get at the tougher children hypothesis.[14] The most sophisticated of these use student-level data and attempt to control for differences in student background through statistical methods, longitudinal analysis, or randomization of assignment. As mentioned earlier, the AFT's decision to release its study was prompted in part by its knowledge that the administration had contracted for a hierarchical linear modeling analysis of the NAEP data.[15] Such a multilevel design, which could take into account student, school, and district background characteristics, was unambiguously a stronger one than the simple cross-tabulation that the union was able to perform. In this case, however, greater sophistication did not lead to different results. When finally released, almost exactly two years after the AFT study, the HLM study confirmed that student background characteristics were extremely important in affecting test scores: factors such as gender, race, English-language status, disability, and eligibility for free lunch accounted for most of the differences in performance across schools. When these characteristics were controlled for by statistical means, average test scores were lower in both reading and math in charter schools than in public noncharter schools (Braun, Jenkins, and Grigg 2006a).

The HLM analysis provided much superior controls for student background than did the original AFT study, but it was, like its forerunner, hampered by the nature of the NAEP data. The NAEP is based on a sample of schools and students compiled on a periodic basis. Although the data are longitudinal in the sense that they can provide estimates of trends at the national and state levels, NAEP cannot track the performance of individual students, because the students who take the test are different every year. As mentioned, a small but growing number of states have developed databases that link student test scores over time, including when they move between charter and noncharter public schools. Some districts have developed the capacity to track performance even when the states they are within do not yet have databases. Tracking individual student test scores over time makes it more possible to deal with both selection biases and maturation effects. Researchers can use what is known as fixed-effects models to take into account unobservable differences between charter school choosers and nonchoosers, presumably capturing any underlying differences that would not be taken into account by simple control on observable differences.

> The key advantage of fixed-effect models is that they remove the need to compare apples to oranges (i.e., students in charter schools versus those students who remain in regular public schools). Instead, they compare an individual student's gains in achievement in years she is in a charter school with years in which she is not. Each student then becomes his or her own comparison group. (Betts and Hill 2006, 13)

Having student-level data over time also enables researchers to study student year-to-year gains rather than simply to compare test score levels.

The major studies using student-level state administrative databases have tended to find that charter schools do worse, at least at the beginning. They also find evidence that this deficit decreases over time. Findings are mixed about how large the initial deficit is and whether it disappears or even reverses. In Texas, Florida, and North Carolina, student-level test scores controlling for fixed effects found that students did worse when they switched to charter schools than they would have done had they remained in their noncharter public school. Hanushek, looking at Texas, found evidence of a school-level maturation process: the longer the charter school had been in operation, the smaller its deficit. When looking at simple test score levels, the deficit for charter schools disappeared for schools in operation for more than three years. When looking at individual student gains, the deficit disappeared for schools operating more than two years (Hanushek et al. 2005). Bifulco and Ladd, looking at North Carolina data, found a larger deficit associated with switching into charter schools. They also found that the test score loss associated with switching occurred primarily in the first year of attendance, but though charter-choosers subsequently made gains comparable to what would have been expected had they remained in public school, they still had not made up the difference even after four years (Bifulco and Ladd 2004). Tim Sass, using Florida data, found that the initial deficit disappeared for schools that had been in operation for at least five years, and those longer-term charter schools began producing reading test scores higher than those of traditional public schools (2006).

Two studies using local district administrative databases offer somewhat more positive findings. John Witte and others analyzed four years of test scores for Milwaukee students, including 8,357 who switched from traditional public schools to charters and 2,623 who switched in the other direction. Using student-level fixed effects to account for differences in their backgrounds, they concluded that white and Hispanic students showed larger math score gains in charter schools. Findings were weaker and more mixed for black students and in other subjects (Witte et al. 2007). Julian Betts, Y. Emily Tang, and Andrew Zau, using data from the San Diego Unified School District, explored student achievement gains using a variety of statistical methods. They found that aggregate charter school performance was improving over time, but less because individual schools were maturing than because the newer generation of schools opening in the city was attracting a different kind of student than were the first generation of charter schools. They also concluded that more sophisticated models, using student level fixed effects, were more likely to show a positive charter school effect (Betts, Tang, and Zau 2007).

In most states, charter schools are required to allocate seats by a lottery when particular grade levels are oversubscribed. This makes it possible, under some circumstances, to use a third strategy for dealing with selection bias, a randomized field trial (RFT). RFTs are frequently referred to as the gold standard because, when carried out perfectly, they make it possible to compare test scores of charter school students to those of noncharter students who do not systematically differ from them in any other way. The randomization of the lottery itself ensures that differences between the groups are random.[16] Hoxby and Rockoff used an RFT design to compare test scores of students who attended three Chicago charter schools to students who applied to those schools but lost the lottery. They found positive effects for those who entered charter schools in earlier grades, but none for those entering at fourth grade or above (Hoxby and Rockoff 2004).

Although RFTs can provide the strongest evidence that a policy intervention is responsible for the outcomes ascribed to it (what researchers refer to as internal validity), they typically leave questions about whether it is appropriate to generalize from those studies to a broader population (external validity). This general problem is exacerbated when, as in this case, there are good reasons to assume that the charter schools studied are not typical. Only those schools believed by parents to be among the most desirable are likely to be oversubscribed. This is a serious limitation and is endemic to the reliance on lotteries. Doing numerous RFTs might allow us to build some confidence, especially if the findings are consistently positive and apply even in charter schools with artificially high waiting lists (for example, if they are the only charter school in the area). However, if the goal is to compare the overall charter school sector to the overall public school sector, the problem will not go away.

Poorly Performing Charter Schools Do Not Necessarily Lose Customers Market-based rationales rely on the power of parental exit to hold charter schools accountable. How sensitive, though, are parents to differences in educational quality? Do other attributes of schools matter to them more? How willing are parents to pick up and move their child if test score performance is not up to snuff? This as an area in which the research literature is still pretty thin and still pretty crude. Studies of parental decision making within various kinds of school choice arrangements have confirmed that parents say that academics are a major concern (Schneider, Teske, and Marschall 2000; Teske and Reichardt 2006). When researchers have looked at parents' actual choice behavior, however, the evidence is more mixed. Buckley and Schneider, for example, found that parents using a Web-based search vehicle for reviewing information on schools in the District of Columbia spent more time and returned more often to information about the demographic characteristics of the students than to other information on test scores, mission, and facilities (Schneider and Buckley 2002). Gregory Weiher and Kent Tedin found that Texas parents who said that academic performance was their primary criterion, frequently selected charter schools with racial compositions more similar to their own and test scores below the schools they were exiting (Weiher and Tedin 2002). Gregory Elacqua, in a recent study of school choice in Chile, similarly found that parents' choice sets—the schools about which they actually collected information—were more closely aligned with social class than academic measures. Even when parents said academics was most important, they frequently did not choose the school within their choice set with the highest test scores (Elacqua 2005). In an analysis of parents' ranked choices within Charlotte-Mecklenberg's controlled public choice system, Justine Hastings and her colleagues found that, though test scores were a powerful predictor of preferences for a small group of families, the average parent valued proximity far more (Hastings, Kane, and Staiger 2005).

It is possible that parental selection and exit patterns will become more closely aligned with academic quality and claimed criteria over time, as they gain greater experience with the exercise of choice and as information about school performance becomes more widely accessible. Evidence of the former can be found in one study of charter school selection in Texas. Hanushek and his colleagues used student-level data in Texas to examine the effects of school quality on the probability of exit. Whereas school quality (measured so as to reflect value-added beyond the family and personal attributes that the students bring with them) had almost no impact on exit from traditional public schools, it did have a consistent and sizable influence on the likelihood that parents leave poorly performing charter schools (2005).

The extent to which families exercise choice based on academic quality remains uncertain, then, but it is clear that families in many instances choose and remain loyal to charter schools that are not performing well academically. The beauty of charter schools, some proponents argue, is not that every school will be excellent but that the charter and choice system will, over time, do a better job at weeding out the bad apples. However, such a weeding-out process, it appears, cannot depend on market forces alone. Rather than flee bad schools, some charter schools families have remained aggressively loyal. When charter school authorizers have announced the forced closure of schools because of substantial management and educational failures, rather than finding half-empty schools steadily leaking disgruntled students, they often have been confronted by angry families asking that the schools be kept open (Mindlin 2004; Rotherham 2005).[17]

Other Consequences of Charters and Choice

Times change, and when they do so do the terms of public debate. During the 1950s through the 1970s, race and integration were the dominant issues around which educational conflict took place. During the 1980s, President Reagan and his supporters made a strong and ultimately successful effort to shift the reference point from equity to excellence. That became the seedbed for the current emphasis on outcomes. Schools, though, historically have been expected to serve many social goals, and integration and academic achievement will not always dominate debate. In the shadows of the controversies about segregation and achievement, less prominent skirmishes have played out about the effect of charter schools on other types of outcomes. Three types of outcomes that warrant some discussion involve innovation and variation, family satisfaction, and competitive effects on existing public schools. Despite many unresolved questions and heated arguments, it is possible to identify some emergent findings that can and should inform public discourse.

Innovation and Variation

Critics of traditional public school systems have disparagingly noted that contemporary schools look and feel much like schools that existed generations ago. Despite rapid and significant changes in society, schools still run on a schedule originally dictated by agricultural cycles; classrooms still sport rows of desks facing forward; a single teacher still stands at the head of the class. According to Milton Friedman, "hardly any activity in the United States is technically more backward. We essentially teach children in the same way that we did 200 years ago, one teacher in front of a bunch of kids in a closed room" (1995, C7). One expectation expressed by some advocates is that disentanglement from stifling regulations will allow entrepreneurial schools to experiment with different ways to conceptualize, organize, and deliver education. John Stossel, a pro-choice enthusiast and television journalist, put it this way in his biting and graphically titled report *Stupid in America: How Lack of Choice Cheats Our Kids Out of a Good Education*:

> Competition inspires people to do what we didn't think we could do. If people got to choose their kids' school, education options would be endless. There could soon be technology schools, science schools, virtual schools where you learn at home on your computer, sports schools, music schools, schools that go all year, schools with uniforms, schools that open early and keep kids later, and who knows what else. If there were competition, all kinds of new ideas would bloom.[18]

The evidence to support this is mixed at best.

Charter Schools Appear Better Able to Tinker with Some Elements of the Schooling Process   Charter schools in many jurisdictions are experimenting with length of the school day, length of the school year, the targeting of particular types of students, nontraditional grade configurations, and the use of technology to support distance learning. Some of these may be salutary, but with the possible exception of the last, they represent incremental changes, not radical reforms.

The notion that children might benefit from more hours of instruction is not new. There are also good reasons to believe that extended school days and school years could especially help low-income students, who, for example, tend to lose more ground over summer vacation than do children in upper class families, who may pepper vacation time with stimulating learning experiences (Alexander, Entwisle, and Olson 2001). Traditional public school systems often have responded by adding time to the school day, providing special weekend tutoring options, expanding summer school options, and even dramatically rescheduling to provide all-year schooling options. According to one study, the proportion of public schools opening before September 1 rose from just over half in 1988 and 1989 to just under three-quarters in 2005 and 2006 (Greifner 2006). Their ability to do so is unambiguously constrained, however, by teacher contracts, parental preferences, and sometimes lobbying by business groups that do not want their access to teen summer and after-school workers to be compromised. In some cases, states have aggressively acted to rein in local districts that have tried to extend the school year (Greifner 2006).

A number of charter schools have emphasized expanded classroom time in their marketing materials. Edison Schools, for instance, indicates that "better use of time" is one of the ten fundamental elements underlying its charter school approach. Its Web site promises "a longer school day" and "a longer school year —198 days — that's about 10 percent more than the average school year."[19] KIPP's Web site points proudly to the fact that "students are in school learning 60 percent more than average public school students, typically from 7:30 a.m. until 5:00 p.m. on weekdays, every other Saturday, and for three weeks during the summer."[20]

Not much is known yet about how the extra time is used, and this probably differs dramatically from school to school. Edison claims that its extra hours provide "more time for fundamentals and for special subjects like art, music, and world language." A more systematic assessment in California provides evidence that charter schools overall may be providing more instructional time in noncore subjects, such as foreign language and the fine arts (Zimmer and Buddin 2006). This could conceivably represent a demand-driven response to parents unhappy with the drilling, overemphasis on math and reading, and general test-score mania they believe has infected many public schools as a result of No Child Left Behind.

Perhaps the most dramatic way in which some charter schools differ from traditional public schools is in their reliance on technology to deliver distance learning and support home-schooling. Cyber or virtual charter schools, in which instruction is delivered through the Internet, operate in at least fifteen states and serve a small but growing percentage of the nation's charter school enrollment. In addition, some charter schools work with home-school families, providing curriculum, supplementary computer-based instruction modules, or online support (Huerta, Gonzalez, and d'Entremont 2006; Zimmer and Buddin 2006).

Estimates of the size of this sector vary. Carpenter estimates that "alternative delivery" charters constitute more than 6 percent (seventy-three) of the total nationwide, but that is probably an underestimate, and in some places the density is much higher (2005). Ron Zimmer and Richard Buddin estimate that there are more than 120 non-classroom-based charters in California alone (2006). Pennsylvania is a national leader in charter schools. As of spring 2005, its eleven schools were serving more than 10,000 students with more than 4,000 students enrolled at one (Chute 2005).

There Are a Number of Bright and Exciting Charter Schools, but Little is Going on in Charters that Has Not Been Piloted Within the Traditional Public School System Rhetoric about stifling bureaucracies aside, many school districts have been experimenting for years with alternative calendars, alternative pedagogies and curricula, alternative organizations, and alternative learning environments. Public systems began experimenting with alternative schools early in the twentieth century, with some aimed at gifted students, some at lagging students, and some designed to provide vocational and technical skills (Smith, Barr, and Burke 1976). A number of charter schools nationwide emphasize expeditionary learning, which encourages hands-on learning, teamwork, and learning adventures outside of the school building, as their innovative curriculum, for example. One of the first expeditionary schools in the nation was a New York City public school opened in 1993, and at least three of the city's new small schools have adopted that learning mode (Herszenhorn 2006). A number of states have programs in place to give performance bonuses to teachers whose students do well on standardized tests; Texas's new plan makes it possible for an individual teacher to receive a cash increment of as much as $10,000 (McNeil 2006).

A generally positive evaluation found a number of interesting efforts among Michigan's charter schools, but concluded that charters overall were "essentially working to create localized variations of practices that are already common within the broader public school community" (Mintrom 2000a, 29). Rather than the so-called laboratories of experimentation that some eager advocates initially promised, a more fitting analogy might be to Japanese industry, which has a vaunted record of taking ideas initiated elsewhere, shaping them, and putting them into the field. As one charter school advocate notes, schools do not have to be radically innovative to provide individual families a wider array of educational options:

> Charter schools are situationally different but they are not necessarily different in a larger sense. . . . A Montessori school, charter school, can be unique in Springfield, Ohio because there isn't any other Montessori

school in town. So chartering enabled a Montessori school to come to be in Springfield, Ohio and in that setting it is astonishingly different from everything else that is there, but the fact of the matter is on the face of the educational planet it is nothing new. [A1]

Whether Overall and Over Time Charter Schools Will Become More Innovative than Traditional Public Schools Remains to Be Seen   There are good theoretical reasons to imagine that charter schools could become more innovative over time. There are also reasons to expect the opposite.

The argument that charter schools will become more and more distinct draws on premises about how politics and markets handle new ideas. The charter school movement in its early years was an upstart: politically vulnerable because it was unproven, challenging to the conventional system and those who were invested in it, and lacking an established constituency of its own. As a market product, it faced a large pent-up demand from families unsatisfied with their current options and eager to try almost anything that offered a better approach. Both political vulnerability and market demand may have encouraged charters to steer charters down a safe, middle-of-the-road path as they sought to establish themselves. Politically, it can be astute to avoid sharply different approaches to education: approaches that might be unsettling to legislators, foundations, and others whose support or at least acquiescence was considered critical. In market terms, strong demand from families who just want something beyond their assigned school reduces the pressure to offer something truly different. In a community lacking any restaurants, the first to open is more likely to be a family-style style place offering burgers and pizza than an exotic, fashionable, and expensive establishment offering unfamiliar fare. In these terms, it would be reasonable to expect charter schools to grow more diverse and more different over time, as the movement becomes more politically confident and as greater competitive pressure forces new entrants to aim for niche markets that want something other than simply a better version of the conventional American school.

The argument that charter schools may become less innovative relies on theories about political and economic dynamics that are only slightly different from those that predict gradual diversification. Theoretical models of both market and political behavior give pride of place to the median consumer or median voter consumer. That is because both tend to assume that preferences are distributed roughly in the shape of a normal curve, with more shoppers and more voters packed near the middle and fewer and fewer as one moves out toward the tails at either end. If most families are looking for a refurbished version of the standard American schools, market forces may draw the center of gravity in the charter school universe toward a fairly uniform set of offerings. Even if many families prefer diverse and innovative options, economies of scale, as well as aggressive political and economic tactics by the larger, corporate providers, could lead to a dynamic akin to what happens when a large discount chain store kills off Mom and Pop stores in the old downtown. Idiosyncratic charter offerings—even those with small but loyal consumers—could be gradually muscled out of the market by their better-capitalized brand-name competitors. There is a familiar pattern, in other sectors, of private firms using their political power to push for regulations that standardize expectations and make it harder for new and different providers to enter the market.

Regulation May Play a Role in Imposing Some Uniformity and Conformity, but it May Also Be that Parents Are Less Eager for Innovation Than Some School Reformers   Research on this issue is scant, but anecdotal reports abound. Charter school founders frequently are motivated by a vision of a very different kind of schooling. Often the impetus comes from teachers who adhere to a more progressive pedagogical philosophy, one oriented less around testing and drilling and more around nurturing and guiding what they believe to be children's innate desire to learn. Somewhat ironically, these charter founders can find themselves doing battle with parents whose image of education is much more conventional. Although in principle choice should allow parents to sort themselves out in a way that better matches their desires with school missions, in practice parents signing up for charters frequently are driven more by their desire to escape their current school than by the specific attributes of the charter school to which they apply. For many, the motivating pressure behind choice appears to be a simple desire for a better version of the standard product.

Family Satisfaction

Parents are Generally More Satisfied with Charter Schools than With the Schools They Left Behind and than Parents Who Remain with Traditional Public Schools   One of the most consistent findings in the charter school literature, and indeed in the research on school choice more generally, has been the expressed satisfaction on the part of parents. These almost always say they are more satisfied after the move (Buckley and Schneider 2007; Finn, Vanourek, and Manno 2000; Goldring and Shapira 1993; Henig 1999; Schneider, Teske, and Marschall 2000).

In markets, consumer satisfaction typically is considered the lodestone. Ironically, the way the school choice debate evolved has had the effect of muting attention to this strong positive outcome. Faced with the fact that public opinion polls showed that most Americans were satisfied with their children's schools, early choice proponents found themselves arguing that satisfaction was a soft standard. What mattered were objective indicators of performance. Satisfaction—if proven and if sustained—would be a powerful factor to take into account in a pluralist system like ours, however. That would be especially the case if, as some suggest, parent satisfaction has the potential to translate into stronger involvement and the growth of social capital within the school community.[21]

What Satisfies Parents Doesn't Necessarily Satisfy Children, However   One of the arguments in favor of choice is that choosers feel satisfied and empowered to take more responsibility for the learning process. Proponents often focus on parents but implicitly assume that a similar process occurs at the student level. Almost certainly, it is satisfaction and engagement on the part of the student that will have the more proximate impact on performance.

The literature on student satisfaction is not as well developed as that on parents. One reason is that much of the choice experience takes place among younger children, including those just entering school, and for whom assessment of satisfaction is more problematic. Among older children who have their own, often firm, ideas about what they want from schools, some evidence indicates that levels of satisfaction with charter schools are not as high and do not comport with those of their parents (Buckley and Schneider 2007; Miron and Nelson 2002).

Initially High Levels of Satisfaction with Charters May Also Dissipate Over Time   Psychological theories about cognitive dissonance would lead one to expect parents to express satisfaction with choices they recently made. To do otherwise would suggest that they had erred, and erred in a way that might impose costs on their own children. "Everyone loves a new car," as Buckley and Schneider observe, but "what happens as time passes? Does the car hold up or do the wheels fall off at 30,000 miles? Often it is only over time that we discover whether love at first sight endures or whether we bought the proverbial pig in a poke" (Buckley and Schneider 2007, 205).

If it is only the first blush of excitement, relief, and commitment that accounts for the high parent satisfaction in charter schools, we would anticipate that the satisfaction levels might begin to fall over time. There is some indirect and direct evidence that this might be the case. Indirect evidence that parental satisfaction is a short-term advantage of charter schools comes from the fact that families often cycle back to the traditional public school system. In Texas, students exit from charter schools at a more than double the rate of exit from the traditional public schools. Some of those exits are out of state or to other charter schools. However, looking at just those schools that offer a higher grade, in a given year 21.1 percent of charter schools exited to regular public schools. By contrast, only 12.1 percent of public school students exited to charter schools (Hanushek et al. 2005).

Direct evidence is scarce at this point, in part because it is challenging and costly to conduct panel studies that follow charter school parents over time. Buckley and Schneider surveyed a sample of charter school and traditional public schools families in four waves. They found that the charter school advantage in parental satisfaction across a range of school outcomes declined over time and virtually disappeared by the end of five years (2006).

Sparking Improvements in Traditional Schools

Some critics of traditional public schools see little if any hope that they can be substantially reformed. John Chubb and Terry Moe's influential critique laid the blame for poor school performance on bureaucratic constraints that they felt were endemic to majoritarian institutions in diverse societies (1990).[22] Others, though, insist that their goal is not to replace the existing system but to provide electroshock therapy that will jolt it into reaction. When students exit to private schools, traditional school systems do not directly lose money; indeed, since the parents of those children are still required to pay taxes to support the schools, arguably the system is left with more money per pupil. With charter schools, on the other hand, at least some of the public funding follows the exiting student. At some point, a strong competitive effect from charter schools should force traditional public school systems to sit up and take notice, and when they do so, some charter school advocates believe that the result will be an improvement of education across the board.

The Jury is Still Out on This Issue of Competitive Effects   Caroline Hoxby has been perhaps the most visible proponent of the notion that market pressures generate positive responses from traditional public schools. Her early work—and subsequent clashes with Jesse Rothstein (as discussed in chapter 4)—looked at this issue in terms of intrametropolitan competition. She has also claimed to find positive competitive effects in the specific case of charter schools. In Michigan and Arizona, two states with a relatively large number of charter schools, Hoxby examined public school performance in districts that faced a high degree of charter school competitive threat, which she defined as those in which charter school enrollment constituted at least 6 percent of overall public school students. In both states, she found higher increases in test scores in schools faced with a charter threat than in those that were not. Hoxby portrayed these differences as unambiguous and large. To those worried that charter schools would lead to declining scores, because they would draw off students and resources, Hoxby suggested that her findings "suggest that the fears of a downward spiral aren't merely overblown. They're simply wrong" (Hoxby 2001, 70). The size of the effects she claimed were large enough to wipe out completely some of the stickiest and most troubling achievement gaps within as little as twenty years. Comparing Detroit, which faced a lot of charter school competition, to its affluent suburb Grosse Point which did not, she concluded: "If Detroit were to maintain its faster rate of improvement, it would close the achievement gap between its students and Grosse Pointe's students in just under two decades." She made the same prediction about Phoenix and its more prosperous suburbs (Hoxby 2001, 73).

Some recent studies have used more precise indicators of competition. Some also find positive competitive effects, though most do not make anywhere near as dramatic a claim. Sass characterizes the literature as "generally quite mixed." Looking at student-level data in Florida, he finds patterns consistent with modest competitive effects, but notes that these could be due to charters siphoning off worse or more disruptive students. "In either case, the evidence suggests that the existence of charter schools does not harm students who remain in traditional public schools and likely produced some net positive impacts on mathematics achievement" (Sass 2006, 118-9). Kevin Booker and his colleagues examine eight years of student-level data from Texas, which allows them to control for student and family characteristics and look at changes in performance over time. They improve on studies that simply assume having charter schools nearby indicates the presence of a threat. Instead they look at how many students—and how much funding—a given district and school have lost to charters. They found that charter school penetration had a positive and significant effect on traditional public school student outcomes. When they broke out districts by performance level, they found the competitive effects gains occurred in the districts with the lowest scores. Although the pattern of their findings is roughly consistent with that offered by Hoxby, Booker and his colleagues are more tentative in their interpretation, noting in particular uncertainty about whether the effects they find would be sustainable or apply in the case of a much broader charter and choice initiative (2005).

Other studies that also use student level data have had different results. Bifulco and Ladd examined whether traditional public schools that are located near charter schools perform better than those that have no charter school competition and found that—at least in North Carolina and given the (still rather low) intensity of charter school competition—the "effects of charter school competition on the achievement of students in traditional public schools appear to be negligible" (2004, 33). Buddin and Zimmer using student level, longitudinal data from six districts in California, similarly found "no measurable impact" on the performance or operation of traditional private schools (2005). They, like Bifulco and Ladd, admit this could change if amount of charter school competition increases

If competition from charters gets high enough, traditional public schools are likely to be affected, but many still disagree about whether those effects would be positive or negative overall. Advocates on both sides argue that it is too soon to judge whether competition from charter schools will radically change the health and effectiveness of the traditional public school systems. Researchers know that the relationship between policies and social consequences is not always linear. It is possible that, bad or good, effects will not become manifest until some threshold level of charter school density is reached. Despite the fact that they have been around for more than fifteen years in some places, charter schools in the greater scheme of things are still a relatively new invention. Empirical analysis can provide us with some indicators of where things seem to be heading, but they cannot penetrate the fog of the future with any degree of certainty. In places like the District of Columbia, where charter school penetration is high, the public system is unambiguously struggling, but arguably is performing better than it was ten years ago. There are at least three credible scenarios about what may happen next. Prodded by charter school competition and other pressures to perform, such districts might turn a corner and begin to reestablish confidence. The steady migration of students from the traditional to the charter schools might continue, eventually resulting in a negative spiral as lost revenues eviscerate any residual capacity to improve. Alternatively, charters and traditional systems might settle into an equilibrium, each demonstrating some successes and some failures and both underscoring the fact that the challenges of urban education transcend the institutional distinctions between the two kinds of schools.

Most researchers would probably agree that, at least so far, the impacts are not as dramatic—positive or negative—as some hoped and some feared. Mobilizing political support requires stirring hearts and minds. It is hard to stir hearts and minds with the slogan "This may help." Some proponents may have believed that charters would be a miraculous panacea, but others probably oversold the product as a realistic response to what they saw to be the heavy challenge of inducing change in a political system that provides so many opportunities to derail challenges to the status quo. Some opponents of charter schools probably believed that they would spark a sudden and unstoppable demolition of a system of democratically responsible "common schools," where children of diverse backgrounds learned together and learned to work well together. Others probably overstated the degree and certainty of the threat out of fear that an equivocal response would open the door for structural changes that would be difficult to reverse. These fears and tactical responses were not silly, but they oversimplified matters in a way that contributed to the polarization of public debate. There are many things about the implications of charter schools that we do not yet know. What we do know is that those implications are more subtle, uncertain, mediated, and gradual than the high-strung rhetoric led us to expect.

From the Trees to the Forest

They say that one should never see sausages made. Even if you like the final product, full disclosure about what goes inside the casing may turn you off the dish entirely. The same can be said about the research enterprise. It is the nature of science that fields of study are subdivided into specialized arenas in which individuals or teams of researchers compete to outdo one another in answering arcane questions and refining instruments and measures. It is the nature of science that knowledge claims are provisional and contested.

Despite the appearance that charter school research is irresolvably polarized and irretrievably stalemated, I have argued that there has been a gradual accumulation of evidence about how charter schools affect such things as segregation, achievement, parental satisfaction, and the like. I now take that argument one step further. Within the subfields discussed, unanswered questions and animated debates continue. That is to be expected, and by and large it is a good thing. To those operating within these arenas, some of the thrill of the chase—the sense of making a contribution—is tied to the pressure to come up with better measures, better designs, better interpretations. Each new study justifies itself by pointing out how it is superior to those that went before. That study in turn becomes the target for others to surpass.

The push-and-pull of this normal research enterprise sometimes obscures broader lessons that become apparent only by stepping back to gain perspective. I offer a handful of such meta-lessons: broad and convergent findings that are emerging across research foci and over time. These are derived in part from my own reading of the literature, but also from my distillation of answers I received, during my interviews, from a set of questions about how the researchers themselves characterized the current state of knowledge about charter schools. We know considerably more now about market-like mechanisms than we did ten years ago. The emerging picture is a more nuanced, tentative, and contingent on time and place than were the interpretations advanced by the most assertive proponents and opponents in the early days of the charter school debate. It does not support the rosy predictions of leaping test scores and contagious competitive effects offered by some of the early advocates, but neither does it reinforce the worst fears of the charter-skeptics about creaming, re-segregation, and dire effects on the schools and students left behind.

Charter Schools Are Not All Alike

When I asked researchers to characterize what we currently know about charter schools, their most common first response was to struggle against the invitation to generalize. More and more, it is becoming apparent that the term *charter school* is a broad umbrella under which are clustered schools that differ among themselves in important ways. Researchers have begun discovering differences in behavior and outcomes between start-up charters and existing schools that convert to charter status; between charter schools associated with a traditional school district and those standing fully on their own; between charter schools started by for-profit firms and those started by nonprofit and social service agencies; between those targeting median students and those seeking to serve niche populations with special needs; between those that are classroom-based and those that provide home-schooling and distance learning. Some of these differences are being found to be relevant to factors such as charter school staffing, recruitment, and test score results (Braun, Jenkins, and Grigg 2006a; Brown et al. 2005; Lacireno-Paquet 2006; Lacireno-Paquet et al. 2002; National Center for Education Statistics 2004).

Although there is broad recognition that type of charter school matters, there has not yet been convergence on a theoretically or inductively derived set of categories that researchers should rely on, despite several recent efforts to move in this direction (Brown et al. 2005; Carpenter 2005). In an innovative effort to develop a workable typology, the Minnesota-based Education I Evolving organization, with funding from the Spencer Foundation, has initiated a wiki-style Web site to enable researchers to try out and help to shape a taxonomy.[23] Regardless of their basic orientation on the school choice issue overall, researchers are in near agreement that there are some very good charter schools and some very bad ones, and that the simple sector-versus-sector comparison is not as stark or illuminating as it was once expected to be.

Time Matters

In the early days of charter school research, all the schools under the magnifying glass were young, and green, and works in progress. Today, the early cohorts have been around for ten years or more. Years in operation can change charter schools in many ways, both for the better and for the worse. There are good reasons to expect positive maturation effects, as teachers and administrators find their way, as funding becomes more regularized and assured, as families become more familiar with different types of schools and better able to select the one that best fits their needs. There are also possibilities that some things may change less favorably. Schools may lose momentum as the original founders burn out or move on, as the early funders begin to pull back on their support, as routines get more routinized, as enthusiasm wanes. Evidence suggests that the passage of time can be associated with changes in student composition, levels of satisfaction, and academic performance.

Place Matters

Some charter schools are in central cities; some in suburbs, and some (a markedly smaller number) in rural areas. Some are in places where the population is booming, some, where it is in decline. Some are in racially and ethnically mixed communities, and others in more homogenous settings. Some are in districts with reasonably strong public schools, and others are not. Here again, the point is not simply that variation exists, but that the evidence is accumulating that these variations make a difference in terms of the way that charter schools behave and perform, their effect on racial and economic composition of student bodies, and the way that existing schools, districts, and political actors respond to charter schools.

Governance Matters

Like so many other domestic policies in our federal system, charter school programs differ based on differing state laws, regulations, and implementation. Some states have passed laws designed to make the chartering process slower and to set a ceiling on charter school expansion. Others have worked as hard as they can to set ground rules that make it easier for charters to form. States differ in the rigor and frequency of their reauthorization processes, the amount of funding they provide, the kinds of rules and regulations they impose, the extent to which they favor certain types of charters, and more. These state differences are meaningful. Charter schooling, as a phenomenon, can look and be quite different depending on where one lives.

Student Background Still Matters. . . A Lot

One of the strongest and most consistent findings in education research is the powerful role of family, community, and peer background as it affects student test performance. The original Coleman Report nailed this point and radically changed the way subsequent researchers have analyzed and talked about school effects. Since then, the battle to account for differences in student test scores has been fought at the margins. The question among researchers is whether some factors relating to schools also matter and in more than a minor way. Debates over how to measure and control for family background historically have bedeviled efforts to gain consensus on whether private schools outperform public schools, and they continue to do so today (Lubienski 2003, 2004; National Center for Education Statistics 2004). The same issues now account for much of the stalemate and polarization around the question of charter school effects. Just to be clear, however: the debate is not over whether family background matters. That is a given.

Despite the fact that researchers know very well that family background and peer effects are powerful, public discourse about education generally and charter schools specifically has recently deemphasized it. Reciting the catch phrase "all children can learn," advocates on both the right and the left have adopted the posture that admitting to the role of class is tantamount to lowering expectations for the poor and to making excuses for the schools. Either in response to this or because they just plain believed it, many early charter school advocates promulgated the belief that charter schools would be able to quickly and dramatically raise test scores above and beyond what would be predicted based on student demographics alone.

Sharp clashes over the methodological details of recent charter schools studies—such as those by the AFT, Hoxby, and NCES—should not obscure the fact that the new charter school research has reconfirmed that class matters a great deal. For example, the challenge that Peterson and Llaudet level at both the Lubienkis and the NCES HLM studies of private schools and public schools is primarily over competing notions of how to control for class, not whether it is necessary to do so (2006). Indeed, in all three sets of studies, various indicators of student and family class and race have stronger and more consistent power to predict test scores than the school sector variables do. That the school sector nonetheless remains the focus of the policy debate appears to reflect a general, albeit problematic, acceptance that inequalities in socioeconomic status are an immutable backdrop against which policy decisions are made (Rothstein 2004).

Even though signs indicate that research is clearing away some misconceptions and generating some convergence in our understanding of charter schools, this does not mean that consensus on policy responses is just around the corner. It does, however, dilute some of the fuel that has been thrown on the fire of the school choice debates. Better research will not eliminate hard lines of ideological conflict. It can, however, potentially soften the edge of disputes, help dissipate alarmist rhetoric and its consequences, facilitate a focus on pragmatic solutions.

Values Matter

Good researchers take steps to limit the extent to which their own values and predispositions are likely to determine their findings. One way they do this is to structure their designs to put their expectations to an especially stiff test. A researcher who believes school choice will not lead to resegregation, for example, might deliberately study a school district with a history of racial tension. A researcher who believes traditional public schools deliver a superior education might deliberately study a district known to be overly bureaucratized and historically low performing. There are myriad choices embedded in research designs and many of these choices have the potential to affect the results. Some choices inevitably are made without deliberation and may reinforce researchers' expectations without their being aware of it. In some instances, undoubtedly, researchers deliberately skew these choices to steer the results in a direction they favor. Good researchers, though, try to prove themselves wrong.

Even when individual researchers do allow their values to infiltrate their work, the enterprise of science has mechanisms to sniff this out. Research is reviewed at many stages, from grant proposals, to conference presentations, to peer review for publication. Studies with strong findings tend to be targets for others to attempt to replicate, using the same data or with different designs and in different settings. It is good practice for researchers to make their data available for reanalysis, and journals are increasingly making that a condition for publication. Studies that are outliers—those that find especially strong effects—and researchers who consistently produce such studies tend over time to be pushed toward the margins of the scientific debates, their results to a degree discounted.

Yet, despite these safeguards, values still matter. Disagreements about them sometimes underlie putative disagreements about facts. Drawing conclusions about the costs and benefits of charter schools almost inevitably involves assigning values to differing outcomes. If it turns out that, given the option to choose, many majority and minority families opt for more racially homogenous schools settings, how much of a slide toward resegregation would we be willing to accept, as a society, in return for greater individual freedom? Would we be willing to accept more homogenous student bodies if it turned out that this contributed to an increase in average achievement? If we were willing to trade those off against one another, how large an increase in test scores would we demand? What about the trade-off between raising absolute achievement versus that of reducing achievement gaps? Or that between preparing students to meet society's definition of a well-educated person versus preparing students in ways that their families find appropriate and worthwhile?

If effects of charter schools were large, unambiguous, and across-the-board of all valued outcomes, questions like these would be moot. If that were the case, research in itself would provide the clear and direct guidance that idealized visions of the policy sciences lead us to expect. We know now that that is not the case. If charter schools have consequences—good or bad—they are incremental, less powerful than consequences flowing from other variables, and contingent on circumstance, policy design, administrative implementation, and local context. This information in itself is valuable. Policy makers need to know that charter schools are neither a panacea nor poison. They need to know that decisions about whether and how much to encourage charter schools require careful attention to the specifics, including the type of charter sponsor, the place-specific need and demand, the public sector capacity to monitor and intervene.

Researchers differ in the way they weight value trade-offs such as equity versus excellence, integration versus choice, family freedom versus majoritarian interests, pluralism versus harmony. The various protective mechanisms that dilute the impact of these value differences on empirical findings are less effective when it comes to how researchers draw implications for public policy. Research methodology, research training, and the collective give-and-take within the research enterprise are calibrated to circle in on findings of fact. The step from what we know to what we should do is a large one, especially when what we know is tentative, complicated, and contingent. When researchers are prompted to take that step—out of a personal desire to be relevant or in response to queries from others—they find themselves on ill-mapped terrain.

Some critics of an idealized vision of the policy sciences argue that research is inevitably corrupted by power, and corrupted to its core. They find the polarized and combative presentation of charter school research to be unsurprising. Interests deeply invested in the existing educational system can be expected to fund and direct research to discredit the charter school challenge. Interests ideologically committed to markets over government can be expected to fund and direct research that will present the traditional arrangements as bureaucratized, unresponsive, and ineffective.

The public face of charter school research is highly politicized, but I have argued here that, below the surface, the research enterprise has been operating more closely than we might have imagined in a manner consistent with what we might like to see. Concepts are being sharpened, measurements refined, stronger research designs are being brought to bear, changes over time are being taken into account, and inflated hopes and inflated fears are being put to pasture. This raises, of course, as many questions as it answers. If the arc of research is converging on several basic findings, why does the public discourse remain so polarized?

One possibility is that public discourse about research is polarized because it reflects deep cleavages in values and ideals among the American public. Mix disparate values in the crucible of democracy and the resultant brew might be too strong to nourish open-minded reflection based on careful consideration of available evidence. That, we saw in chapter 2, is the lesson some have drawn in rejecting the naïve vision of scientific research as the antidote to politics. The sources of polarization may not lie in the democratic politics per se, however, but instead in some of the mediating institutions that shape research and determine how it is disseminated to the public. The next two chapters consider how research funding and the modes of communicating research may contribute to the politicization of research by pulling research and researchers toward simplified messages and filtering out presentations of evidence that acknowledge complexity, contingency, and uncertainty.

Chapter 6

Follow the Money: The Role of Funding in the Politicization of Education Research

We have been wrestling with a puzzle. Research has been converging on an understanding of charter schools that provides a mixed, nuanced, and somewhat complicated picture; one that does not fit neatly into the simple narratives of the political right or political left. The public face of charter school research, however, is still marked by personalization, politicization, and polarization. The high stakes ideological and political battles discussed in chapter 3 help explain why partisans engage in hyperbolic, take-no-prisoners, brook-no-compromises tactics. Why and how, then, do researchers get drawn into this maelstrom?

"Follow the money" is a somewhat cynical slogan, but cynicism at times is a reliable guide. If you want to understand why things happen the way they do, sniffing along the trail of material incentives can be a reasonable place to start. Advocates on both sides of the charter school debate frequently refer to the funding sources of researchers whose findings they disagree with as a way to discredit them. To critics of market visions of school choice, the pro-voucher conclusions of Paul Peterson are thrown into disrepute by the substantial funding he has received from conservative foundations: nearly $2.5 million from the John M. Olin Foundation alone.[1] To advocates of choice, the funding bête noires are the teachers' unions. When Carnoy and others published their book reviewing the methodological weaknesses of charter school evidence (in which they criticized the AFT study but also charged several signers of the *New York Times* ad with blatant hypocrisy), Michael Petrilli, then second in command in the United States Department of Education's Office of Innovation and Improvement, referred to the book as a "200-page press release" from what he termed "the union think tank."[2]

This chapter probes the possibility that money—in particular structural changes in the way education research is funded—affects how the research agenda is shaped and the ways that research is brought into play. I begin by presenting three sharply contrasting perspectives, building on the approaches discussed in chapter 2. The first is an ideal-

128

ized vision in which government, foundations, and research institutions are aligned to maximize knowledge and constructively harness it to legitimate visions of the public good. Juxtaposed to this are two perspectives that emphasize the politicization of research. One, nurtured and disseminated by elements of the political right, sees government, foundations, and universities as part of a liberal "education blob" that steers the research enterprise to shield from scrutiny a traditional public education system that is oppressive, ineffective, wasteful, and corrupt. The other, nurtured and disseminated by elements of the political left, argues that an active and focused conservative movement has hijacked or selectively displaced elements of these institutions in a self-conscious effort to dismantle, disparage, and privatize a democratically controlled and publicly implemented system in favor of one oriented around individualism, unfettered markets, and religiosity.

In conventional parlance, to charge that funding has led to the politicization of research is to assert that it has corrupted the basic enterprise of research at its core. That is, that it has led to a situation where ideology displaces norms of good scholarship, the selection of research designs and methods is dictated by anticipation of what will produce favorable outcomes, and data are nudged and fudged until they conform with partisan platforms. The evidence presented in this chapter does not support the charge of politicization so baldly defined. The need for funding is less pervasive, the pattern of its availability less ideologically structured, and the formal and informal protections against scientific abuse more resilient than presumed in the harsher caricatures of either the right or the left.

It would be wrong, though, to conclude from this that funding is not an important part of the story behind the polarization of research. The government and foundation community have been reluctant to fund education research at all, and especially wary about funding research on the volatile issues of choice, but in doing so have left the field open for influence by a smaller number of funding sources that are self-consciously using research as an ideological advocacy tool. Rather than corrupting the core process of research, the political impact of funding is felt most consequentially at the agenda-setting stage—where it affects what aspects of school choice and charter schools get studied, how, and by whom—and at the dissemination stage, where it affects which findings and interpretations are most likely to be emphasized and which studies get the greatest exposure.

The Politicization of Research Funding: Three Perspectives

Researchers want money so that they can do their jobs. Some want it because techniques of data gathering can be costly. Some want it because their jobs depend on their raising soft money to help support the institutions in which they work. Some want it because funding can buy them time to get their research and writing done more quickly and well. Some want it because funding can help them ensure that their findings are attended to and because obtaining funding in itself can confer status and boost professional advancement.

Let us suppose—both because it helps focus our discussion and because it is almost certainly true—that most researchers are neither devils nor angels. Some, more than others, might be personally opportunistic, ambitious, or rigidly partisan and willing to bypass norms of honest scholarship in pursuit of those ends. Some, more than others, might be dedicated pursuers of truth, willing to follow evidence where it leads them, convinced that knowledge, though volatile, in the end empowers and ennobles. Most, we can presume, are distributed, like the rest of us, somewhere in the murky middle: wanting to do good, wanting to be right, flawed, selectively closeminded, occasionally duplicitous, frequently misled and misused. Against that backdrop, while institutions—formal ones such as laws, regulations, and policies, as well as informal ones such as social values and professional norms—may affect individual researchers' behavior only at the margins, their impact can add up to significant societal effects

An Idealized Vision: Funding Through the Prism of an Apolitical Policy Science

We can imagine a system in which a society's need for useable knowledge and researchers' needs for funding are harmoniously aligned. This is a vision akin to the view of the policy sciences discussed in chapter 2. The idealized vision is not so idealized as to naïvely presume that researchers, left to their own devices, will consistently and accurately fill democratic societies' needs for usable knowledge. In this system, democratically elected officials would play a significant role in setting the research agenda. Based on their understanding of the public interest and competing demands on the public purse, they would tackle broad decisions about how much of the government's dollars should be addressed at answering deeper theoretical questions, how much applied research focusing on more specific policies and program needs, and how much to regular data collection enterprises—like the United States Bureau of the Census, the National Assessment of Education Progress (NAEP), and the Schools and Staffing Survey (SASS)—that constitute elements of the national infrastructure for research. Based on their understanding of the extent and nature of societal opportunities and threats, they would make broad determinations about how much of the nation's investment in research should go to education as opposed to security issues, or space exploration, or housing policies, or the environment.

Where the broad parameters of public investment in research would be set by publicly responsible actors and institutions, the determination of which specific projects were worthy of support would rely heavily on some form of peer review. Assessment of the research design, data, and qualifications of research teams would be made by those with expertise in those areas, and the process would be shielded from partisan interference and political patronage.

This idealized vision assumes there are forces within the research community that inculcate and enforce norms of good science and objectivity. Universities, academic disciplines, and social norms of scholarship create pressures on researchers to meet exacting standards. Being right, being sophisticated, acknowledging uncertainty, and building on the work of others generate payoffs that compensate, at least in part, for the lower visibility and less immediate impact that typically go along with slow, careful research and the long simmering process in which findings get presented first in informal settings, obscure academic conferences, and then eventually in scholarly journals after a time-consuming process of peer review.

Democratically responsive public institutions set the broad parameters for research in this idealized vision, but there is both room and need for foundations as alternative sources of funding. Retaining some privately financed research options is valuable as a check and balance against the risk that government will monopolize knowledge and turn research into a tool for expanding its power. Even in the best of all worlds, furthermore, some ideas are too speculative or too contentious to warrant public investment. Free to be more daring and to explore areas in which there is nothing approaching a democratic consensus, foundations have the potential to be a socially valuable source innovation and testing ground for unconventional ideas.

Aspects of our current system of research funding have evolved with this vision in mind. Federal budgets approved by Congress each year steer millions upon millions of dollars into research designed to better understand the causes of societal problems, to identify promising points for intervention, and to assess existing programs to see if they are working as intended. A portion of this funding ends up going to field-initiated proposals, in which researchers come up with a topic and plan that federal agencies find compelling. However, more is given in response to specific requests for proposals (RFPs), through which agencies stipulate topics and often precise elements of design and measurement and then invite researchers to compete for the grant to carry out the project. Often governmental research funds are allotted by contract rather than grant, which gives public officials an even stronger control over the content, process, and dissemination of results. For many of these re-search awards, agencies rely on—sometimes by choice, sometimes by congressional mandate—assessment of proposals by other researchers who score proposals according to their scholarly merit, quality of de-sign, and track record of the individuals or organization that would perform the study. To increase the likelihood that reviewers will give objective analyses, untainted by personal relationships, the review process is usually set up so that reviewers remain anonymous to those who submitted the proposal.

When critics on either the right or the left charge that funding is part of politicization of research, they typically are not rejecting the value of this vision as a normative ideal. Rather, they are claiming that these mechanisms are too feeble, symbolic only, or have been recently under-mined. They also are arguing that there are considerable, and growing, amounts of funding that fall outside the purview of these checks and balances.

Mothers Milk for the Education "Blob": Research Funding as a Tool of the Left

Nothing about research is inherently liberal or conservative, left or right. At the high point of the Great Society, however, it certainly did not seem that way. Although not linear, the expansion of government, and especially the growth of the national government, seemed inex-orable at the time. Many on the left saw this as a natural outgrowth of growing knowledge and sophistication. Universities, progressive foun-dations, and cosmopolitan public leaders were using the guiding light of science to steer a path away from parochialism and ignorance. As more and more was learned about the factors that account for poverty, racism, and destructive economic cycles, society was more and more drawn to harnessing that knowledge to a public sector campaign to promote the collective good. Many on the right saw the same set of ac-tors and the same use of research, but interpreted the driving force in a quite different way. Rather than collaborating in a noble quest to make the world better for all, they saw researchers and foundations as part of a political dynamic that ratcheted up the size of government by discov-ering more and more problems, proposing government programs as the solutions, and then laying claim to funding to feed those programs and to evaluate them. This cycle, they felt, was self-serving and self-reinforcing. When evidence suggested that programs were not work-ing, the response was to propose bigger and better programs (and big-ger and better evaluations) rather than consider the possibility that public intervention might be inappropriate.

Several streams fed the conservative suspicion of research. One was a form of cultural populism that saw academics as cultural clones of the Eastern Establishment Ivy League elites who dominated government and society. These elites looked down their noses at the average, middle- and working-class folks who paid taxes to support the weighty programs the researchers dreamed up in the name of the poor. During the latter half of the twentieth century, this cultural aversion to academic research was supplemented by an elaboration of the concept of iron triangles, one that, ironically enough, had been invented and honed by social science academics. As initially formulated, the theory of iron triangles was offered to explain why government programs, once enacted, were so much more likely to grow than to disappear. Rather than assuming that this was explainable by the out-and-out merits of the programs, political scientists argued programs stuck around because of the political constituencies that formed around them: tight networks comprising politicians, who championed the programs and used their reputed benefits to stake a claim for votes; bureaucrats, who owed their jobs to the programs and who used their inside knowledge to build a case for their expansion; and organized interest groups consisting of program beneficiaries. Researchers, under this scenario, were not so much independent forces as hired guns, readily available to serve in the interest of an expanding national government. Adopted as an explanation for dominance of the traditional model of public education, this perspective pointed a finger at the so-called education blob, an undifferentiated mass including teacher unions, education schools, and liberal politicians, who assumed they knew more about what was good for children than the parents of those children did, and put their own interest before those of the students.

From the vantage point of conservatives at the time, private foundations appeared to be another important piece of the constituency for governmental growth. Symbolic of the problem was the Ford Foundation, and especially its Gray Areas antipoverty project that provided a testing ground for ideas later incorporated within the federal War on Poverty. "Ford was the first—but far from the last—foundation to conceive of itself explicitly as a laboratory for the federal welfare state," according to Heather MacDonald of the conservative Manhattan Institute. "In this vein, the foundation measured the success of Gray Areas by the number of federal visitors to the program's sites, and it declared the passage of the Economic Opportunity Act of 1964, which opened the War on Poverty and incorporated the Ford-invented community action agencies, to be Gray Areas' 'proudest achievement'" (1996). According to MacDonald and other conservative observers, Ford's activist ideology permeated the foundation world.

Then, and still, most of Ford's funding was targeted on action projects, not research. However, think tanks and universities also received considerable foundation support, and according to this interpretation were the breeding ground for new programs and the rationales attached to them. MacDonald describes a process by which foundation staff, under the cover of their claims to special expertise, wrested control of giving from the instinctively more conservative capitalists who created the endowments to begin with. The result, as she portrays it, was a flow of dollars in the form of grants to universities for research that worked to bolster the creation of a welfare state that the original founders would have considered anathema.

The major early foundations were critical, too, in underwriting the first think tanks: "universities without students" (Weaver 1989, 564) that collected top scholars and gave them the time and platform to more systematically focus on the issue of how ideas and knowledge could promote social reform. The Rockefeller and Carnegie foundations, for example, were major funders of the research organizations that merged to form the Brookings Institution in 1927.[3]

Government funding, from this perspective, was a major source of sustenance and glue to the cluster of liberally inclined researchers and research institutions in and out of government. "By selecting topics for research, and by funding particular organizations to undertake that research, administrators can use federal money to produce data that tend to favor the expansion of [their] programs," wrote the Heritage Foundation's Stuart Butler (1985, 20-21). As federal grants grew in number and size, universities expanded units that could compete successfully for them, gradually becoming more dependent upon the large indirect costs component, more eager to claim successful grantsmanship as a mark of competitive excellence, and more aggressive in pursuing and enticing those researchers who were good at providing the kinds of research the government wanted to fund. New think thanks and other private research organizations emerged to fill the gap that universities could not, in part because the latter were often too slow, too oriented around more theoretical issues, less likely to reward researchers whose focus was highly applied, and less comfortable with contracted work that might put limits on public discussion and publication. Military and security related research was a major driving force in the emergence of a new set of think tanks during the middle of the twentieth century, with the RAND Corporation standing out as the most prominent.

The new departments, policy schools, and institutes in the universities, and the growing think tank world, according to the conservative view, did not passively feed on the growth of government. Instead, they created the ideological rationale and added interest group muscle for its further expansion. A revolving door between government and the research world ensured that members of the two arenas thought alike, maintained close bonds, and could readily find common interests. To the extent that military needs ebbed after World War II, these research interests proved adept at helping to transplant the model—government grants and research contracts supporting researchers and their institutions which, in turn, lobby for new and bigger programs and more and more elaborate research—to the domestic policy world. The War on Poverty program, from this vantage point, is understood less as a governmental response to the needs average citizens who want help than as a new benefit program for the research establishment.

Research Funding as Weapon for the Conservative Right Wing

Because they saw research and governmental growth as inherently linked, traditional conservatives typically tried to cut funding for policy research and or keep it tightly controlled. A new breed of conservatives reacted differently. Social science in the past research may have tended to support the liberal agenda, but that was because liberals had been more adept at shaping the research enterprise. If research can be harnessed to an ideological agenda, they reasoned, two could play at that game. During the 1970s, a newer generation of capitalists began to put their money into efforts to reshape the political and policy agenda and did so with an eye toward making sure that their intent was not hijacked by more liberal offspring and foundation staff. These conservative philanthropists—people like Joseph Coors, Richard Mellon Scaife, John M. Olin, Harry Bradley—joined forces with conservative advocates in a broad and somewhat coordinated effort to turn the same tactics and mechanisms that had been used by liberals to build the welfare state into what Butler (see chapter 3) referred to as a mirror-image coalition designed to shrink government and install markets as the dominant means for addressing social needs (1985).

Today, many observers on the left appear ready to concede that conservative activists have gained the upper hand. From their perspective, public and private research funding today are skewed heavily in the direction of conservative policies, and universities and think tanks, responding to the money trail, are seduced to support a right-wing agenda, including educational vouchers and charter schools.

The National Committee for Responsive Philanthropy (NCRP) was founded in 1976 by a coalition of nonprofit leaders from "organizations involved in minority rights, urban affairs, tax reform, environmental action, public interest law, housing, women's rights, community organizing, service to the handicapped, children's rights, consumer rights and citizen participation activities, in addition to scholars and observers of the funding community."[4] NCRP has issued a series of reports monitoring the activities of conservative foundations. These reports argue that conservative foundations have employed a focused mission, overlapping membership to coordinate activities, and a self-conscious strategy of political marketing to leverage substantial influence. "It would be difficult to argue that the political right is not winning in this country, as it dominates at all levels and branches of government," one NCRP report concludes. "The many foundations and nonprofit organizations reviewed in this report have undoubtedly helped advance, market and strengthen the conservative agenda in all policy realms" (Krehely, House, and Kernan 2004, 42). According to one conservative foundation leader, school reform is "the No.1 issue for free-market conservative think tanks" (24). In contrast, as we shall see in this chapter, most of the older, more mainstream and generally more liberal foundations have shied away from this issue.

Conservative foundations have used targeted resources to support scholars whose writings challenge the notion that government can or even tries to promote the public well-being and to buck up the notion that free markets and individualism provide not just liberty but prosperity and justice as well. Some of this conservative funding has gone into efforts to discredit universities as bastions housing the enemy. The Olin Foundation, for example, provided funding support to Allan Bloom, whose 1987 book *The Closing of the American Mind*, with its provocative subtitle "How Higher Education Has Failed Democracy and Impoverished the Souls of Today's Students," was one of the first widely selling conservative attacks on universities (DeParle 2005). David Horowitz has written withering critiques of liberal think tanks and academia at large. His 2006 book, *The Professors: The 101 Most Dangerous Academics in America*, names names in attacking academics he believes are proselytizing for the left wing. From 1989 into 2006, his organization, the David Horowitz Freedom Center (formerly Center for the Study of Popular Culture) received more than $15 million in grants from an array of conservative foundations including Olin, Scaife, Bradley, Carthage, and Hume.[5]

There is no question that at least some on the right quite strategically thought about how to "recapture" research institutions from what they perceived to be their pro-governmental bias. One window into their thinking is found in a 1971 memo from Lewis Powell, then soon to be a Supreme Court justice, to officials at the United States Chamber of Commerce at their request.[6] In the memo, Powell bemoans the broad antibusiness and anti–free-enterprise culture in the nation and the complacency of business in the face of what he considers to be dangerous attacks. "American business 'plainly in trouble'; the response to the wide range of critics has been ineffective, and has included appeasement; the time has come—indeed, it is long overdue—for the wisdom, ingenuity and resources of American business to be marshaled against those who would destroy it." Although there are multiple causes, Powell identifies academia as the central source of the problem.

> The social science faculties usually include members who are unsympathetic to the enterprise system. . . . Such faculty members need not be in a majority. They are often personally attractive and magnetic; they are stimulating teachers, and their controversy attracts student following; they are prolific writers and lecturers; they author many of the textbooks, and they exert enormous influence—far out of proportion to their numbers—on their colleagues and in the academic world.

The Chamber of Commerce, he proposed, should mobilize substantial resources to mount a counterattack. This could include "establishing a staff of highly qualified scholars in the social sciences who do believe in the system" and using contacts on university boards of trustees to pressure the institutions to hire a more ideologically diverse faculty.[7]

Similar notes were sounded by William Simon, United States Secretary of the Treasury under President Ford in the mid-1970s and later president of the Olin Foundation. "Funds generated by business . . . must rush by the multimillions to the aid of liberty . . . to funnel desperately needed funds to scholars, social scientists, writers, and journalists who understand the relationship between political and economic liberty," he wrote in his book *Time for Truth*. Business interests need to "cease the mindless subsidizing of colleges and universities whose departments of economy, government, politics, and history are hostile to capitalism" (1978, 228-30).

These calls to arms were heard and heeded. Conservative foundations used grants to entice universities to initiate centers and programs that undertook research, trained students, and provided fellowships and internships with markets and individual freedom as their focus. George Mason University (GMU) was a favored target. According to the progressive National Committee for Responsive Philanthropy, GMU (or the legally distinct George Mason Foundation) received $8.5 million from twelve conservative foundations from 1992 through 1994 alone. Most of the funding went to support the work of the Center for Market Processes,[8] the Center for the Study of Public Choice, the Institute for Humane Studies,[9] and the Law and Economics Program and Center (National Committee for Responsive Philanthropy 2004).

Where universities were resistant or inflexible, the funding was used to create alternative institutions. These included new think tanks, both nationally and at the state level, as well as residential fellowships for scholars to allow them time to write and new journals to ensure that the ideas and research these scholars were generating would not be

blocked by liberal gatekeepers in the academic journals. No less significant were the special publications and training seminars, run by Heritage and others, to expose rising conservative politicians to the research they could use to attack the policy status quo, articulate their
own stance clearly and consistently, and defend a new agenda that portrayed economic growth and markets as better than governmental programs as a way to solve social problems.

Table 6.1 summarizes the three perspectives and how they differ on
key dimensions. The rest of this chapter delves more deeply into government, foundations, and research organizations looking at their role
generally and in the specific issues of charter school research. These institutions shape the array of incentives to researchers and the conditions under which research questions are identified and research projects are carried through. A naïve vision of research as independent of
and elevated above the pull and tug of politically defined interests simply cannot be sustained. The views from the right and left are too crude
and one-sided in their turn as well. Education research, I suggest, is a
contested arena, and neither the right nor the left has unambiguously
and irretrievably gained the upper hand. It is true, however, that the
right has been more self-conscious and aggressive in its recent efforts:
building new institutions that create research tied to advocacy goals
and making sure that research is widely disseminated. Funders that
might have hewed to a more objective, pragmatic, or open-minded approach for various reasons have tended to stay on the sidelines. From
the standpoint of those who would like to see evidence drawn into mature and thoughtful democratic deliberations, the concern should be
less one of which side will win the latest set of skirmishes and more one
of deciding how we can reform institutions and norms so the static of
short-term maneuvering and partisan politics does not obscure the signals that serious research can bring to bear.

Who Needs Funding and Where Do They Get It: Mixed Evidence in the Charter School Arena

In the gloomiest scenarios of politicization, desperate researchers are
tempted by the apple of funding and in return make sure that their
findings fit their funders' political needs. The first dent in the simple
politicization model is the discovery that, though external funding can
be critical for some and make life and work easier for others, the need
to chase research dollars is not universal and many researchers are
buffered from the money chase.

Given the powerful role attributed to funding in both the conservative and liberal versions of the follow the money argument, it is inter-

Table 6.1   Three Visions of Research and Funding

	Idealized	View from the Right	View from the Left
Defining attribute	Harmonious alignment	Research as part of the Education Blob	Privatization and assault on the state
Government	Democratically selected officials set agenda, invest in infrastructure	Public monopoly seeks to defend itself	Conservative Republicans use new power to control access to data and steer research toward pro-market policies
Foundations	Source of intellectual pluralism; testing ground for innovative ideas	Traditional foundations as providing ideology and manufacturing evidence for social intervention	"New wave" foundations as legitimizers of markets
Research institutions	Norms and traditions nurtured by universities provide powerful informal limitations on abuse	Research as tool of governmentally defined elite; universities dominated by an elite that is hostile to markets and culturally out of step	Researchers as aspirants/tools of deep-pocketed private sector elite; new wave think tanks as counter-institutions

Source: Author's compilation.

esting to discover that pursuing external funds was relatively unimportant for a considerable portion. I asked each of the choice researchers I interviewed: "Given your position and the kinds of research you do, how important a priority is it (relative to others) to obtain external funding? Extremely (5) to not at all (1)." As indicated in figure 6.1, the responses were rather polarized. The largest fraction among them gave the answer a 5, the highest ranking of importance; yet just under half gave it a 3 or less.

For some respondents, particularly those who engage in research that involves qualitative research in multiple settings, the need for funding is so pressing that they almost could not conceive of answering anything but 5. "My mother was a teacher. My father worked for the government so I have to pay the mortgage. I am not sitting on some endowment or trust fund. It is everything. Getting people to fund and pay for it" [A3]. For others, the situation is different.[10] "I've been lucky," one

Figure 6.1   Importance of External Funding

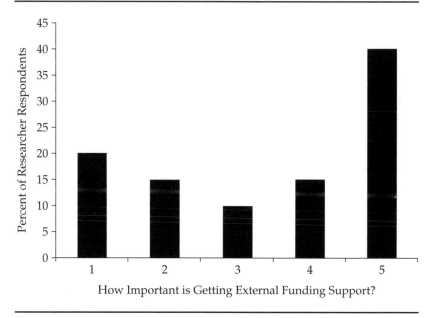

How Important is Getting External Funding Support?

Source: Author's compilation.
Note: 1 = lowest importance; 5 = highest importance.

researcher critical of market-oriented choice claims, "because I don't have pressing needs for money. I can wait until something comes along" [R18].

That some researchers are sheltered from the day-to-day pressure to nail down external support does not necessarily mean that money is not influential. For example, it might be that some researchers are sheltered precisely because they are in institutions generously supported by funding sources with an ideological goal in mind. To get better insights on the phenomenon, we need to probe more deeply into why money matters more to some than to others and whether the availability of funding systematically differs for researchers with differing orientations on the choice and charter school debates.

Why Is External Funding More Important to Some?

There are at least three reasons why some researchers are less oriented toward external funding than others. The first has to do with the kind of research they typically do. Different kinds of studies carry different price tags and, though many researchers are flexible enough to employ more than one kind of research design, most have a limited number of approaches for which they have been trained, with which they feel most comfortable, or on which they have built their reputation. Some tend to do studies that require hiring research assistants, interviewers, contracting with survey research firms. As one researcher who said external funding was extremely important explains:

> I am extreme on that, I think, because I do big studies. You know big Ns and big numbers of schools. And if I don't have the research team around me, I can't do that. I mean I am not a single researcher going out there and doing a school. I could never do it. . . . Now there are some things that I could do without this. But in these big evaluations of charters and vouchers, you have to have funding or you can't do them. [R10]

Others, however, tend to do more theoretical work or focus their empirical studies on secondary analysis with available data sets. "Actually, I'd say it's [external funding] not that important," says another. "I'd say it's probably about a two. A lot of the stuff that I'm interested in doing I don't think requires a lot of funding at this point" [R19].

A second factor has to do with where researchers do their work. Some work in soft money centers,[11] either independent research organizations that make their money by selling their research expertise or discrete units within universities that have little or no budgetary support from the broader institutions and for which finding external funds is critical. Among the researchers I interviewed, some in these soft money settings were especially attuned to—and anxious about—external funding. Asked to report the importance of external funding, on a scale of 1 to 5, one answered simply, "Five. My salary is paid by grants. We have no money" [R7]. Respondents who depend on soft money either for themselves or to pay others for whom they are responsible, often can tick through the names of program officers at various foundations indicating what kinds of things they do and do not tend to respond to.

Other researchers fret less than others about external funding because they receive substantial institutional support that buffers them from the need to pursue external funding on their own. Some of these work in settings covered by large endowments or where they can rely on others to raise the funding. "I'm on hard money, so I don't need to raise my salary," a faculty member in a well-endowed university observed. "And the other reason I think is that I'm very lucky to be at [name of academic affiliation], where the resources are pretty widely available."

> Q: So, if you have a research assistant or something like that on a project . . .
> A: I don't have trouble finding money to pay for that. I got a start-up fund when I started. I don't really need a lot more than that. There's a survey research center here that, if I needed, I would probably have to

raise some money if I wanted to run a survey through that, but I wouldn't have to raise the full cost. So, it makes all of this a lot cheaper. I've gotten some external grants, but I've been able to wait for the low-hanging fruit and just go for that and use that. [R18]

Others are in similar circumstances.

Not very important would be the answer . . . I have a unique circumstance here in that I have an endowed center and the endowment basically will cover my salary and so I basically only have to raise money basically to pay for two assistants. If I didn't raise money then my assistants wouldn't have a job. But I would still have a job. [R3]

A third reason researchers vary in their perceived need for funding is potentially more consistent with the theory that money matters. Some have funders practically knocking at their door. "I am basically looking for money to fall in my lap and there are foundations out there who know who I am," one researcher relates, "and who basically support the kind of work I have done in the past and who are willing to say, yeah, if you want to explore such and such a topic, we will give you x dollars to do that and so I don't have to go spend time submitting reports and stuff" [R8]. "No matter what I say there is someone out there who will fund it and I know this," says another. "As it turns out in education policy, there is lots of money available no matter how one approaches the issue" [R11].

Both of these researchers are strongly identified with the pro-choice arguments. If money is flowing freely to those who tend to generate studies either clearly favorable or clearly opposed to charters, vouchers, and choice, there could be implications for the polarization of the debate. Findings could drift toward the poles because researchers sense what will sell. They could also do so even if the researchers themselves are immune to the pull of funding; if, for example, the availability of funding makes those who get it more productive or makes it more likely that their findings will be packaged and disseminated in a way that gathers attention.

Before I began my interviewing, I coded respondents as to whether they tended to be seen as more favorable or critical toward charters, vouchers, and school choice.[12] Consistent with the argument that funding is more readily available to proponents of choice, those generally more favorable toward choice are somewhat less likely to say they need outside funds (figure 6.2), two-thirds of those generally critical of choice express a high need (4 or 5), and more than half of those generally supportive of choice do not. To get a better sense of the funding environment, we need to look more closely at

Figure 6.2   Expressed Need for Funding by Orientation Toward School
Choice

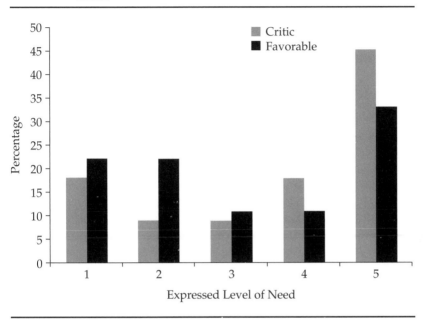

Expressed Level of Need

Source: Author's compilation.
Note: 1 = lowest level of need; 5 = highest level of need.

both the public and private sectors and the ways in which they make
resources available.

Federal Funding of Research in Policy, Education, and Charter Schools

When it comes to funding research, the federal government is the ele-
phant in the room. In 2005, considering all agencies combined, the federal government spent about $103 billion on research and development.[13]
About half of that was for development—defined as the process of taking
new ideas and converting them into "useful materials, devices, and systems or methods" (Meeks 2005). Research itself, defined in the same
source as "the systematic study directed toward fuller scientific knowledge or understanding," accounted for about half. Measured in constant
dollars, federal spending on research nearly doubled between 1970 and
2004.[14] The National Science Foundation, a major arm of the federal government's research funding enterprise, according to one estimate "funds
some 52% of all social science research done by U.S. academics and some
90% of the work by political scientists" (Mervis 2006, 829).

There are good reasons to want government to fund the nation's social research agenda. Generation of new knowledge is, or at least can be, what economists refer to as a public good. Public goods have characteristics that make them awkward for markets to handle efficiently. Market transactions work best when those who stand to gain and lose are party to a transaction, because they can barter based on their assessments of the profit they stand to gain, the price they will have to pay, and the risks that things may not turn out the way they hope. The wider the potential benefits coming from new knowledge, the more difficult it can be to identify those who will gain and dun them for their share of the costs of generating that knowledge. In such cases, societies will tend to underproduce the good in question unless government, with its broad taxing power, is brought to bear. Because new knowledge can be a public good, citizens and leaders often decide that investment in research and the development of new ideas is a legitimate and even necessary undertaking for government.

Looked at in relation to the issues of polarization and politicization of research, though, the federal government's role can be portrayed as threat as well as a salvation. There is a saying that knowledge is power. If that is the case, allowing those who hold the reins of power in government to direct billions of dollars of research opens the possibility that they will use it in order to further cement their position and control.

Compared to spending on research in the private sector—whether by for-profit corporations or not-for-profit foundations—however, research spending in the public sector is open to more scrutiny and oversight. Especially when it comes to grants by units of government with a specific charge to further research, there are formal and informal mechanisms in place designed to minimize abuse and maximize quality by giving professional researchers a role in review. The National Science Foundation (NSF), for example, is overseen by a twenty-four-person governing board, most of whose members are university-based researchers or administrators. The roughly 40,000 proposals that NSF reviews every year are subjected to competitive, confidential, merit review through an elaborate process involving scoring by independent review panels comprising experts in their fields.[15] Reviewers are instructed to judge proposals based on the twin criteria of intellectual merit and broader societal impacts.[16]

The United States Department of Education (ED) supports research through grants and contract and by supporting an array of data collection activities designed to build the nation's education research infrastructure. Since 2002, the main unit responsible for the department's research enterprises has been the Institute of Education Sciences (IES). Education research in the United States has long been looked at as intellectually fragmented and methodologically weak, with federal efforts overly influenced by the political muscle of organized interests with a stake in maximizing public funding and protecting from scrutiny the basic structure of the current system. The formation of IES represented an effort to upgrade the ED research effort, making it more scientific and evidence-based.[17]

As with NSF or the National Institutes of Health (NIH), research within ED maintains certain procedures that are intended to buffer it from undue political manipulation. IES is overseen by a fifteen-member National Board for Education Sciences, which has among its duties helping to shape a research agenda, reviewing procedures for technical and scientific peer review of the activities of the Institute, and helping to ensure that activities of the institute are "objective, secular, neutral, and nonideological and free of partisan influence and racial, cultural, gender, or regional bias."[18] The research areas of highest priority to the institute are in curriculum, instruction, assessment, teacher quality and "the systems and policies that affect these conditions and their interrelationships" including "policies that support the ability of parents to improve educational results for their children through such means as choice of education services and provision of school-related learning opportunities in the home."[19]

Review panels for federal research are not an infallible means of eliminating political concerns. The White House and key members of Congress have influence over the setting of the research agenda. One former NSF program officer cites as an example a speech the president's science adviser made in which he talked about the need to do more studies on the subject of science itself. "Folks at NSF heard that as a signal" and began to develop some initiatives looking to work in the area. They issued a "dear colleagues" letter saying that they were looking to fund work on the "science of science policy" They do this to show the administration (or at times Congress) that they are "playing ball" (personal interview). Division directors have some discretion in whom they select as program officers, and program officers can in theory nudge the process through their selection of panel members and reviewers. Reviewers' scores are taken very seriously, and both formal process and informal norms make it very unlikely that a project would be funded if reviews are decidedly negative. Defining the precise cutoff between what gets recommended and what not, however, requires making choices among similarly scored proposals and program officers might lean one way or another based on their own predilections or their perception of what the agency or administration would prefer. Panel members and reviewers may bring their own political biases which they self-consciously or unconsciously allow to be expressed in language of methodological critique.

Partisan and ideological politics can of course infiltrate the grant-making process, but the institutional arrangements make such manipulation more difficult and the impact of a partisan reviewer marginal. One school choice researcher, who had recently had a large grant denied by a private foundation because of one very negative review, drew a sharp distinction between the foundation and journal world, where you can be sabotaged if there is "somebody out there" who wants to block you, and the current IES procedures, which provided more protection against a single negative reviewer [R10].

Federal funding would appear to be a logical target for researchers interested in studying school choice and charter schools. Similarly, its formal (albeit fallible) processes for ensuring objectivity and high quality research might make it an important counterweight to polarization pressures coming from political partisans and organized interest groups. That said, the impact of NSF and ED on the charter school debate is less significant than might be imagined. Among the researchers interviewed for this study, federal funds are not a major source of support. I asked them "roughly speaking what percentage of the research you do is supported by the following?" The choices were government,[20] foundations, support from their home institution,[21] or advocacy organizations or clients. On average, federal grants and contracts constituted only 13.2 percent of their normal funding stream (see figure 6.3).

Why Hasn't Federal Funding Played More of a Role?

There are both supply-side and demand-side explanations for why federal funds seem not to loom large in the charter school research environment. The former have to do with decisions by political leaders about how much money to allocate toward social science research, education research, and school choice research. The latter have to do with decisions by researchers about whether to pursue federal funding.

Less Than Meets the Eye

"No one ever died because of the lack of education research." This is the response that Christopher Cross, a former United States Assistant Secretary of Education, recalls receiving during the 1970s, when he asked a staff member for a Senate committee that oversaw appropriations for health, education and welfare why education research funding was as low as it was (2006, 6). The comment reflects a reality. When it comes to making a claim on the federal purse, education research is seen by many to lack urgency.

Despite the fact that government injects substantial funding into re-

Figure 6.3   Respondents' Sources of Research Support

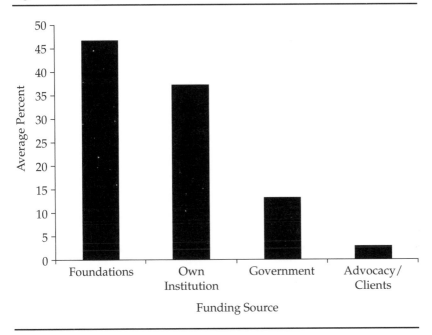

Source: Author's compilation.

search and development, for several reasons the amount available for studies of school choice and charter schools is less than meets the eye. Government support for research in the social sciences generally and funding for research on education policy in particular has been a much more minor affair than spending on such things as health, life sciences, military technologies, and the like. Most (about 60 percent) of the federal R&D budget goes to defense. For every $100 spent on research, less than $2.25 goes to the social sciences and less than 41 cents goes to research within the Department of Education. Figure 6.4 shows historical federal outlays for the Department of Education as compared to those for the National Institute of Health and the National Science Foundation.

Tight Specification

Not only does the federal government spend less on social science research generally, and education research in particular, what it does spend tends in some ways to be more tightly defined and controlled. Compared to federal funding in some areas, education research is more

Figure 6.4   Federal Outlays for R&D, Education vs. NIH and NSF, 1967 to 2005

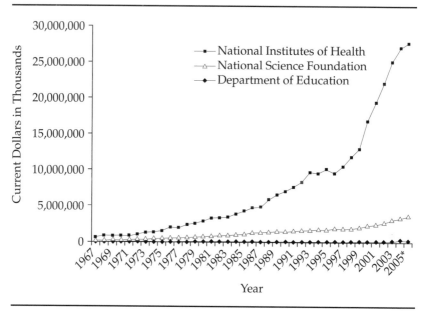

Source: Author's compilation; Meeks (2005).

likely to be applied than basic and more likely to take the form of contracts than grants. In each case, the difference narrows the degree of discretion left in the hands of researchers, reduces the role of peer review and other formal protections for scholarly autonomy, makes the funding somewhat less attractive to university-based researchers, gives researchers not based at universities some competitive advantages, and increases the ability of program administrators to shape the study and influence the dissemination of findings.

From 1979 to 2004, the amount of money the Department of Education devoted to applied research increased by about 113 percent and expenditures on program development increased over 40 percent. Basic research spending, during the same period, increased only a little over 12 percent. Basic research accounts for just about $3 of every $100 of research funded by the department. By comparison, it accounts for just under $50 of every $100 spent on research by the federal government overall and about $1 in $3 within the social sciences (Meeks 2005).

As components of research, applied research and development fall more within the zones of competence and oversight of political and bureaucratic decision makers than basic research, where the special expertise of the researchers themselves is more likely to be recognized and deferred to. There is nothing wrong with public officials wanting to make sure that citizens' tax dollars are spent on research that is closely harnessed to real world needs. To the contrary, as conceptualized in the idealized perspective, this is just the kind of thing that public officials are supposed to do. However, if public research funds are overly tethered to distinct applications, there is a price to be paid. Our review of the research in chapter 5 suggests that some of the early conflict and uncertainty in assessing charter schools was attributable to fundamental confusion in the way researchers and others thought about charters—about distinguishing among types, about maturation processes over time, about interactions with local context. Basic research is more likely than applied research to provide insights that have to do with underlying theories and conceptualization. These, in turn, are arguably most important when dealing with new approaches—especially those, like choice and charters, where impacts are expected to be systemic and indirect. In addition, because the process controls on basic research are designed to meld the distinct needs of government with the research community's conceptions of what constitutes quality and importance, basic research arguably is less vulnerable to direct political manipulation. This is a disadvantage, perhaps, to whatever party is dominant at a given time. It can be an advantage, however, from the societal standpoint, where there can be a hunger for independent findings that may not fit conventional wisdom or that challenge reigning policy orthodoxies.

Complementing its increased emphasis on applied over basic research is the Department of Education's frequent recourse to contracts as its vehicle for funding research. Contracts allow the originating agency much more leverage to specify the research question, research design, implementation, interpretation, and dissemination of results. Although there are more grants than contracts for education research, contracts tend to be much larger and to account for a greater proportion of the expended funds. In its March 2005 biennial report to Congress, IES provided a list of all grants, cooperative agreements, and contracts greater than $100,000 that received any funding from FY2002 through FY2004. Based on this,[22] I generated a database comprising 544 awards worth about $2.5 billion.[23] Contracts accounted for just less than one-third (32.4 percent) of the total number of awards, but contracts on average were more than three times as large the number of dollars and accounted in total for about 60 percent of the funds awarded.

Research conducted under contract to government agencies typically is more narrowly defined and administratively constrained than research conducted under competitive grant programs. As one researcher puts it: "from the federal government, it really depends on whether it's a grant or contract. If it's a contract, you have the whole review process and everything is very bureaucratic and it's very, it's more difficult to release reports" [R17]. Research grants often give researchers broad discretion about how to work their way through the many decisions that emerge as one moves from research design to implementation, analysis, and dissemination of the findings. Contracts, though, can impose very restrictive oversights designed to ensure that the study, its findings, and the manner of its release meet with the perceived interest of the sponsoring agency. One school choice researcher who receives federal support emphasized the relative absence of direct oversight or interference once the study was funded, but stressed that this was because the funding was via grants rather than contracts. "I know people who do have contracts. . . and they fight a great deal over all of those things. And that is not the case with the grants" [R15].

The constraining aspects of government contracts can be especially clear when the topic is politically volatile. Two relevant examples include a congressionally mandated study of the scholarship (voucher) program it initiated in the District of Columbia and the NAEP-based, HLM study of charter schools discussed earlier. In the case of the voucher study, an advisory panel comprising unaffiliated social scientists was established to work with the contracted researchers—a step meant at least in part to ensure that standards of objectivity and rigor were applied and political interference limited—but the Department of Education also put severe restrictions on any discussion of the results as the multiyear study unfolded. Members of the advisory committee were required to sign confidentiality agreements and when results were presented to them it was typically in Powerpoint displays and tables that were collected at the ends of the meetings to ensure that the figures would not be leaked.[24] In the case of the NAEP-HLM study of charter schools, as discussed in chapter 4, stakeholders on both sides of the debate knew that the basic analysis had been done months before a final document was approved and released. Even though the AFT study and the initial, statistically less sophisticated, Department of Education analysis were dismissed by many as too methodologically primitive, the department held tight rein on the release of the more sophisticated analysis for months, despite pressure from the AFT, which anticipated that it would essentially confirm its own earlier study.[25]

The Rise of Think Tanks. . . the Marginalization of Universities?

For government and some foundations, think tanks and private research organizations have emerged as an attractive alternative to university-based researchers when it comes to policy research. This may be especially the case in the education world, where the normal unwieldiness of academia arguably is exacerbated by the idiosyncrasies of education schools and what policy makers see as their almost obstinate indulgence of abstraction and narrative in preference to quantification, rigor, and contemporary standards for scientifically based research. When funders want answers, soon, and especially when they want to retain a measure of control over the design and dissemination of results, these private, nonuniversity organizations are emerging as a preferred partner.

Table 6.2 compares university to counterpart recipients using the data on IES grants, contracts, and cooperative agreements. Both won roughly equal numbers of awards, but the awards of nonuniversity recipients were, on average, 1.8 times as large. Universities were grant specialists; their awards were about fifteen times more likely to be grants than contracts. Nonuniversity research organizations were equally likely to receive grants and contracts. Most of the funding to nonuniversities went to a handful of large think tanks. The top five received fifty-nine awards for a total of just less than $888 million.[26]

The large research organizations that effectively compete for federal contracts lower their profiles when it comes to controversial issues and public attention. That is partly because their clients want them to be discreet. Whether government or private sector, the organizations paying the bill for contract research often want the results delivered to their ears only—or, at the very least, first. It is also because these organizations themselves have an incentive to avoid getting visibly entangled with volatile political issues. Political regimes come and go. Democrats held the dominant hand in Congress when most of the think tanks mentioned got their start. Although their fortunes have ebbed and flowed, they have stayed viable through shifts in the political climate. One way they do so is by resisting the impulse to become overly identified with an ideological point of view. As an example, RAND told its education researchers that they should not sign the CER-sponsored advertisement criticizing the AFT charter school study.

The emergence of private research organizations means that academic institutions continue to lose the dominant claim on research they once enjoyed. If that translates into quicker, better, and more usable research, that could be fine from a societal perspective. There are risks, however, that bear on the issue of politicization of research in the public arena. Tight reins on research from government funders may not always steer the research toward broad public ends; under some circumstances they may steer it instead based on narrower partisan goals of those holding power. Tighter restrictions on the discussion of research, and self-editing by research organizations that depend upon the favor

Table 6.2   IES Awards to University and Non-University Organizations

	Grant	Contract	Total
Non-university			
Average amount	$2,393,503	$7,971,897	$5,450,157
Number	132	160	292
Percentage	45.2	54.8	
University			
Average amount	$2,668,539	$7,909,483	$3,001,297
Number	236	16	252
Percentage	93.7	6.3	

Source: Author's calculations based on data included in U.S. Department of Education (2005a).

of funders, could reduce and selectively filter the flow of information into public venues. The displacement of universities as research partners may also loosen the influence of the institutional procedures associated with academia that, among other things, evolved to buffer their faculty and its research endeavors from political influence and to reinforce norms of scholarship relating to public presentation of findings, peer review, and freedom to explore ideas that are unfashionable.

School Choice Research as Political Hot Potato

A fourth reason federal funding is not higher on the radar screens of school choice researchers may have to do with the government's general reluctance to get involved in topics that are so highly visible and ideologically infused. Education research, as we have seen, is less well funded than other areas of federal research and also more tightly controlled. When the federal government does fund research on school choice, the studies tend to get prominent attention because of their size, their national scope, and the expectation that federal policy makers will pay more attention to research results they have sponsored than to studies done under the auspices of others.

Despite—or perhaps because of—the subject's prominence in national debates about education reform, by far the bulk of education research is focused on matters other than school choice. A search of NSF's electronic file of grants awarded, using the terms "school choice OR vouchers OR charter school"[27] generated only twenty-one grants that appeared to be genuinely dealing with these issues over the twelve years from 1994 through 2005. The amount awarded was about $3.5 million. This may not seem insignificant but pales in relative terms when one takes into account the fact that the agency makes roughly

10,000 awards every year and has a budget is approaching $6 billion per year.[28]

A full explanation for this pattern undoubtedly would be complex. Probably one important factor is a general and more or less self-conscious orientation on the part of elected officials—a mistrust of softer social sciences and a greater eagerness that the benefits show up concretely and immediately. This in turn is especially apparent in the world of education policy, which rightly or wrongly has earned attention for being particularly ideological, particularly abstract, and particularly weak in research design.[29] It becomes particularly sensitive when the topics involved are volatile, because even politicians who respect the power and objectivity of research in the physical and biological arenas often feel differently about researchers in these softer areas.

Politicians' Wariness About Soft Research

When it comes to research for understanding social problems and policy, education is the Rodney Dangerfield in the room: it simply gets no respect. Early in May 2006, Senator Kay Bailey Hutchison voiced reservations about social science research that provides an insight into the thinking of at least some of those who are responsible for determining the nation's support for the policy research enterprise. Expressing support for President Bush's proposal to increase NSF funding, she made it clear that her support was for funding in the hard sciences and studies most likely to result in advancements in science, mathematics, and technology—research that will improve national competitiveness in global markets rather than research intended to help her and other elected officials make wiser and more informed decisions. "I want NSF to be our premier agency for basic research in the sciences, mathematics, and engineering," she emphasized. "And when we are looking at scarce resources, I think NSF should stay focused on the hard sciences" (Mervis 2006, 829).

Political leaders' skepticism about the value of social science research is nothing new and its appeal is not limited to the Republican Party. From 1975 through 1988, Senator William Proxmire (Wisconsin, D.) regularly issued a Golden Fleece Award to draw attention to what he considered to be "wasteful, ridiculous or ironic use of the taxpayers' money."[30] Social science studies were among the more frequent and publicly noted winners. The first award, for example, went to an NSF project that had the goal of elucidating "why people fall in love." In making the award, Proxmire indicated that such matters were better left to "poets and mystics, to Irving Berlin, to thousands of high school and college bull sessions." Others went to such things as a National Institute of Mental Health funded study of what went on in a Peruvian brothel; a study, commissioned by the Federal Aviation Administration, of the physical measurements of airline stewardesses, including the "length of the buttocks;" a Justice Department study to determine why prisoners try to escape (Severo 2005).

Because the public harbors its own suspicions about so-called ivory tower researchers and pointy-headed elites, it's relatively easy for some politicians to demagogue on the issue of silly research. Funding social science and policy research presents legitimately tough questions even for public officials who sincerely want good information, but are aware how difficult it may be to make and defend the journey from tentative and contingent evidence to sound decisions. Officials who blindly defer to researchers, under the dubious assumption that good studies make good policy, are being no less simpleminded than those who blithely paint targets on researchers' backsides. Even the best policy research—arguably especially the best—comes with certain "ifs, ands, and buts" attached. Because sensible policy makers know that they cannot easily draw the right inferences from the available evidence, they are aware of the risk that research will be used by others to goad, sway, or deliberately mislead them.

Historically, politicians have been especially sensitive to the threat that discretion they grant to researchers will be used by them to surreptitiously push political agendas of their own (Moynihan 1969). Normally, the charge that research is soft is meant as a challenge to its weaker research methodologies. It may be, however, that this different sense in which social and policy research is soft—the sense in which it is manipulable for political or personal gain—has more to say about why federal funding in these areas is less bountiful and more tightly overseen.

Demand-Side Explanations for the Limited Federal Role

These supply-side considerations—limited education research funding overall, tight constraints, funder wariness of sensitivity about hot-button issues, politicians' skepticism of social science research—reduce the odds that school choice researchers will succeed in obtaining federal support and raise the costs of pursuing and conducting such research as well. Demand-side factors also play a role. For various reasons, some school choice and charter school researchers simply find it more attractive to pursue nongovernmental sources of support.

In explaining why in many instances they did not even pursue more federal support, respondents mentioned a number of things. Some suggested that the work required to assemble a credible proposal was great and the chances of receiving the funds too low. "It was the hardest proposal I ever wrote and spent a lot of time on it and it didn't get funded," said one [R2]. Another, who "occasionally" goes after government grants generally avoids them "just because they are such a hassle to go through the procedures for them" [R11]. "I am always amazed at people who are willing to go through the process of trying to get an NSF grant," notes a third. "You know I did that when I was an assistant professor and I think there is a certain cachet that goes along with getting an NSF grant but for God's sake you know it just takes so much time and then maybe you won't get it" [R8].

Others referred to what they saw as a methodological bias at IES that reduced their prospects for succeeding. As part of an aggressive effort to increase the methodological rigor within the education research field, IES has emphasized randomized field trials as the gold standard for quality education research.[31] This has led at least some researchers to conclude that it is not even worth their time to apply for federal funding unless they are able and willing to go that route. This is true despite the fact that some of the best quality research on charter schools is being done using nonexperimental techniques but taking advantage of student-level data available in some states, as discussed in chapter 5. "There's a reason I'm not getting federal money right now," suggests one researcher who employs sophisticated quantitative, but not experimental, analysis and who often serves on federal research review panels. It is "because I'm not doing much random assignment. . . . That doesn't mean all the funding from the Department of Education is in that direction, but they clearly have a strong bias in that direction right now" [R16].[32]

Others were deterred by what they considered political factors that limit their access. Researchers whose work tends to be critical of market-oriented reforms more often expressed this view. "These funding agencies at any time have a general stance," says one, who "can't conceive of getting a grant from the U. S. Department of Education" on choice related work [R1]. "And partly because of the politics," says another. "You know you can't say anything bad about charter schools." [R2].

If federal funds were the only game in town, factors like these might not be enough to keep researchers from aggressively pursuing federal funds and accepting the methodological and oversight restrictions that can come with it. There are alternatives, however. Private foundations also provide support, and, as we have seen, choice researchers are much more likely to say they get their funding through this route than through government support. Foundation grants tend to be smaller, but have other advantages. Unlike the Department of Education or NSF, foundations are for some considered an avenue to easy money. One researcher, as quoted earlier, likened foundation funding to dollars falling into his lap [R8]. Another researcher did not deal much with foundations until switching to education as a focus. "It seemed to me that when I got into education that there were more foundations with more money. And so I started thinking about foundations, and I had not thought about them much before" [R16].

This privatization of school choice funding may be important to understanding the polarizing forces that we have seen are so prominent. These other avenues carry fewer protections for the integrity of the core research enterprise and may increase the probability that results will be framed less tentatively, with fewer caveats, with more sharply drawn policy implications, and more aggressively injected into public debate.

Foundations and the Privatization of Education Research Support

The foundation world is crowded and diverse. Some foundations are huge. The Bill and Melinda Gates Foundation, the nation's largest, had assets of about $30 billion in 2006, and, with the addition of the Warren Buffett bequest, will roughly double in size. Others are tiny. The Siders Foundation, in Bloomington, Minnesota, had assets of about $16,000 and total giving of $19 in 2005. Some are broad and with an ambitious focus. The Ford Foundation's goals are nothing less than to "strengthen democratic values," "reduce poverty and injustice," "promote international cooperation," and "advance human achievement."[33] Some are narrow and parochial, limiting funding, for example, to a particular area (such as theatrical arts) in a particular community. Some are run by professionals and with huge staffs; some are amateurish and driven by family board members who may be whimsical or inattentive.

Why have some foundations become major players in promoting charter schools and funding charter school research, and, more important, what difference does it make? Government funding is hardly a guarantee that research will be well aimed and well constructed to meet public goals. What government does is influenced, for better or worse, by politics. And politics can be the breeding ground for partisanship, patronage, and playing it safe. At least potentially, though—as envisioned in the idealized version and as pursued with some seriousness of purpose through the formal processes of peer review, requirements for public information, and restraints on administrative staff control—public funding has the advantages of being more transparent, of incorporating well-tested checks and balances to limit manipulation, of being designed to sift through conflicting interests to find and define broader and more unifying ones.

Is the role of foundations in the charter school debate best understood as a complement to public funding, a source of venture capital in a still new and developing arena? Or is it part of the explanation for the political polarization that is the central focus of this book? Have right-leaning and left-leaning foundations used their largely discretionary funds to pull scholarship away from the core methods of scientific investigation, the institutionalized values and buffers provided by universities, and the professional checks and balances provided by disciplines, journals, and peer review?

There are two main story lines to relate. One is populated primarily by conservative foundations ardently dedicated to the goal of promoting market-oriented alternatives to government. For some of them, charter schools are a valuable piece in a strategy that is self-consciously political at its core. The Walton Family Foundation in 2004 gave about $66 million for K-12 schooling, "outpacing the educational philanthropy of Ford, Carnegie, Kellogg and other venerable foundations" (Hassel and Toch 2006). About eight out of every ten of these dollars supported charter schooling: either by funding schools directly, funding advocacy and support organizations, or funding research.

The other is a story populated by what I will call, for lack of a better term, more mainstream foundations. This includes many of the venerable foundations, but also some newer ones like the Bill and Melinda Gates Foundation. These foundations are not outside or above politics, but—compared to the conservative advocacy foundations—their politics are less partisan, more diffuse.[34] They, too, want to change the world, but their primary point of attack is civil society—the array of nonprofits, community groups, and nongovernmental organizations that constitute a sector that is collective, like government, but private like the market. Many of these foundations would prefer to reform public institutions than to replace them. They are wary of the market-oriented thinking that, as described in chapter 3, has come to dominate the public framing of the charter school issue. For reasons I will explain, however, these foundations have shied away from a head-to-head engagement on this issue. They have not funded a cadre of charter-skeptical researchers to balance out the adamantly pro-choice team assembled by the conservative foundations. Nor, by and large, have they stepped up to the plate as supporters of an objective, rigorous, and open-minded research agenda that might seriously wrestle with questions about how government, markets, and various mission-oriented providers might best combine to meet the nation's educational needs. Instead, they have placed their chips elsewhere, some deemphasizing K-12 schooling generally, others assiduously limiting their focus to reforms that do not directly engage the school choice debate.

The stories about these two types of foundations have somewhat different trajectories, but they share three themes. First, contemporary foundations—whether oriented toward political advocacy or societal change, whether fellow travelers of the right or the left, whether measured against government or against the foundation world of fifty years ago—are defined by a mission and seek to maximize their impact by keeping that mission manageably constrained.

Second, with few exceptions, supporting research is an instrumental, not a primary, goal . . . if it is a goal at all. Foundations, for the most part, do not want to fund research that is untamed: research that could question or complicate their core missions or guiding principles. This instrumental orientation has different consequences when it plays out in conservative advocacy foundations and in the more mainstream foundations. For the former, promoting market-based solutions is a core part of the institutional mission; funding research on choice, vouchers, and charter schools is accordingly complementary to the organization's overall goals. For the latter, choice and charters are more likely to be seen as a complication and distraction.

Third, where they do see research as complementary to their enterprise, foundations tend to put a heavy emphasis on dissemination. This is both because they want to show their trustees that they are having an impact and because they see the route to impact as coming through changing minds. Research, for their purposes, must be simple, clear. Like other groups interested in having an impact, today's foundations have been influenced by the clear and consistent advice from Madison Avenue and public relations firms to rely on simple messages, product branding, and repetition. Pursuing the objectives of getting attention and changing minds is not necessarily in opposition with fidelity to the norms and procedures of rigorous research, but it does generate tensions that are not always resolved in the favor of the research enterprise.

Education Research Funding: How Much and to Whom?

Mapping the activities of the foundation community is challenging. Possibly the most used and complete data is a directory compiled by the Foundation Center, "the nation's leading authority on U.S. philanthropic activity" (Hassel and Way 2005, 178). For the years 2000 through 2003, the Foundation Center's directory includes 331,186 grants from 533 foundations.[35] Overall, the database includes information on almost 85,000 foundations. Fifty-nine of these have assets of $1 billion or more; a little over 24,000 of them have assets of $100,000 or less.

Most foundations do not give money designated for K-12 education. To get a picture of foundation giving, I compiled data on grants made from 2000 through 2003 in which the substantive focus was K-12 education. This generated 25,384 separate grants, less than 8 percent of the total number of grants in the database for those years. Not surprisingly, given the variation across the foundations, these grants were of many different sizes and types. The BB&T Charitable Foundation in North Carolina, for example, gave one grant of $10 to a local public school district, and Publix Super Markets Charities in Florida gave $25 to a Catholic school in the state. Some grants were huge. The Bill and Melinda Gates Foundation accounted for five of the seven largest, each more than $20 million. The Walton Family Foundation also gave two separate grants of more than $20 million each, both to the Children's Scholarship Fund, a private voucher program in New York City.

Among those foundations that give for K-12 education, research per se is not a high priority. Some grants specifically indicate research as the designated use. I coded these as research-oriented, but added also any grants in which the word *research* appeared somewhere in the text of the grant description.[36] Even using this generous definition, only 1,581 grants—about 6 percent of all those related to education—could be characterized as having a research component. From there, the universe was further trimmed. All grants in which recipients were located outside the United States were removed, as were all one-time anomaly grants—those less than $50,000 in which recipients appeared only once in the entire database. The result was a database of 1,280 grants awarded by 192 foundations to 563 organizations for a total of $401,984,124. Figure 6.5 shows the distribution of the grants by the amount awarded. One out of three (32 percent) was for $50,000 or less, more than half (55 percent) were $100,000 or less, and fifty-four (less than 5 percent) were for more than $1 million.

Education research grants from foundations go to a wide array of organizations. They include private research organizations and universities, but also units of state and local government, other foundations, and even individual schools. Some recipient organizations focus exclusively on education. Others include education among a wide array of concerns. Table 6.3 shows the distribution of grants by the type of recipient organization. Nearly two-thirds (65.4 percent) went to organizations for which research is a primary focus. Universities were the most prevalent recipient (18.8 percent) and won largest share (27.3 percent). Research organizations with a general (not education-specific) focus were the second most common recipients (15.5 percent); research organizations with an education focus were slightly fewer in number, but received somewhat more grants and grants that were on average larger. Public general purpose governments (states, localities) and education-specific governmental units (state and local departments of education) accounted for a much smaller number of grants. The grants to state departments of education (ED), however, were on average the

Figure 6.5   Number of Foundation Grants for K–12 Education Research, 2000 to 2003, by Size

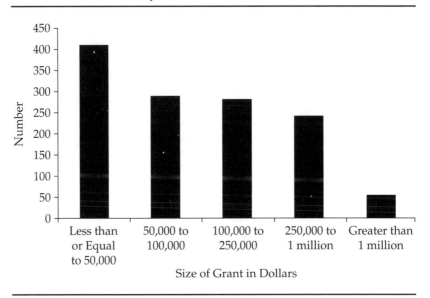

Source: Author's calculations.

largest of all foundation grants and local EDs had the largest share of the grants going to governments.

Included in the *other* category are eleven grants to individual schools. These were few grants and generally small. This is not because foundations do not fund individual schools; they frequently do. Rather, it is because those grants are typically for programs that have no research component. Three out of every four of the research grants going to schools went to traditional public schools. Charter schools, however, make up much less than one-fourth of the nation's schools, indicating that they on average had a greater likelihood of winning grants of this type. Charter school grants, in addition, tended to be larger than those to traditional public schools.

Trends Over Time   The data reveal no evidence of consistent trends in the number or amount of education research grants awarded by foundations from 2000 to 2003. The number of grants rose slightly until 2002 and then fell in 2003. The average size of grants decline from 2000 through 2002 and then rose in 2003. Given the small number of years included and the relatively small differences from year-to-year, it is hazardous to speculate about what to make of this pattern. There were no

Table 6.3 Foundation Grants for Education Research, 2001 to 2003

Type	Number of Organizations	Percentage of Organizations	Number of Grants	Percentage of Grants	Average Size of Grant	Aggregate Grants
University	106	18.8	350	27.3	$338,955	$118,634,250
Nonprofit, not research, educ focus	81	14.4	120	9.4	$594,110	$71,293,200
Research organization, educ focus	71	12.6	255	19.9	$255,837	$65,238,435
Another foundation	56	10.0	102	8.0	$543,783	$55,465,866
Research organization, general	87	15.5	233	18.2	$211,931	$49,379,923
State or local DOE	47	8.4	64	4.8	$302,037	$19,330,380
Nonprofit, not research, general focus	73	13.0	103	8.1	$133,042	$13,703,326
State or local government	7	1.2	10	0.8	$115,185	$1,151,850
All others	35	6.2	43	3.3	$181,095	$7,787,085
Total	563		1280		$314,050	$401,984,315

Source: Author's compilation.

consistent changes in the type of organizations receiving the grants during this period.

Foundation Funded Research on School Choice   Overall, very few education research grants were explicitly targeted to the study of school choice. Only thirty-nine of the 1,280 grants supporting K-12 education with a research component (3 percent) had the words *choice, vouchers,* or *charter schools* as the designated subject or elsewhere in the grant description text. Neither the number nor the amount awarded systematically increased or decreased between 2000 and 2003. By far the largest grant was $10 million from the Walton Family Foundation to Parents in Charge, an organization founded by Ted Forstmann to encourage parental influence on their children's education. Significantly, although research was mentioned in the descriptive summary, most of the funds did not go into research per se. Although the grant description is not detailed enough to determine precise uses, it appears that most of the funds were used for public outreach and to support the private voucher program. Between 2000 and 2004, Parents in Charge spent more than $5.5 million that appears to have gone to advertising agencies and about $6 million for the Children's Scholarship Fund.[37] Nonetheless, Paul Peterson's later research on this program became an important part of the public debate about vouchers and choice, with Peterson concluding that vouchers significantly improved the performance of African American students and Alan Krueger, reanalyzing the same data, coming to a different conclusion (Howell and Peterson 2002; Krueger and Zhu 2004).

Foundations, Funding, and Ideology

The idealized vision of foundation funding sees it as a source of intellectual pluralism, a testing ground for innovative ideas from throughout the ideological spectrum. Liberals fear and argue that private funding of education is dominated by conservative advocacy-oriented foundations that steer findings toward simplistic pro-market conclusions. Conservatives fear and argue that both progressive and many mainstream foundations fund research designed to discredit choice, in general, and more market-oriented forms of choice in particular.

To assess the ideological dimensions of education research funding, all individual grants were coded as coming from funders who were Conservative, Mainstream, or Progressive in their orientation.[38] Conservative foundations combined to provide fifty-seven grants, 4.5 percent of the education research grants in the sample. The progressive foundations were considerably more active, accounting for 28.4 percent. The conservative foundations offered more money per grant, however: their average grant was 1.4 times as large as the average for the progressive foundations. In the aggregate, progressive foundations provided 4.5 times as much.

In reviewing these figures, it is important to bear in mind that the data depend on whether grants were identified in the Foundation Center directory as having an education research element. They do not include grants given exclusively for program development, or advocacy, or any of a number of possible uses that need not involve research. Moreover, they do not include grants that are not identified or allude vaguely to such functions as "continuing support." This is important given that a review of the grants in the directory suggests that conservative foundations are more likely to characterize their gifts very broadly. Because of this, it is reasonable to surmise that the figures I present may understate the actual research activities of the conservative activist foundations to a greater degree than those of other foundations.

Figure 6.6 shows the distribution of grant activity by funder orientation over time. There is no evidence that foundations are getting either more or less active in an ideologically meaningful sense. Rather, all three types of foundations appear to be responding in a generally similar pattern: increasing the number of grants through 2002 and decreasing the number but increasing the average size in 2003. If politicization

Figure 6.6   Number of Education Research-Related Grants by Funder Orientation Over Time

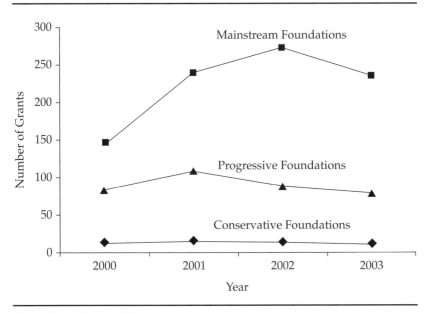

Source: Author's compilation.

of research is related to foundation activity, we will have to look deeper to find the mechanism.

On one issue, however, there *is* an important difference related to foundation orientation. As indicated in figure 6.7, grants by conservative foundations are much more likely to focus on school choice. Nearly one of three (31.6 percent) education research grants by the conservative foundations dealt with school choice, vouchers, or charter schools, compared to about three in 100 (3.3 percent) for progressive and one of 100 (1.1 percent) for mainstream funders. When it comes to education research, conservative foundations have been much more focused on the choice debate. Others are spreading their funding over a much wider array of research questions.

Here, then, is a possible insight into how conservative foundations seem to be dominating the debate around choice and charter schools despite their smaller number and scale. Chapter 3 suggested that choice and charter schools were especially explosive issues precisely because of the way that had come to be aligned with the larger ideological battle over whether government or markets represented the better option for meeting social needs. Other areas of education research—studies of curriculum, teacher burnout, class size, small schools, and the like—

Figure 6.7   Education Research Grants Focusing on School Choice, By Funder Orientation

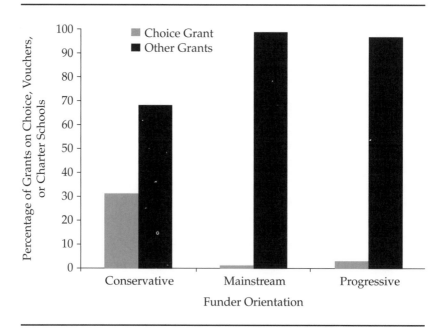

Source: Author's compilation.

may have a more certain and immediate impact on children and classrooms. However, conservative foundations, it appears, may be more strategically emphasizing research that can be used in the bigger battle about how big or small should government be.

Why Studies Get Funded: The Importance of Foundation Mission

The way that foundations think of themselves and their organizational missions tells us more about what studies will get funded than does the innovativeness of researchers' ideas or the intricacy and sophistication of their research design. I asked respondents to tell me about the "factors that in your mind determine whether you get funding," asking them to score, from 1 to 5, a series of factors and then giving them a chance to mention others that they felt were important as well. Figure 6.8 shows the average score that researchers assigned to each of the seven factors I presented to them. The two most important were Funder Priorities and the researchers' Personal Reputation. One respondent

Figure 6.8   Researchers' Perceptions of What Determines Funding

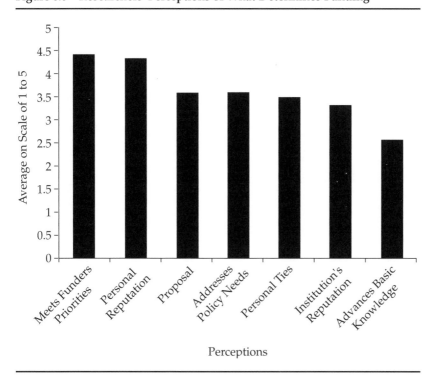

Source: Author's compilation.

took pains to emphasize that, though he rated some other factors a 4, "the only thing I hesitate about" is that funder priorities are "so important that [they are] more than one notch above the others" [R3].

Next in importance, and roughly equally scored, were the quality and style of the proposal, the extent to which the study addressed policy needs, and researchers' personal ties to the funder. Least important was the extent to which the study had the prospect to advance basic knowledge. Not a single respondent said that meeting basic knowledge was extremely important; by way of contrast, no fewer than three of the twenty researchers gave each of the other factors the highest score.

The way respondents answered this question was related to the particular mix of funding that they received. Table 6.4 shows the correlation between the relative importance respondents gave to each criterion and the percentage of their funding that came from their own institution, governmental entity, or private foundation. With a small sample and simple bivariate analysis like this, one has to be cautious in interpreting results, but the pattern is intriguing. For those relying most heavily on internal resources, the nature of the proposal is least important; indeed, some of these researchers are able to tap into their institutional funds without writing a formal proposal at all. The more respondents rely on governmental support, the more important they perceive the proposal, consistent with the belief that government funding prospects depend on a review on the merits of the question and design. The more respondents rely on foundation support, the more it is that the specific priorities of the funder are seen to make a difference.

Open-ended interview responses make it clearer what this means. Respondents see foundations as having very specific program interests. With very few if any exceptions, foundations have little or no interest in funding research for its own sake, no matter how clever, and poten-

Table 6.4   Perceived Funder Criteria

	Percentage of Respondents' Support		
	Own Institution	Government	Foundation
Policy needs	−0.31	0.25	0.10
Basic knowledge	0.10	0.30	−0.22
Funder priorities	−0.24	−0.37	**0.46**
Proposal	**−0.48**	**0.48**	0.16
Personal reputation	−0.04	−0.27	0.25
Institution's reputation	−0.05	−0.23	0.17
Personal relation with funder	0.33	**−0.56**	−0.02

Source: Author's compilation.
Note: Bolded coefficients meet or barely miss meeting the .05 test of statistical significance.

tially knowledge-producing that research might be. Matching a proposal to a foundation that considers it within its limited area of interest is a big part of the battle of winning support and sometimes necessary. This is not due to narrowmindedness or indifference on the part of foundations, but from their self-conscious strategy to maximize their impact by working within well-defined niches and by treating research as a means for pursuing their mission, not an end, however worthy, in and of itself.

> What's happening now is they're picking up in niche areas. They're not doing broad, blanket contracts or grants. They're saying, "Well, we're going to have our impact in this area and this is what we're going to focus on, and they're going to focus all their resources in one particular area." [R17]

Foundation representatives tell a similar story. "The work in our foundation, and the work in most of the larger foundations now," one observes, "is focused, targeted around a set of social goals," going on to observe that "the more strategic of the foundations go beyond that."

> They put metrics around this. They have strategic plans. They have theories of action that determine funding, the entire area and sub areas within. They mobilize grantees and others who are focusing in the same direction to talk about it and think about it and to have sub goals, yearly goals, short range goals, long range goals. [F2]

Some school choice researchers make it a point to emphasize that, in their experience, foundations are not much interested in research at all. That may be true. "We consider ourselves entrepreneurial," one program officer emphasizes. Basic research "has a time line for delivery of knowledge that is so long, and when it actually comes out the links between what is found and what the implications are for practice is so attenuated it is like 'so what is the point.' So I will take it on myself to say that I have discouraged us from doing a real aggressive research agenda" [F1].

Equally true, however, is that some foundations do care about research, but care about it in a very instrumental way. Research, to them, is not an open-ended search for more and better understanding of the conditions and policies they are addressing; it is a way to better focus and better promote an agenda. The same funder quoted above had observed a shift in the foundation's stance vis-à-vis research, a shift from an emphasis on producing knowledge that others might see as useful to one of wariness about the ways that research they produced might actually interfere with their programmatic concerns. When "philanthropy is trying to effect a certain set of social outcomes, trying to pull certain kinds of policy levers and other levers, trying to mobilize some power constituencies, to start putting their resources in certain direction, the pressure builds, right, to be able to send consistently positive messages." Research can be too unpredictable, its messages too mixed. "And a fear grows up" that research results might be used by others in ways that undermine the organization's core goals, that revealing for example that some initiatives are not working as well as planned "might be too damaging, might cause the whole thing to collapse" [F1]. As a result, "without anybody being particularly cynical or malicious in any way," foundations find themselves asserting a tighter control over research design and implementation, and reserving the discretion to keep findings in-house: "treating educational research as an analog to quarterly reports and annual reports."

Within the corporate world of philanthropy this orientation toward "strategic giving" is even more self-conscious than among foundations that proclaim broader social goals; giving simply because a project or recipient is worthy is seen as unfocused, anachronistic. To get bang for the buck corporate foundations, in particular, feel they must coordinate all their giving around a sharply defined focus and a plan for leveraging change (Epstein 2005). Research is important to some; less important to others. But in almost all cases, and seemingly increasingly, research is seen as a tool that must support the foundation's mission, not as a value in and of itself.

Foundations, Strategic Focus, and Consequences for Research and Public Discourse

The increased emphasis foundations put on incorporating research into a more focused strategy for pursuing their missions appears to be endemic. Sometimes referred to as the new philanthropy, it is commonly linked by illustration to newer foundations. Sometimes this narrative attributes the focus on strategic giving to a Silicon Valley mindset that is entrepreneurial, confident, and impatient. Sometimes it is attributed to deliberate plans by wealthy donors to sustain individuals and institutions that will singlemindedly pursue conservative, market-oriented policies. Whether or not it originated in one or both of these places, the impact has rippled throughout the foundation world. Researchers across the school choice spectrum are adamant in insisting that they do not shape the core elements of their research to meet any funder's mission, but do admit to selecting which foundations to approach based on the niche foundations have defined, and to spinning the way they pitch their proposals to underscore alignment with the foundations' stated goals. Although my research cannot establish this with certainty, this appears true regardless of the researchers' view of choice, the age or size of the foundation, or the foundations' ideological or social mission.

The strategic focus of foundations has consequences for the way research gets framed and introduced into public discourse. Significantly, these consequences do not depend on any presumption of nefarious collusion between researcher and funders to manipulate, steer, or distort the research itself.[39]

A first consequence involves the importance of selective attraction in bringing together researcher and foundation. Researchers who look toward foundations as a source of funding have relatively clear ideas about whether some sources are ideologically or otherwise likely to be unresponsive to them and their ideas. Most of the foundations are also relatively informed about researchers; rather than rely on researchers to come to them, they often pursue particular researchers because they like their work or trust them to produce studies that will be useful to them. "I've never funded anything that came in over the transom," one foundation officer notes [F4]. The resultant fit between foundation mission and researcher orientation can be, in such instances, as much a meeting of minds as it is an example of money leveraging a particular result. Even though this sorting process is not specific to funders of one ideological disposition, that conservative foundations disproportionately target the choice issue means that its impact may be ideologically skewed in favor of promarket findings.

A second and related consequence is that foundations can exercise selective oversight. In particular, they are free to concentrate on the front and the back ends of the process—setting an agenda and recruiting researchers on the front end, and finishing and disseminating results on the back end—and exert only the lightest of touches when it comes to monitoring the research process itself. Most of the school choice researchers who receive foundation funding emphasize how little attention they receive from program officers between the time they receive an award and the time that the research is almost complete. One relates, "actually, it is an amazing process how little contact there is really between funders, me and funders. They never...I mean sometimes I can come out with results and I won't hear from them after that either. That is quite odd; quite common" [R11]. Another explains: "I have never had anybody even email me or call me and say what are you finding. Nothing" [R8]. Researchers report that some program officers pay more attention than others, but this is driven more by the degree to which the program officer is personally interested in the topic or concern about monitoring costs and enforcing deadlines than an effort to exert control.

Well, I would say it is a huge mix, it depends on the program officer. Some of them are more into accountability for the dollars, which I think is important and which comes partly from your financial report and then your narrative report, about what all these people did and what all these people wrote but then there are some people who are just more interested in the results. [R2]

Foundations may apply a light hand when it comes to the details of the research, but they often care a great deal about how the findings are interpreted and framed. Here are reports from two researchers—one strongly identified with the pro-choice side of the debate; one a noted choice skeptic—each of whom produced findings that in some ways did not fit what their funders might have preferred. The former had support from a conservative, pro-voucher foundation but produced a finding that did not fit neatly into the preferred market-oriented arguments: "They were pissed at me and they hated the book which was pretty funny, but they were incredibly lax about reporting and stuff."

> Q. They didn't want to know along the way what you were going to say?
> A. I think I filed like a one-year report or something, and I suspect nobody ever read it. I think I gave them . . . at that point the argument of the book had taken shape in my mind and so I gave them a one page and I suspect nobody ever read the damn thing. [R5]

In the other case, the choice skeptic was funded by a generally progressive foundation but one in which the program officer who inherited the project was a strong charter school supporter. Asked about oversight, this researcher said,

> I don't see a lot of oversight in terms of findings. I don't feel like they are evaluating the findings at all. . . . So we kind of came out with a report that was more about the questions that the previous regime [in the foundation] was interested in asking and not what the current regime wanted to ask. But, you know what I mean; I spent the money as I said I was going to spend it and they never said "boo" to me. I mean I got the final report and I am sure [the program officer] hated it. [R2]

Although the foundations did not try to squelch the findings, in each of these cases, the researchers involved recognized that they would be likely to face serious obstacles getting funding from these sources again.

A third consequence has to do directly with translating research into the public arena and shaping the presentation of findings to make it more likely they will be heard and understood. What the foundations do care about is getting final reports, conferences, and—more generally—the results broadly disseminated. Most foundations ask researchers to include a dissemination plan in their grant proposals, and for some this is given as much emphasis as their insistence on a clear and appropriate research design. Some researchers indicated that foundations seemed to them to be much more willing to sponsor conferences at which research might be discussed than to sponsor research per se. One foundation officer sees this emphasis on creating attention in the media to be of relatively recent vintage:

> The one thing that I think might have changed in the more recent past is the importance of communications. . . . And that probably has to do with the technological revolution and the importance that people give to media and marketing and the, what do they call them, the soundbites. [F5]

Some of this emphasis on dissemination is content neutral. That is, most foundations want to see studies they funded talked about, and in some instances that is just as important as what the studies claim to find. In other instances, it is related to a desire to please donors and board members. At least some foundations feel pressure to prove to skeptics in Congress that foundations deserve their exemption from taxation because of the social benefit they provide. In some instances, it is because the foundation has a broader strategy of changing public minds and public policy, and regards research that is not picked up in the media as akin to the proverbial tree falling in a forest where it cannot be heard.

Linked to this concern is an intense interest in how the research results are presented in terms of style, simplicity, and focused message. A number of years ago, when working with some foundations on the release of some research, I was asked to attend a media training session. Numerous matters were covered, but one item was repeated over and over again. Keep the message simple—no more than two or three bullet points—and stay on the message regardless of what questions might be asked. This notion—that research findings must be clipped and molded to present a clear message—is evident also in this reflection by a foundation program officer.

> I have learned that as much as policy makers and others clamor for the evidence, the capital "E" evidence, their standards of evidence are fairly loose, because they really don't have time to read technical appendices, right? So you know a lot of research that a really critical observer might dismiss can be distilled down into a PowerPoint, put in front of a congressional committee and sold. So our advocacy people know that and our advocacy people are trained and socialized professionally to think in terms of sound bites, power points, things that they know and communicating those things in ways that will resonate. [F1]

Another observes that program officers sometimes resist the pressure to engage in what they see as oversimplification, but rarely win straight out.

> I'd say the program officers try to push back and say, no, but it's not that simple. And then the communications people say, yeah, but you've got to be able to say it so that people understand. . . . And for the most part I would imagine that stuff that comes out, nobody's totally pleased with it. You know, the communications folks would've loved it to be punchier and we would've loved it to be more nuanced. So you kind of go somewhere in the middle. [F5]

There are at least three distinct notions that fuel this mantra of keeping the message simple. The first has to do with theories about the limitations in the capacity of the public to understand complex messages (Jones 1995). The second has to do with theories about how to attract the attention of the media and to crack their standards for what is and is not newsworthy. The third has to do with estimations of what competing interests might do to blunt, twist, or spin messages that are not straightforward and declarative.

In the long run, and for the sake of serious and informed public discourse, it makes a difference whether estimates of the public's limited interest and capacity are accurate, whether the media really does tend to favor studies that make strong and confident claims over those that admit limitations and uncertainties, and whether findings that admit ambiguities inevitably lose traction in high stake political debates. In the short term, however, it seems to be that the keep-it-simple mantra is infiltrating the arena in which research results are communicated to broader audiences. Those funding and disseminating research increasingly are hiring public relations firms to coordinate their strategies for influencing public policy. This is not necessarily nefarious. In a crowded arena, those who want to get their message heard feel pressure to work with professionals to craft that message accordingly. It can, though, work to screen some kinds of studies in and others out of public discourse based on factors other than their methodological strength.

A fourth consequence has to do with the disproportionate impact of small amounts of money when considered within narrow program areas. Because foundation niches are becoming more finely honed, on any particular policy question—like that of charter schools—a relatively small number of foundations can have a large impact. In the charter school and school choice arena, this has played out most advantageously for the conservative foundations with a strong advocacy mission. Like Avis, the rent-a-car agency that claimed to try harder because it was number two, these market-oriented foundations, and the think tanks they helped spawn, adopted a sharpness of focus and commitment that arguably enabled them to alter the public agenda more effectively than some of their more established predecessors, despite their smaller size. School choice, moreover, emerged in 1990s as a key tactical focus of many of these organizations: a thread they felt they could pull upon to more quickly unravel the Democratic constituencies they saw as their competition. As a result, some scholars likely to promote a market agenda found it quite easy to gain substantial and relatively unconstrained support. The findings of these scholars were more aggressively disseminated, often repackaged by professionals in communications and public relations, and given a sharp, clear, and consistent policy message that sometimes was missing from more critical studies or those that gave full attention to the complexities, uncertainties, and context-specific nature of their findings.

Disparate Engagement: Why Mainstream Funders and Think Tanks Are on the Sidelines in the School Choice Debate

There is one more, especially puzzling, feature relating to the money trail that needs to be addressed. The more mainstream foundations and centrist research organizations and think tanks are substantially larger than their conservative counterparts. Conservative activists are convinced that they also are more hostile to their agenda, more inclined to favor liberal solutions and governmental programs, more enmeshed within conventional wisdom, and more protective of the status quo. That may be true. Yet among researchers and within the attentive public, it is the pro-choice foundations—Walton, Bradley, Olin, Hume, and others—and more conservative think tanks—Heritage, CER, Manhattan Institute, and those in the State Policy Network—that seem to be playing the stronger role in sponsoring research and getting it into the public forum. Part of the explanation relates to the generally more aggressive posture of the more conservative organizations as has been mentioned already and is documented elsewhere (Hacker and Pierson 2005; Micklethwhaite and Wooldridge 2004; National Committee for Responsive Philanthropy 2004; Rich 2004, 2005). Just as important may be explanations for why the more muscular mainstream institutions have not really joined the fight.

Four factors may be in play. First, some of the larger mainstream foundations appear to have soured somewhat in their view of how important research is to their mission. A core group among the conservative foundations have a strong appreciation of the value of research, at least as a political tool. In contrast, Rich discusses how the Ford Foundation shifted from a heavy emphasis on research to seeing it as something as a digression, a drain on resources that might be better used to provide direct services to those in need. "Through the 1950s and 1960s," he writes, "the Foundation was itself staffed primarily by academics, and the ethos at the Foundation was to fund research on public problems, rather than actual programs intended to solve them." In the late 1970s, however, the ethos changed. As one program officer at the time later recounted to Rich, research came to be regarded as "just a bad word. We've studied too damn much, let's get on with doing things" (Rich 2004, 61).

A second factor may relate to these mainstream foundations' reticence about privatization. Foundation program officers tend to be critical of teachers' unions and wary of the notion that providing more money is the answer to school reform. At the same time, they also are very strong supporters of the ideal of public education. Asked to respond to the statement that "public education is the nation's most critical democratic institution and should be protected at all costs," 92 percent of program officers in foundations active in K-12 grant making reported that this was very or somewhat close to their own view (Loveless 2005, table 3). Some, out of frustration with a history of failed school reform efforts, gradually decreased their giving in that area. Some of the program officers at these foundations initially were very wary of charter schools. They saw them as an extension of the voucher movement and therefore as potentially a threat to public education more generally. Although, over time, some have become more open to the notion that charter schools might be in some instances a progressive force, there is residual reluctance to put scarce resources into a speculative and politically controversial area. "I've seen [the movement toward charter schools] as part of a pattern to privatize education. And I don't think my views have changed" [F5].

A third factor relates to the general movement toward niche strategies discussed earlier. Whether out of frustration with school bureaucracies or simply as an extension of their strategic emphasis on narrowing their focus to better leverage change, some foundations have identified particular kinds of education activities they would support and cut back on the scope and open-endedness of their giving in the area. The Pew Charitable Trusts, for example, made a decision to focus its education funding on pre-K giving. "Rockefeller's not going to do any education reform or K-12 at all. And that's different," a program officer at a different large foundation observes. "They're moving to higher ed more. And then to the other things that they're doing. They have a new president and she's sorting it out. But it's clear that they're not going to be doing education" [F5]. Others are banking on small schools or better professional development for teachers. One researcher who has been critical of privatizations, and who, as a result, the most conservative foundations would be unlikely to fund, would normally look to the larger mainstream foundations as an alternative but finds that their narrow niche areas make them uninterested. "But the problem there is that those organizations and here I am thinking of Carnegie, Rockefeller, Ford Foundation, Pew, MacArthur, Hewlett Packard, just to name that is seven, we could add to that list, they tend to support projects in areas where they have a program and the programs now are predominantly educational leadership and teacher quality. There are some others but so what we do is we find ourselves shut out" [R1].

This points to the fourth factor—political skittishness— contributing to the sidelining of the mainstream foundations. This gets expressed in two ways. Some of the mainstream foundations have long and deep ties with progressive groups and nonprofit organizations that themselves are very sensitive on issues relating to what they see as conservative assaults on public institutions. Some of these groups would see funding research on charter schools as bringing attention and legitimacy to a phenomenon they would rather see fade away. With more than enough meritorious projects to consider, the generally liberal program officers at these mainstream foundations may see little reason to make grants that other recipients see as ideologically misguided. Significant, too, is the sense on the part of at least some mainstream foundations that conservatives in Congress are looking over their shoulders. "The reasons for the reticence of the more progressive foundations to get sucked into the fray is not just internal," one program officer who was not formally interviewed for this study suggested to me: "We have been targeted by the right wing as too politically biased, so there is a degree of fear operating as well" (personal interview).

What does following the money tell us, then, about the polarized way in which charter school research enters the realm of public discourse? On the one hand, the story seems less dramatic than either the liberal or conservative views of funding as systematically "buying" evidence that could be strategically used to further a political agenda. Researchers, as a group, appear less desperate for funding than some presume; many rely on generally low-cost research methodologies, have institutional resources they can draw on, or find it relatively easy to find external support. Much of the federal support has been indirect, through its funding of databases such as NAEP. Direct federal funding, as in the instance of the NAEP-based NCES-funded charter school reports (Braun, Jenkins, and Grigg 2006a; National Center for Education Statistics 2004), has been important precisely because these studies carry an extra stamp of legitimacy. Federal funds, however, have been a less prominent feature than might have been expected, partly because of historical and systemic factors that have pared down the government's support for basic education research. Mechanisms designed to limit political interference in federal research funding arguably have further narrowed the range of funding in this contentious area and ensured that studies, when funded, are tightly controlled and so moderate in their interpretations as to border on being bland. The most publicly discussed research has been privately funded.

To say that money does not directly and blatantly drive the research process, however, is not to say that money does not matter. Although the relationship with funding is nuanced, it does help to explain the puzzle we have been wrestling with. What is involved seems to be akin to what political scientists sometimes refer to as nondecisions (Bachrach and Baratz 1963). That is to say, a key factor is what has not happened. Federal government sources with institutionalized processes for peer review and other forms of quality control have not been prominent. Neither have the larger, mainstream foundations that might have been less committed one way or the other to charter schools, and therefore more generally interested in funding research the results of which might be unpredictable. This is partly because of the particularly contentious nature of the issue, but also largely explained by systemic changes at the federal funding level and in foundations as both have become more interested in applications than basic research. That has left the field open to funders with a more advocacy orientation.

These more advocacy-oriented funders do not tend to directly stick their nose into the mechanics of the research process itself. They make their decisions about what to fund less on the basis of the strength of the research design than on their estimate of their trust in the researchers, and this facilitates a sorting out of researchers and funders based on political proclivities. The researchers have an investment in maintaining the core integrity of their research. Where they give up some independence—sometimes reluctantly, sometimes willingly, and sometimes simply due to lack of attention—is more in dissemination: how studies are packaged and translated and conveyed to others whose political motivations are much less inhibited by the need to be attendant to norms of scientific research, and its resultant caveats, uncertainties, and complications.

With our attention then increasingly focused on the translation of research into public discourse, we turn in the next chapter to the role of the media: traditional mass media, nontraditional new media, and scholarly channels for communication.

Chapter 7

How Research Reaches the
Public Ear: Old Media and New

I definitely had the sense talking to reporters that they didn't want to report nuance about this; they wanted to report fraud or this guy's picking a fight with a giant or something. I mean, they wanted a story.

[R18]

[Reporters] want sort of these pithy, succinct statements that again are usually gross simplifications of the truth and they will try to get you to say something like that so that they can write it down. And they want balance. But the thing is they don't want balance from you.

[R8]

Ambiguity doesn't sell newspapers.

[A3]

Education is as polarized as any issue (intelligence, the war, religion, etc.) these days. And the tougher the truth, the stronger the spin.

[J2]

Other things were happening on August 16, 2004, the day before the *New York Times* ran its front page story on the AFT charter school report. Here is a sampling of the stories the *Times* ran deeper in the paper on August 17. On page 10, it reported that an American journalist had been kidnapped, at gunpoint, in Iraq.[1] On page 14, it revealed that the *Times* had gotten access to an email in which a senior officer for the Central Intelligence Agency bitingly attacked the agency and the commission investigating the 9/11 attacks for "a failure to punish ''bureaucratic cowards'' in the intelligence agencies."[2] On page 18, it reported on a new scientific study that found that if the use of fossil fuel continued at its present pace, summertime high temperatures could increase by 15 degrees in some inland California cities, "putting their climate on par with that of Death Valley now." In cities like Los Angeles, it found, the number of days of extreme heat could increase by four to eight times. It projected that heat-related deaths in Los Angeles, which it said averaged 165 annually during the 1990s, could double or triple under the moderate scenario and grow as much as seven times under the harsher one.[3]

Front-page placement, in the upper part of the page—what newspaper journalists refer to as "above the fold"—is not easy to come by. "This is not an easy sell," one journalist reflected in discussing the *Times* decision to run the AFT story on its front page.

> Reporters refer to their pages as real estate. This is the most expensive. You know, Central Park West, Upper West Side, Upper East Side, Fifth Avenue real estate in the business. Front page of the *New York Times*. It is like going through a condo board. You have to really, really sell that story. You have to really convince the board that you deserve this condo, that you deserve this real estate. So somebody either did a great selling job or a whole lot of people fell in line. I mean this is not something that [only] a few people get to decide. [J1]

Other major newspapers devoted their front pages that day to stories that had nothing to do with the charter school study.[4] Even after the story was broken and even after it sparked a sharp response, The *Wall Street Journal* for instance, did not cover it as a news story. It did on August 18, however, include an op-ed piece on page A10 titled "Dog Eats AFT Homework," in which Paul Peterson and two younger political scientists from Harvard (one being one of Peterson's students) argued that "the AFT's report tells us hardly anything about the relative effectiveness of charter schools" and suggested instead that the real story should be the finding, regarded as favorable to charter schools, that rather than creaming, charters are serving high proportions of the nation's neediest students.

What determines whether and how news media report on policy-relevant research? And what, if any, difference does it make in shaping the contours of public understanding and discourse? Is the important issue in the AFT charter school study case the study itself? Do the critical issues have more to do with the way the study was communicated to attentive citizens and policy elites? Is this a cautionary tale about the danger to democracy when a few key media can dictate public discourse based on their judgment and their understanding, both of which may be flawed? Are the researchers who complain about media coverage just shifting blame for a polarization process for which they share responsibility? Do the important lessons have more to do with much broader and more structural aspects of the way research moves from computer output to the public's ear?

The intense reaction to the *New York Times* report shows that the traditional print media remain an important battleground for defining issues. Absent that coverage, the AFT study would have been talked about, to be sure, but it lacked the rigor or rich data to rise above the background noise of numerous studies addressing the question of whether school choice works. In this chapter, I explore what determines when research cracks the surface of the major media. Is it a reflection of political bias, as charter school proponents charged when they criticized the *Times* for giving the AFT such prominent coverage—and as school choice opponents charge when they react to the *Journal*'s often favorable coverage of pro-voucher studies? Do the major media possess the expertise to make sound judgments about research quality? Are they locked into a template of reporting that induces them to balance each reported finding with an equal and opposite rebuttal? How is the dissemination of research being affected by the new media of blogs and emailed compilations of "the latest" news organized and framed by interest groups on both the right and the left?

This chapter focuses primarily on the print media—and within that group primarily on major newspapers—to gain better understanding of the role they play in shaping public discourse about charter school research. The role of the print media is changing and almost certainly losing the dominance it once held as a conveyer of political and policy news. "The press is no longer gatekeeper over what the public knows," but newspapers continue to be the point of first reference for the most attentive members of the American populace (Project for Excellence in Journalism 2007).

Researchers themselves believe that the media encourage them to oversimplify their views, and that even when they present nuanced positions it is their blunter quotations that more likely make it into print. Advocates believe that the major newspapers have politically defined agendas that shape news and editorial coverage of school choice research. Journalists admit that they can have a hard time convincing editors that readers want or need to know about studies that present mixed findings or lack sharp and immediate implications for public policy or parent decisions. My analysis goes beyond the common complaints that the media may exacerbate polarization by examining the specific mechanisms involved.

As was also the case in analyzing the role of research funding, the story that emerges here is a subtle one. There are differences, for example, in the way that the *New York Times* and *Wall Street Journal* present research on charter schools, but they are not sharp and do not deeply penetrate their news coverage. Although some articles feature the battling experts format in which two scholars on competing sides present starkly different readings of the evidence, this is less common than the folk wisdom among researchers suggests. One of the most important findings here is like the Sherlock Holmes story of the dog that did not bark. In Arthur Conan Doyle's famous story, "Silver Blaze," Holmes solves the case by remarking on the "curious incident" of the dog that had not barked (which led the detective to suspect that the crime was committed by the dog's owner). Paying attention to what has not happened, in this instance, leads to less focus on the polarized presentation of research by the media and more attention to what is missing. This is the kind of deep and sustained coverage that would be needed if intelligent readers were to be given the chance to wrestle with the complexity of the issues as they emerge. A second finding relates to the pressure of time: the need for journalists—especially as they are increasingly faced with competition from the new media—to get their stories out quickly, and as a result to turn to researchers who are quick and sure to respond to their hurried calls. A third relates to the blurring boundaries between serious studies, with strong designs and analyses that have been battle tested in peer review, and quick turnaround reports that are rushed into the field and rushed into press release to meet politically defined deadlines. Here, as in the case of funding discussed in chapter 6, I suggest that we may be paying some price for the disengagement, withering, or transformation of institutions designed to digest, moderate, and exercise quality control.

The Media as Battleground

Social scientists may disagree about how much power and importance to ascribe to the media.[5] To mobilize the manpower and money and effort she did to counterpunch in response to Diana Schemo's *New York Times* article, however, Jeanne Allen presumably thought that something significant was at stake.

Conventional wisdom certainly presents the media as important shapers of American knowledge and beliefs. This is underscored on television every weekend, when journalists on new shows interview other journalists about the hot issues of the day. It is echoed on talk radio where right-wing callers deride the liberal-dominated media, and in left-wing publications where progressive analysts bemoan the way conservatives control the news through mastering sound bites, orchestrating photo-friendly debates, and using—in some cases even hiring—sympathetic journalists to run stories that cast them in a favorable light.

The importance that the Bush White House and Department of Education put on managing the media was highlighted by a series of revelations regarding the use of federal contracts to plant letters to the editor, op-eds, and seemingly straight news stories that would promote the administration's position on school choice and No Child Left Behind. *USA Today* reporter Greg Toppo wrote in September 2005 about a *Dallas Morning News* op-ed written by a woman who described herself as an angry parent and criticized the local school board for failing to act forcefully in taking up the reform challenges laid out in NCLB.

> Appearing 23 days before the Nov. 2 election, her piece read like an ad for President Bush's 2002 education reform law, a cornerstone of his domestic policy. But what readers never knew was that, for all practical purposes, it was an ad—paid for, in part, by taxpayers, through a grant from the Bush administration. . . . In 2003 and 2004, Garcini's nonprofit group, the Hispanic Council for Reform and Education Options (CREO), received two unsolicited grants, totaling $900,000, from the U.S. Education Department, to promote school choice and tutoring options for Hispanic children. But in two op-eds in the *Morning News* and a third that appeared in two Spanish-language publications earlier in 2004, Garcini never disclosed, as was required by law, that CREO had received the government grants.

Nor was this an isolated incident. Earlier, Toppo had broken the story that the Department of Education had paid $240,000 to Armstrong Williams, an African American commentator, to write favorable op-eds and run supportive segments on his syndicated television show. The Inspector General's Office within the ED investigated thirteen grants the department had awarded to communications firms for public relations purposes. In addition to the two grants to CREO, three, totaling $1.5 million, were made to the Black Alliance for Educational Options (BAEO) "to actively support parental choice and increase educational options for black children through a 'multi-layered media campaign'" (U.S. Department of Education 2005b). The Greater Educational Opportunities Foundation received $745,000 for similar activities promoting NCLB and school choice. In all but one of the cases, the investigators concluded that the groups receiving the funds failed to disclose, as required by law, that federal funds were used in producing the materials they generated. The official report on the investigation raised a number of concerns about whether procedures were properly implemented and whether the department had been sufficiently vigilant in attending to how these funds were used. But Representative George Miller, the California Democrat who had requested the report, was less diplomatic in his assessment:

> This report shows that, in case after case after case, grantees—without disclosing who was paying them—took taxpayers' money and used it to promote controversial policies. Department officials allowed this practice to continue with such frequency and such consistency that they cannot now claim that they were ignorant that it was happening. Either the

Department is grossly incompetent when it comes to awarding grants
and contracts, or it is misleading investigators and engaging in a cover
up of the misuse of taxpayer dollars. (Toppo 2005)

The Bush administration's appreciation for the power of the media
did not manifest itself only in efforts to place favorable opinion pieces.
It also targeted basic news coverage. A public relations firm under contract to the Department of Education produced videos featuring a fake
journalist "reporting" news favorable to the department's initiatives,
and distributed the videos to local television news stations, many of
which ran them on the air. The same firm carried out a system of monitoring education coverage by print and electronic news outlets and individual reporters, and scoring them according to how favorable they
were toward the administration's No Child Left Behind initiative.
When the coverage was neutral or negative, the firm suggested in its
proposal to DOE, "we will determine what it might take to change their
position."[6]

Considerable research supports the notion that media style and content can influence what individuals think and how communities shape
their policy agendas. As one review of the literature puts it: "The days
of belief in 'minimal effects' by the media are over. A large body of evidence now indicates that what appears in print or on the air has substantial impact upon how citizens think and what they think about . . .
how they attribute responsibility for policy problems . . . and what policy preferences they hold"[7] (Page 1996, 23). Research has shown, for example, that simply altering the race of individuals shown in a news
story about poverty can alter viewers' expressed beliefs about whether
poverty results from the choices of the individuals or from societal
forces (Iyengar 1990).

At least some of the recent research suggests that the impact of the
media may work as much through stimulating deep emotional responses as through any kind of rational processing of information. In
one study, using MRI scanners, neuroscientists investigated what happens in the brain when subjects are presented with information that
seems to put their favored candidates in a bad light. Republican and
Democratic partisans were asked to read material, including a doctored
quote attributed to George Bush supporting Enron's Kenneth Lay, and
one attributed to John Kerry indicating that he favored overhauling Social Security. They were then given additional material suggesting the
two had subsequently reversed their field. Rather than change their
minds, both groups of respondents made excuses for their favored candidate. Measurements of brain wave activity showed, though, that the
regions of the brain that were most active were those normally involved in making emotional judgments about things like forgiveness,

and not those normally associated with reasoning and calculation (Carey 2006).

Jeanne Allen presents a somewhat nuanced view as to the power of media. On the one hand, as the CER rapid response indicates, she saw the *Times* article as potentially affecting parents and policy makers at a critical time. As discussed in chapter 4, CER felt it was important to counter the AFT report immediately, lest the impression it set take root and linger. This concern was heightened by awareness that, in the era of the Internet, old studies and old articles do not fade away; they remain on the Web poised to come up whenever a student, researcher, reporter, or government staffer conducts a Google search on the topic of charter schools. Although the cost of the advertisement would be substantial, measured against the potential impact it seemed to Allen like a good— even necessary—investment.

> And that [cost of the ad] is not something I take lightly. But to be able to hit potentially thirty million people over time with an advertising drop that changes the dynamics of the debate, it would have cost us in human and other terms, probably half a million dollars to fight it over the next year. (personal interview)

Allen also warns against overestimating the mass impact of research reported in national newspaper like the *New York Times*. First, for average Americans, she suggests, local newspapers and stories about local schools are what hits home the most: "we were trying to get a gauge on how much do people really pay attention and we know from a lot of our work that even really informed people are reading the *Bethesda Gazette* before the *Washington Post* to get community news" (personal interview). Second, even when they do read about reports, members of the public may weigh other sources, including what they hear from friends and neighbors, more than they do national studies based on national data. CER hired a private firm, the polling company, inc., to conduct a survey that would gauge how people respond to unfavorable reports about charter schools. Respondents were told that "recently there have been reports based on information collected by the federal government of students' academic performance in conventional public and charter schools. These data show that students in charter schools are sometimes slightly behind students in other public schools academically." Given two options—one suggesting that the reports troubled them; the other suggesting that "there is other more reliable information about charter schools besides government based data"—CER's survey suggested that people were willing to discount reports attributed to the government if convinced that there were other and contrasting findings available (the polling company n.d., 6).

In the CER case, the seeming tension between skepticism about the influence of the *Times* and the rapid and expensive mobilization to counter its article can be resolved in two ways. The first has to do with timing, the second with the distinction between mass and elite publics. Social scientists who raise questions about the impact of the media typically take great pains to distinguish short-term effects, which are commonly found, from long-term changes, which are more difficult to nail down. Allen, like a number of others I interviewed, took pains to emphasize that in real world politics short-term shifts in belief and behavior have the potential to bring about policy changes that have genuine staying power. This might be the case, for example, if the coverage comes during an election campaign or in the period in which policy makers are debating critical legislation. In this case, the *New York Times* article on the AFT report came less than three months before Election Day, right before the ramping up of campaigning and public attentiveness that typically occurs after Labor Day. Charter proponents did not worry that the Bush administration itself would turn sour on charters based on this account, but it was reasonable to worry that some politicians out on the stump might reshape their stance on the issue if they sensed a turn in the evidence or in public support.

By responding with an advertisement in the *Times*—as opposed to mounting a counter-attack through other channels—the Center for Education Reform may also have been acknowledging that a key zone of combat involves shifting, even subtly, the center of gravity among key and uncommitted elites. If CER's primary target had been so-called Middle America, other media outlets would have been less expensive and more targeted. The advertisement in the *Times* was meant more for the eyes of Washington-based policy makers and other media elites, not so much to change their minds as to reduce the likelihood that the AFT study would prime them to become generally more skeptical toward charter schools. It was too late to stop the report itself. But not too late to provide a metaphorical morning-after pill to lessen the probability those bad ideas would be fully implanted.

Charters and Choice in the News

From 1980 through 2004, five major newspapers—the *New York Times, Wall Street Journal, Washington Post, Boston Globe,* and *Los Angeles Times*—published more than 4,300 articles dealing with school choice, or vouchers, or charter schools.[8] As indicated in figure 7.1, newspaper attention to choice did not really take off until the 1990s. Early in the decade, attention was on other forms of choice, predominantly vouchers. The charter school issue soon swamped discussion of vouchers and other forms of school choice, however. In 1993, fewer than 17 percent of

**Figure 7.1   Number of Articles on Choice Vouchers and Charters in Five
Major Newspapers, 1980 to 2004**

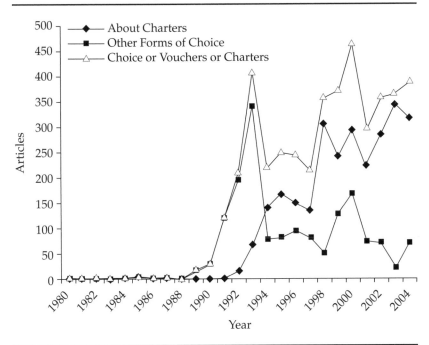

Source: Author's compilation.

the total choice-oriented articles and commentaries mentioned charter schools,[9] but the very next year that proportion went up to almost 65 percent. Since then more than seven of ten choice articles have discussed charter schools.

Many of these were short articles or mentioned the phenomenon only briefly. Sometimes the five papers were running articles reporting on the same event. By far the bulk of these articles made no mention at all of research.

To get a deeper look at how newspapers use research and whether this varies by their perceived pro- or anticharter school editorial stance on charter schools, I constructed a database including news articles and commentary in two of the publications—the *New York Times* and the *Wall Street Journal*—that explicitly cited experts or referred to empirical evidence in ways that were conducive to drawing conclusions about whether charter schools are working or not.[10] Neither the *Times* nor the *Journal* devoted as much attention to choice and charter schools during this period as did either the *Boston Globe* or the *Los Angeles Times*,[11] but they are worthy of closer investigation for at least four reasons. First, as self-consciously national media, the news coverage of these two papers is likely to be less driven by local events.[12] Second, they are more likely than the others to be read by national policy makers. Third, the differences in the political leanings of their editorial stances—with the *Times* generally more liberal and the *Journal* more conservative—provide an opportunity to test the extent to which editorial stance may infiltrate news coverage. Finally, the very different reactions of the two papers to the AFT report—the *Times* giving it front-page status followed the next day by an editorial that also raised questions about charter schools, and the *Journal* leaving the story uncovered but running an op-ed the following day sharply critical of the AFT report—makes it important to assess whether these were idiosyncratic differences or reflections of broader tendencies that would infiltrate their general coverage of the issue.[13]

A first and important finding is that in-depth discussions of research on charter schools is extremely rare. Even if we eliminate articles that mentioned school choice, or vouchers, or charter schools only in passing, fully 87 percent of the articles in these major newspapers discussed the phenomenon without including any substantial reference to research on their consequences. Eighty-eight articles[14] did include serious discussions of research: forty-six in the *Times* and forty-two in *Journal*. How did they present the research? How did they use experts? Were there substantial differences in news coverage in these outlets with sharply differing editorial stances on the subject?

Valence of Headlines and Article Content

To capture the tone of the articles—whether they reported research on choice and charter schools as generally positive, negative, or mixed or neutral—I asked two research assistants, doctoral students familiar with educational research literature, to code the articles on a three point scale from −1 to +1.[15] The rule of thumb they were to use was whether a proponent of charter schools would be likely to welcome the article (+1) or be distressed by it (−1). Each independently coded all of the articles based first on headlines alone; after that, they read the entire article and coded it based on content. In general, there was solid agreement between the coders (in 78 percent of the cases the two gave the article the exact same score), but sometimes they disagreed. We handled this by adding together the two sets of scores and creating, thereby, a 5-point scale. Articles that both coders recorded as negative received a −2; if both scored it as positive the final score was +2. Disagreements in various combinations could produce scores of −1, 0, or +1.[16]

Coding for both headlines and content is important. Some readers may form opinions based on a cursory reading of the paper, with headlines being very important in shaping their views of what the paper says. If that is the case, then the discretion exercised in distilling what might be complex and mixed findings could be politically important by shifting the weight of public opinion among sizable groups of citizens who are relatively inattentive to this issue. If newspapers pull debate to the poles by assigning headlines that oversimplify what might be nuanced discussions in the body of the articles, this would show by having fewer headlines than articles coded 0 and more at the extremes. Norms of professional journalism and idealized notions of the role of media in an open democracy suggest that coverage of news should be untainted by the ideological dispositions of the owners, even though the latter may be freely reflected in the editorial pages. Both the *Times* and the *Journal* take pains to institutionally buffer the news component from the editorial stance and the reporters for these papers for the most part are fierce defenders of their freedom to "write it as they see it." Reporters do not typically write their own headlines, however, and it is conceivable that any institutional ideological bias might creep into the process at that point. If that is the case, we might discover that the ideologically pro-choice *Journal* heads its choice-based stories in ways that shade toward more favorable interpretation than would be derived from a reading of the content alone, whereas the *Times*, charged with being ideologically resistant to choice in favor of the traditional public school model, might tilt things the other way.[17]

The overall ideological leaning of the paper matters.[18] Figure 7.2 presents the results for both sets of codes. Whether measured by headline or content, the coverage in the *Times* was more likely to present the research discussed in a way that charter advocates would consider to be negative and, even more markedly, the coverage in the *Journal*, especially in content, was likely to show choice, vouchers, and charters in a positive light. Barely fewer than two of three (61.9 percent) of the *Journal* pieces had a clear pro-choice tilt (+2) as coded based on overall content as compared with just over one in four (26.1 percent) in the *Times*.

To highlight more clearly the differences between headline and content coding, I created a difference score by subtracting the percentage getting each rating based on content from that based on headlines. Thus, for example, if 20 percent of the *Times* articles coded by headlines and 10 percent of the *Times* articles coded by content were scored −2, the result would be +10. Table 7.1 summarizes the results and juxtaposes those with the pattern of differences between headline and content we would expect with each of the possibilities: general tendency toward polarized headlines, ideologically specific tendency to exaggerate based on editorial stance, and general tendency for headlines to blur information.

Figure 7.2   Valence of Choice Coverage, Coded by Headline and by Content

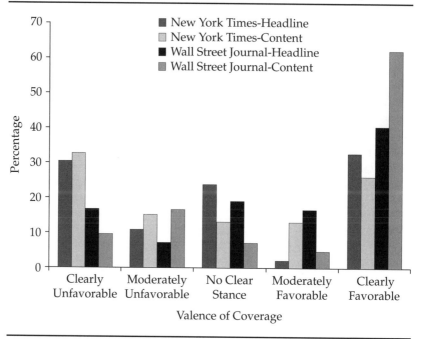

■ New York Times-Headline
□ New York Times-Content
■ Wall Street Journal-Headline
▨ Wall Street Journal-Content

Source: Author's compilation.

The results challenge the notion that polarization results from headline drift— the discretion that newspapers have in attaching headlines to stories. If anything, the content of the articles points to a more polarized media presentation than the headlines do. The *Times* headlines are slightly less consistently critical of choice than the article content and the *Journal* headlines appear to substantially moderate the favorable tilt

Table 7.1   Assessing Three Predictions About Headline Bias

	Headline Content	Least Favorable	−1	0	1	Most Favorable
Predictions						
	Bias toward extremes	+		−		+
	Bias toward editorial stance of the papers	+NYT/−WSJ		−		−NYT/+WSJ
	Blur sharper content	−		+		−
Results[a]	NYT	−2.18	−4.35	10.87	−10.87	6.52
	WSJ	7.15	−9.53	11.91	11.91	−21.42

Source: Author's compilation.
[a] Headline minus content.

to their articles' content, in neither case what a headline drift toward the editorial stance of the paper would predict. Nor is there consistent evidence that headlining distills mixed research findings into a simpler pro- or con stance. The clearest pattern is the higher concentration of 0 scores—indicating mixed or neutral tone—when the articles are coded based on headlines alone.[19]

Further probing suggests that the relatively high pro-choice valence of the *Journal* article content is probably not an indication that the ideologically pro-market stance of the paper's editorial operation has infected the core news operation. Rather, it seems to reflect the structure of the paper and its coverage—which makes news articles by staff reporters less prominent than other formats that are less constrained by the norms of professional journalism regarding balance and objective analysis. Figure 7.3 shows that differences in the types of articles discussing research on charters and choice in the two outlets are distinct. Half of the *Times* articles were straight news stories but only about one-fifth of those in the *Journal*. In contrast, the *Journal* was much more likely to provide coverage on school choice in the form of op-eds, editorials, letters to the editor, and book reviews.

The apparent pro-choice leaning of the *Journal*'s overall coverage is linked to this difference in their relative use of editorials, op-eds,

Figure 7.3   Type of Coverage of Charter and Choice Research

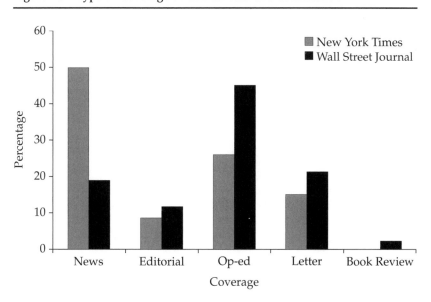

Source: Author's compilation.

columns, and letters—as distinct from news articles—as vehicles for discussing the research literature on charters, vouchers, and school choice. Across both papers, as one might expect, these non-news formats are much more likely to use research to stake out a position on one side or another; while only about one in three straight news pieces was unambiguously pro- or anti-choice in its overall tone, nine of ten editorials and op-eds took polar positions. This different reliance on news versus other formats is not particular to this issue; it reflects the differences in format of the two papers overall. The consequence, however, is that more of the *Journal* content is generated outside the news division, where its journalists are professionally trained to delve into the issues fully and arrive at an informed position. In principle, a newspaper could opt for such an overall format and then take pains to ensure that the editorials, op-eds, and letters it offers are neatly balanced. But this is where the editorial zone of discretion comes into play. Figure 7.4 makes it clear that the *Journal* overwhelmingly favors strong pro-choice pieces in its editorials and op-eds, and that its straight news coverage of choice research is extremely balanced.[20] Letters to the editor, which also play a more prominent role in the *Journal* than the *Times*, appear to be the forum relied on to air some more critical perspectives on the school

Figure 7.4   Valence of Expert Comments

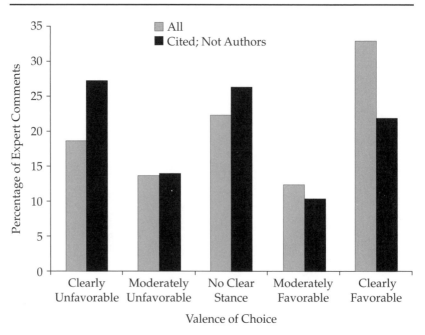

Source: Author's compilation.

choice research front. This pattern becomes even clearer when we look more closely at the use of experts in the two papers.

Use of Experts

How do the media choose and use social scientists in presenting information about school choice and charter school research? One possibility is that the media, confronting an area as complex and politically charged as this one, would work hard to find researchers noted for expertise, rigor, and relative balance, rather than those clearly identified with either the pro- or antichoice contingent. This is what we might hope to find if the media are playing the role assigned to them in the idealized vision of a scientifically informed democracy. Most citizens would have neither the time nor expertise to read and fully process original research papers. Responsible journalists, though, could act to some extent as their surrogates—wrestling with the conceptual and empirical issues and ferreting out the best advice and input available to help them digest and simplify without becoming simplistic. Rather than fueling the flames of polarization, the media in this way might help sift out the ideological spin and steer public discourse toward a more nuanced and realistic reading that acknowledges both complexity and uncertainty.

Another possibility is that the media serve as an echo chamber, picking up and magnifying the polarized elements of the research debate. This could be the case, for example, if journalists formulaically structure their articles to highlight sharp disagreements and the drama of head-to-head conflict among talking heads representing the polar extremes. "Although news reports largely represent the genuine contours of American politics," Lawrence Jacobs and Robert Shapiro suggest, "the media's organizational, financial, and professional incentives prompt them to exaggerate the degree of conflict in order to produce simple, captivating stories for their audiences" (2000, 8). Brian Jacob and Jens Ludwig, noting that news articles often "are limited to a recitation of competing arguments from those who hold different views," observe in an aside that "one friend of ours, frustrated by this media practice in his own area of expertise, once complained to a newspaper reporter, 'How come when NASA launches a rocket into space from Cape Canaveral, you don't feel obligated to call the Flat Earth Society for a rebuttal?'" (2005, 58). As one researcher interviewed for this study put it, journalists "are usually calling you because you are balancing off of somebody else who is not balanced, right? And so they are really trying to get an exaggerated statement from one side or the other" [R8].

A third possibility should be considered: one that shifts the focus of responsibility off journalists and more to the researchers and advocacy groups that are most vocal in attacking the media for bias when it covers stories differently than they would have wished or overlooks research they would like disseminated. We already have seen that some of the claims of polarization and bias in coverage are overstated, and that to the degree they occur differences in slant are more evident in uses of the opinion sections of the papers than in basic news coverage. Rather than simply representing the proactive imprint of journalists, editors, or owners, a polarizing use of experts by the media could also come about if researchers and advocates are aggressively pressing to get the media to feature their particular spin. "We are increasingly in a time when the research world is putting itself forward," one journalist observes. Reporters used to be advised by editors not to trust anything that had not been peer reviewed. "That has really changed quite a bit and now a number of researchers go directly to the media" [J1].

> They have their own press operations. If they are financed by foundations, the foundations want that research to be out there. They want the work that they have financed to have impact, so they push researchers hard to do press. And you know it causes some problems. I mean if you connect that—the fact that researchers are being more up front and seeking out coverage and hiring press operations and there is a number of publicity outfits that are solely in the business of placing research stories in the paper—if you connect that with journalists' sort of lack of knowledge about research and it becomes the person who is the best salesperson who gets their story in the paper. [J1]

In that instance, we might find evidence that some researchers are more prominently featured in op-ed formats which they initiate and which give them more discretion to shape the argument than is the case when they are interviewed by journalists who may quote them selectively or not at all.

For this analysis, an expert is defined as anyone featured in one of the *Times* and *Journal* articles providing substantive discussion of school choice research.[21] In nine of the eighty-eight articles, no specific expert or study was named. The remaining articles produced a total of 161 separate quotes from, references to, or pieces written by experts. In eleven of these cases an institution (for example, "in a Harvard study") was mentioned, but no person.

Table 7.2 provides descriptive information about the use of experts. The first thing to notice is how frequently particular experts are referred to. Many are called, but few are called often: eighty-nine experts appeared at least once, with sixty-nine of these (77.5 percent) appearing only once. Twelve experts appear more than twice. Only 13.5 percent of the experts, they account for a little more than 40 percent of the appearances. The second important thing to notice is that many of the experts who appear do not wait around until their phone rings. In about one of three cases, and these are op-eds or letters to the editor, the expert is the

Table 7.2   Appearances by Experts

Number of different experts	89
Experts appearing more than twice	13.5%
Appearances in which expert is the author (op-ed or letter)	34.8
University affiliation	46.3
Think tank or private research organization	18.8
Union–advocacy	17.5
Bureaucrat–administrator	13.8
Elected official	3.8

Source: Author's compilation.
n = 160 appearances.

author. In the other cases, the experts are quoted in an article written by someone else.

One hypothesis about polarization suggests that it is exacerbated when people who are not scholars are allowed to wrest the mantle of scholarly authority from researchers who are embedded in research institutions where formal peer review, informal norms, reputation for rigor, and professional rewards and sanctions all work to reinforce adherence to scientific procedures and careful inference. What we see here, though, is that, at least in articles that are substantively focused on research, experts who appear are most likely to be identified by university affiliations. Researchers with think tank affiliations are the second largest group. In about one of three cases, the person providing expert commentary is an advocate or public official.

Earlier I presented information on the valence of the articles. Figure 7.4 does the same for appearances by experts. Here, as before, it turns out to be important to distinguish between articles, on the one hand, and op-eds and letters to the editor, on the other. When all appearances by experts are taken into account, the valence clearly tilts toward the pro-choice side: 32.9 percent unambiguously favorable to choice in tone and 18.6 percent unambiguously unfavorable. When we filter out proactive appearances, in which the experts exercise the initiative to write an op-ed or send a letter to the paper,[22] the balance is much more even, tilting only slightly toward the critical side.

Figure 7.5 separates articles in which multiple experts are cited. As noted earlier, critics charge that journalists sometimes create an overly polarized presentation of research by deliberately seeking experts at alternative poles of a debate. Forty-two of the articles refer to or are written by a single expert. In half of these, the voice of the expert is moderate. In seventeen (40.5 percent), the expert takes an unambiguously pro-choice stance. In comparison, in only four (9.5 percent) is the expert's stance unambiguously critical of choice (–2). In forty-four cases the articles use multiple experts. When the articles feature multiple experts, these experts are

Figure 7.4 Valence of Expert Comments

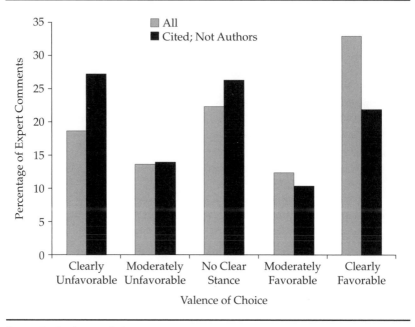

Source: Author's compilation.

Figure 7.5 Use of Multiple Experts

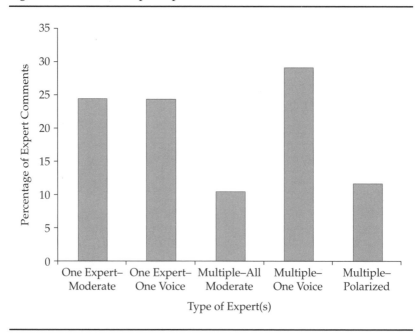

Source: Author's compilation.

almost always quoted to support either a pro- or an antichoice perspective; in only nine articles overall (10.5 percent) did the article feature multiple experts all taking a moderate position. Most of the time when multiple experts are cited in a single article, they are reinforcing one another with either a favorable or unfavorable reading of the research evidence. A starkly polarized use of researchers, featuring at least one taking an unambiguously positive and one an unambiguously negative stance, was relatively rare, occurring in only 11.6 percent of the articles.

To the extent that the media contribute to a polarized public discourse, then, it is not by consistently presenting clashing warriors. Articles that take the Witte vs. Peterson or Hoxby vs. Rothstein format, as discussed in chapter 4, are exceptions. Instead, it appears the media may indirectly contribute to the polarized public face of research by shying away from stories in which experts admit shades of ambiguity and by overfeaturing articles (particularly op-eds) that use research to support a strong pro- or anti-school-choice stance.

A more concrete sense of what is going on can be gleaned from looking directly at the experts and the ways in which they make appearances. Table 7.3 lists the experts who appear three or more times in the substantive articles about choice and charter school research. Eight of the twelve, including the seven *most* visible, are strongly identified with a pro-choice position. The other four have been generally identified as critical. None of the twelve was a passive responder, waiting to be called by a journalist. All were proactive enough to write at least one, and in most cases more than one, op-ed or letter that provided a substantive discussion of the school choice literature.[23] This suggests that newspaper airing of expert reviews may be in at least two senses reactive. First, in a large proportion of the cases, the appearances by the experts are self-initiated, involving the newspapers' decisions about whose letters, columns, and op-eds to publish rather than whom to proactively seek out for interviews. Second, the evidence is consistent with the possibility that newspaper journalists seek out for quotation researchers who have previously identified themselves, through op-eds and letters, as willing to take strong stands and to make themselves available to the press. Nine of the twelve most visible experts appear in our data as authors of op-eds or letters to the editor before they appear as interviewees in an article written by someone else.

Man Bites Dog: Why Doesn't the Media Present More In-Depth and Objective Analysis of Charter and School Choice Research?

The mainstream media have been under attack. Some commentators, noting a seeming fascination with grisly murders and Hollywood ro-

Table 7.3   Experts Appearing Three or More Times

No. of appearances	Name	Stance Re Choice	Named Affiliation	"Self-initiated" (Op-ed or Letter)
14	Paul Peterson	proponent	Harvard	42.86%
10	Jay Greene	proponent	Manhattan Institute (5), Harvard(4), U. Houston (1)	70.00
7	Chester Finn	proponent	Hoover (1), Hudson (3), Fordham Institute (3)	75.00
6	Jeanne Allen	proponent	Center for Education Reform	20.00
5	Joe Nathan	proponent	University of Minnesota (Center for School Change)	40.00
4	Milton Friedman	proponent	Hoover Institution	100.00
4	William Howell	proponent	Harvard	75.00
3	Alan Krueger	critic	Princeton	66.67
3	Amy Stuart Wells	critic	UCLA (2)/Teachers College(1)	66.67
3	Bruce Fuller	critic	University of California Berkeley	33.33
3	Caroline Hoxby	proponent	Harvard	33.33
3	Richard Rothstein	critic	Economic Policy Institute	66.67

Source: Author's compilation.

mances, charge newspapers and television with being overly sensationalistic. Others, comparing the somewhat staid and steady flagship newspapers and network news with the innovative rough and tumble of the Web, level the charge of boring. The left sees the media as tool of right; the right sees the media as a tool of the left. On charters, as we have seen, proponents of choice attack the *New York Times* for being a willing collaborator of a self-interested teachers' union. Critics of choice argue the *Wall Street Journal* is a blindly ideological mouthpiece for privatization and deregulated markets in education and elsewhere. The battering takes a toll. Only about 15 percent of the American public have "a great deal" of confidence in the news media, and more than one of three say they have "not very much" or "none." Asked "In general, how much of the time do you think the media tells the truth," only 5 percent say "all of the time" and 40 percent say "some of the time" or "hardly ever."[24]

Our analysis of the coverage of school choice research suggests that the most sensationalistic critiques are overdrawn. When we isolate news coverage by professional journalists—as distinct from expressions of viewpoint by others using the pages of the papers—the *New York Times* and *Wall Street Journal* are providing relatively balanced assessments. The charge that journalists exacerbate polarization by writing articles that consistently pit adherents from one extreme against those at the other did not get much support.

To say that the media are not as bad as some claim is not setting a very high standard. Arguably, in complex democracies such as ours, the media should be expected to play a much more constructive role in shaping informed civic discourse. Issues relating to education, to science, to medicine, to national security, to taxation and regulation involve tough technical issues and require serious study. Few, today, still hold to the notion of an Athenian style democracy in which citizens collectively deliberate and set the course of the polity. That we necessarily depend on representative rather than direct democracy, and rely heavily on bureaucracies with technical know-how, however, does not mean we should be resigned to relegating citizens to passivity. Even the most minimal role for citizens—as holders of the switch that can "throw the rascals out" if elected leaders fail to perform—requires knowing how well elected officials are doing. Knowing that requires more than taking a reading on how you and your family are doing. It requires having some informed sense of which conditions are susceptible to government intervention, what other factors are involved, and how trade-offs are implied between gains in one area and those in another and between benefits and costs experienced today and those that will come due tomorrow. The most heroic among us might venture to learn about the issues that concern us directly from the research literature without mediation through the media.[25] These are the exceptions. Although they might succeed in a few areas of substantive interest, they are almost certainly fooling themselves if they think they can bypass the media for information across all of the issues that affect their lives. For most citizens, key information must come filtered through intermediaries. The mass media are critical.

Judged against this higher standard, the media's role in communicating research about school choice and charter schools has to be considered disappointing. Substantive coverage of research is relatively rare. When offered, it tends to present research as if it supports one policy stance or the other. Use of experts relies heavily on a relatively small group of strong voices who tend to represent extremes. As a result, it is rare that the careful reader gets exposed to in-depth analysis, researchers not publicly committed to one side or the other, and competing perspectives put head to head in a way designed to discover common ground rather than portray an ideological stalemate.

Why is this? Is the expectation that the media bears responsibility for meeting this heroic standard a legitimate one? Would newspapers that offered in-depth coverage of research survive in today's markets? Given the public's fascination with Hollywood and drama, and its relative impatience with complication, analysis, statistics, ambiguity, and uncertainty, do we get, by and large, the coverage that we want and deserve?

Reporters' Training

Failure to grapple with the more complex issues involving education research could result from any of a number of factors. First, education journalists, particularly outside the more prestigious outlets, tend to lack training in research or deep experience with education policy issues.

Richard Colvin is a former education writer for the *Los Angeles Times*. Since 2002 he has directed the Hechinger Institute on Education and the Media, housed at Columbia University's Teachers College. The stated mission of the Hechinger Institute is to promote "fair, accurate and insightful reporting about education." One way it does this is to hold seminars, at which researchers and policy makers discuss their work with education journalists, broadcasters, and their editors. Colvin has thought a lot about why education reporting is not as good as it should be. Most education reporters are in the suburban offices and they essentially cover school board meetings, "so you might often think of them as school reporters or even school board reporters as opposed to education reporters" (personal interview).

> So the job is not all that satisfying. If you can imagine staying up until 11 or 12 or 1 o'clock in the morning at a contentious school board meeting in the suburbs arguing about whether you are going to buy Astroturf for the school football field. That is not that intellectually interesting. So there is turnover on that level.

When reporters graduate up to the central office of larger newspapers, they still may not be expected to cover the nitty-gritty aspects of education policy and research. The big city school beat "is often covered as politics as opposed to covered as education, and there is not a lot of coverage on teaching and learning . . . so the subset of people who are actually doing that, who are actually writing about the core technology of education is pretty small" (personal interview).

Part of the reason that turnover is high and expertise shallow is that, within the walls of most newsrooms, education is considered a low status beat. Even when it leads into what might seem like big-time stories, education policy is still seen by some as tantamount to covering PTA meetings and budget hearings. As one journalist recalls:

I was there when Congress was debating No Child Left Behind so you would think that that would be the one time when you know it would be a huge national story. [But] with the exception of a couple of times when it was really urgent news coming out . . . it was very much a second-tier story. It might be the top story on a given day, but as soon as something real and important happened—you know, where Alan Greenspan coughed or something happened at the White House or the Pentagon or the State Department or whatever—it was always moved down. [J4]

In more recent years, one or two major newspapers have assigned education articles to prominent journalists who have established solid reputations covering other areas. But even here, another education journalist sees a distinction between being a smart person and good journalist, on the one hand, and really understanding the ins and outs of education issues on the other.

> You wouldn't find somebody covering dance... in the *New York Times* who didn't know something about dance. Or covering science. You know John Noble Wilford [science writer at the *Times*]; that is what he does. You are not ever going to have him cover education or cover something else. He covers science. That is what he does. But . . . I don't know of a newspaper in this country that, although there are certainly education specialists, I don't know of a newspaper that would only hire somebody who had a deep knowledge of education to do this job, including the *New York Times*. [J1]

Sorting through the debates that pit one set of researchers against another calls for knowledge, not just knowledge about education but also about research methodology. For researchers—and often for advocates as well—methodological critique can be the favored weapon in public discourse. When Jeanne Allen sought to counter the *New York Times* charter school story, the advertisement was crafted to emphasize proper social science research design. When a group of researchers wrote a book challenging many of the ad's signers on the grounds of hypocrisy, they did it by showing how the signatories, too, had violated methodological norms in their own work (Carnoy et al. 2005). To do anything more than call the play-by-play, a journalist has to have some independent ability to evaluate competing claims. Yet, Colvin notes, "they don't know very much about research. . . . I mean they talk to researchers and they evaluate what researchers say based on their instincts rather than some sort of formal body of knowledge; it is really a weakness among journalists in general" (personal interview).

But is it realistic and appropriate to expect journalists to learn more about research methods? Colvin thinks so, because without such capacity they are at the mercy of others:

Yeah, I would argue that they definitely should. Increasingly education writers are getting hit with "research" all the time, every single day. We have done surveys of editors and reporters and they have very little confidence in their own ability to discern good research from bad research. And because they don't trust their own ability to do that, they tend not to write about research. They also recognize that education is a field that is rife with advocacy and they can't identify readily whether people are advocates or not so they are just shy about the whole thing. They want to know more and they think it is really important but they just don't trust their abilities. (personal interview)

Lacking the skills to sort research wheat from research chaff, the typical education beat reporter might find it easier to sidestep the tougher issues altogether.[26] Rather than assess whether some studies are more reliable than others or deal with methodological intricacies, they might simply present multidimensional debates as stylized point-counter-points, in which representatives of two extreme positions state their case and denigrate that of their opponent. This may be more likely at the smaller media outlets, where the reporters covering education typically are less experienced, highly focused on more parochial school board agendas, or generalists only occasionally conscripted to focus on hot issues in education policy. Even the top-notch reporters at high profile outlets like the *Times*, however, might not have deeper expertise in education issues, and might show less interest in the intricacies of education research than in the narrower subset of stories that play into broad national policy debates. As one education journalist told me, "when you get into these statistical issues, there are so many pitfalls and turnabouts and it just drives you crazy, so I prefer to avoid them when I can" [J3]. Another, when asked how he deals with an issue in which there is conflict among legitimate researchers answers: "Truthfully? I end up not writing about it a lot of the times, just because I don't have a comfort level that is great enough" [J4].

Tough Editors in Tough Times

A second set of reasons why media might tend to undercover research or use experts to frame the debates in terms of their extremes has less to do with the abilities and knowledge of the news staff and more to do with the norms that editors enforce, either out of a particular notion of professional balance or a pressing sense of what sells papers in a competitive market. Editors might not want their writers untangling issues relating to research in controversial areas, fearing that they might get it wrong, and that they are likely to be criticized regardless of whether they get it wrong or right. Editors and reporters, one journalist notes, have very little confidence in their own ability to discern good research from bad research. And because they don't trust their own ability to do that, they tend not to write about research because they tend not to be able to sort it out. And they also recognize that education is a field that is just rife with advocacy, and they can't identify readily whether people are advocates or not so they are just shy about the whole thing. [J1]

Adding to the picture is the fact that newspapers these days face tough financial pressures. In May 2006, a generally pro-newspaper analyst at Merrill Lynch characterized them as "a stinker of an industry" (Saba 2006). In July 2006, the *New York Times* announced cutbacks in staff and the physical size of the paper. Space devoted to news was expected to fall by about 5 percent. "That's a number that I think we can live with quite comfortably," the executive editor said, "adding that the smaller news space would require tighter editing and putting some news in digest form" (Seelye 2006b, C1). Other papers, such as the *Washington Post*, *USA Today*, and the *LA Times*, had made similar moves, and the *Times* reported that the *Wall Street Journal* also was planning to do so (Seelye 2006a; see also Project for Excellence in Journalism 2007).

A big part of the problem is that newspapers are losing circulation and advertising revenue to alternative forms of media, and profit margins are too low to satisfy owners—a double-whammy as far as covering research is concerned. Staff cuts put strain on the person-power an editor can afford to allocate to in-depth analysis.[27] One journalist told me that, before the AFT charter school report had erupted, he had raised the issue of improving the newspaper's editorial staff's expertise with statistics. Other journalists at the paper were supportive. "They said, we wish we could do this better, but we're racing and we're not trained to look at things in minute numbers." So he raised the possibility of hiring a specialist who could provide support and scrutiny across all kinds of issues. "I suggested . . . wouldn't it be great to have a numbers editor, just a person whose job is to review any piece that is based on statistical evidence." His superior "very much thought it was a good idea, but this was at a time when newspapers were cutting back, not adding" [J5].

What the Public Wants

To the extent that the pressure is coming from competition, the tight economic situation helps support the sense that television news and the Internet may provide more exciting content and may make editors even less likely to risk boring their readers with stories that do not have sharply defined characters, good visuals, drama and heat.

Our bias [at this journalist's paper], we think the stories that really sell papers are, you know, political scandals . . . that is our brand . . . scandals, big crimes investigations. Generally we judge stories by how hard they are to get, and education stories are relatively easy because teachers are so open and forgiving. [J3]

Against this backdrop, cool objectivity, attention to nuance, serious effort to instruct, and caution in drawing premature conclusions are not the criteria that reporters apply when looking for researchers to interview. One education journalist has email addresses of "maybe one hundred or two hundred experts." What makes some experts more attractive than others? "There are some I trust more than others. There are some that are more quotable than others. There are some who are more likely to respond to my emails than others." Asked what more quotable means, this journalist replies, "similes, metaphors," and some sort of dramatic tension [J3]. Another refers to the "parking lot test" for what will stand as a good story:

> My approach is that I sort of demand this of people who are pitching to me and so I demand it of myself when I am pitching to an editor. I use what I call a parking lot test . . . Where, this is a screen writer's trick, and that is if you want to make a movie, you have to be able to stand on one end of a parking lot and yell to a guy at the other end what the movie is about and other variations, like the elevator pitch . . . You know, boil it down very quickly to where people can understand it and get excited about it. [J4]

This real or perceived need to capture the attention of a busy, distracted, and somewhat indifferent readership adds another burden on education research stories because they fail to lend themselves to gripping visual elements. "It's hard to make education sexy," one journalist observes. Editors often reject research or policy-oriented pieces that they initially expressed an interest in because the reporter could not find an individual person—a teacher, or principal, or other compelling figure—to hang the story on.

> Or, my god, the photographs . . . There are a bunch of people sitting in a classroom. That's a lousy picture. How do you get a good education picture? And that kind of thing will move something from page one to page seventeen. [J5]

Journalists' Skepticism Toward Research

Journalists who would like to provide more in-depth coverage of education research face tough editors and a distracted audience. Other constraints are more self-imposed. Some education reporters think research is not just a hard sell, but also—at least often—self-contradictory, trivial, and off-point.

The sense that I get is that it is almost like everybody is staring at a Rorschach. . . . We don't know very much about charter schools yet and they haven't been around for very long. The findings keep contradicting each other, and so it is like everybody is staring at the same picture and pulling out something to suit their needs. You know, one study on one side will say it is promising research that warrants more study and on the other side they will say that this shows that charters are a failed reform. So, yeah, I think that does exist and it sort of drives me crazy. I mean, I think it drives a lot of reporters crazy, just because it doesn't seem to move the discussion any further. [J4]

In some cases, the skepticism is directed specifically at education research as opposed to research in general. "I think education research stinks." one journalist says. "I think it's awful. I think it's ill funded. I think it's got an infirmity that's unique to the field, which is that it's field practitioners who do it, which does not occur in other fields" [J6]. Reflecting on what appears in some of the education journals, this journalist likens them to "an exercise in Alice in Wonderland. The issues they're talking about are marginal fringe issues. It's all sort of reconstructionist history and gender-oriented politics and, God, it's awful. It's awful!"

One of the journalists who chose not to write about the AFT report or the subsequent backlash made a very self-conscious decision. For this journalist, the problem was not just research per se but also the broader policy debates in which the studies are enmeshed.

I am terribly impatient with stories at that level. One of the reasons why I didn't get up and fight [to get in a story on this topic] is because I see myself as a classroom reporter. I think the most interesting stuff going on in education is inside schools, and all the policy stuff I think is too often just people with agendas beating up on each other and looking to look good. And it is like, you know, gang fights. Your purpose in life is just to beat the other guy, and you sort of lose sight of what you are there for. [J3]

The story lines that interest researchers can be the very ones that journalists see as unworthy. Social scientists, for example, wrestle with the issue of representativeness. They warn about the problems that come from drawing inferences based on charter schools that may be unusual, either unusually good or unusually bad. But at least some journalists feel that it is simply not their mission to write about the average school. What is both newsworthy and informative, they think, are the schools that are doing very well or very badly. The journalist quoted above favors stories that focus on a successful charter school to writing about charter schools in the abstract.

[A story about a successful charter school] is an exemplar of a lot of things. That is why it is interesting. It is an exemplar of what is the power of longer school days. What is the power of smarter schools? What is the power of a principal having the power to hire and fire teachers? [J3]

Part of the métier of scholars is to draw general principles out of accumulated concrete experiences. Part of the métier of journalists is to find individuals and concrete stories that somehow represent more general phenomena. Although the two goals may seem complementary, in immediate terms they often clash. Reflecting on why he was surprised at the *New York Times* coverage of the AFT report, one journalist at another paper said

> I don't remember any real people in it. I don't remember any students. I don't remember any parents. That's also typical of *The Times* coverage. . . . They quote a lot of experts. They don't really make a strong effort to see what—no, I shouldn't say always, because they do sometimes—but they tend to write their stories from the point of view of experts and providers of the service. They don't tend to write it from the point of view of the consumer. [J6]

Later this same journalist elaborated:

> I think it's only through real people that you can tell compelling journalistic tales. You can write about policy until you're blue in the face and you'll never write a compelling story. If you tie policy issues to real people, you have something that's compelling and motivating and provocative.

This general journalistic interest in putting a human face on a story may be exacerbated among education writers, many of whom end up on the beat precisely because they were interested in the tangible interchanges that characterize teachers in classrooms.

Avoiding Trouble

When the issue is sensitive, as in the case of privatization, school choice, and charter schools, an additional factor can be journalists' awareness of political tripwires, which create a risk that articles they write will be carefully scrutinized by activists who may not hesitate to complain, not only to them but also to their editors and publishers. Part of the problem is that journalists have come to see all research as politically motivated. "My impression is that just about everybody who proffers research has an axe, and it is a well-known axe," one suggests. "You have to take it with a grain of salt" [J6].

A different journalist encountered a backlash after writing about research in a controversial area of education policy. "That was sort of the story that really got the troops out. I mean I got such a response from that—before I even wrote it, by the way. I mean, people heard I was going to write about it and I started getting phone calls" [J4]. Reflecting on an aggressive letter-writing response to a school choice related story, another speculates that less seasoned reporters "might have been frightened off" about writing about choice and charters in the future [J2].

Internalized Lessons: What Researchers and Advocates Think They Know About Communicating with the Public

The term *ivory tower* is used disparagingly to refer to the penchant of some scholars to retreat into the sheltered world of academia with little apparent regard for the problems of the real world and how their knowledge is or could be put to use to address those problems. Undoubtedly, the characterization fits many scholars. However, at least among those researchers who have chosen to engage with hot policy issues like charter schools, there is a general desire to see their work ripple beyond the tower walls. When asked to score, from 1 to 5, the importance to them of reaching an audience beyond that of other scholars, two-thirds of those interviewed for this book offered a score of 4 or 5 (figure 7.6).

Researchers who want to contribute to public debates about important issues understand that they need to simplify if they want to reach a broader audience. Speaking to a fidgeting crowd of citizens, speaking on the phone to a reporter who seems to quickly lose interest, addressing policy makers who keep pressing for the bottom-line— experiences like these can lead researchers either to retreat into their more comfortable ivory tower or to learn new tricks. These tricks were not only not taught in their graduate school training, they were often actively proscribed: incorporate illustrative stories, sidestep methodological technicalities, offer clear findings without caveats, draw straightforward policy implications.

Researchers see the media as important because they play a gatekeeper role in getting ideas and evidence to policy makers, foundations, and others. The following quotes (along with some of those leading off this chapter) show the consensus among researchers that reporters or op-ed editors want them to simplify their responses in ways that sharpen the storyline.

> You have to drastically reduce the complexity of the statistics. And that comes with the turf. That I don't object to because I realize that people aren't going to have those skills, but what I do object to is that you lose

Figure 7.6   Importance of Reaching Beyond Scholars

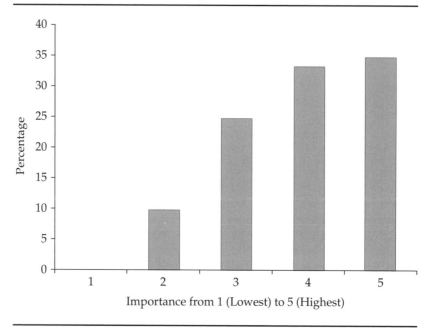

Importance from 1 (Lowest) to 5 (Highest)

Source: Author's compilation.

track of the nuances and the cautions, they want you to overstate the results. [R10]

I think they focus on what they want to focus on . . . I mean, the work that
I do is contextual and it is complicated, and so I am simplifying it first of
all for them, and then they simplify it from what I give them. [R19]

If you are talking to an audience of teachers or parents or even journalists, you are talking to people who are not interested in the methodology.
They are not interested in the kinds of things that social scientists are interested in, and so I think you have to boil it down to the basic ideas. And
you have to be more willing to tell stories and give examples. [R8]

Most researchers express at least some frustration with this pressure
to simplify for other audiences. Their overall reactions differ dramatically, however. Some simply give up trying. Some ignore most phone
messages or email inquiries from reporters, recognizing that reporters
are often on tight deadlines and that failure to respond quickly will be
enough to make the problem go away. Some respond when called, but
avoid proactive steps such as trying to place op-ed pieces in newspapers. "It requires a level of kind of simplification, one notch beyond
where I am comfortable," one researcher reports. "And so I have tried
it and I had a horrible track record writing op-eds. And I said to hell

with it, it is not really my thing" [R5]. Some accept the tensions as inevitable consequences of trying to maintain relevance, but express anxiety about whether they are managing to find the right balance.

> Obviously, if you are going to talk in simple terms to an audience, you are going to have boil down what you know or what social science knows, and any time you boil things down you are going to be leaving stuff out. There is no other way to do it, and so then the question is are you presenting the findings in a way that is misleading. Because the obvious tendency will be, say, for a choice supporter to exaggerate through simplicity, right? So you simplify in an exaggeratedly positive way. And the same thing happens on the other side. When the truth is much more qualified. So I try to guard against that. But it is hard. I struggle with it. [R8]

Still others regard the challenge in a more positive light, as indicating an additional skill which they should master, a way to convey complicated ideas more simply, without crossing the line at which comprehensibility becomes false clarity. This may be an easier challenge for advocates to embrace than for researchers who have been schooled in the norms of scholarship. "It is all about how you present the information," one advocate argues. "How you make it real, just how you talk about it. So it is not saying different things, it is just saying it differently" [A3].

Straight to the Public: The New Media and Bypassing Peer Review

Complicating the task for journalists, policy makers, and the attentive public are forces that may be marginalizing traditional avenues for screening and legitimating research. New technologies have expanded the range of avenues through which research can reach the attentive public. Some researchers regularly use their own Web sites to post works in progress and solicit feedback. The National Bureau of Economic Research (NBER) online working paper series, for example, has become a favored vehicle for economists to get their work out and widely read more quickly than could be expected through the traditional journal route. Think tanks and advocacy organizations regularly distribute electronic newsletters disseminating their own studies or summarizing the work of others. Some, like the Public Education Network's *PEN Weekly NewsBlast*, which has 46,000 subscribers and an estimated 240,000 readers, offers short summaries and links with relatively little analysis.[28] Others, like the Thomas B. Fordham Institute's weekly *Education Gadfly*, which goes to about 7,000 recipients,[29] combine short reviews with more editorial copy. Andy Rotherham's blog, *Eduwonk*, gets about 1,200 to 1,400 visitors every day and about 10,000 different readers every month.[30] As one indicator of the scope of the emerging virtual world of education policy communication, *Eduwonk* includes ninety-seven links to other education blogs, twelve links to sites providing education news and analysis, and thirty policy and political blogs that cover education as well as other issues.[31]

This has altered the relationship between research and policy in at least two important ways. The first has to do with timing, the second, with quality control.

In an earlier era, the normal cycle for policy research included submission to a peer reviewed journal, double-blind review, often requirements for revision, nine months or more from acceptance to publication, and then—if the researcher, funder, or university public relations office was eager for impact—dissemination of a press release. Researchers who worked in similar areas might hear about forthcoming work at conferences, if they happened to attend the right ones and the right panels, but except in special cases there was often a reluctance to publicly cite and respond to conference papers until they had been vetted through the slower and more meticulous processes of peer review.

Today's new technologies mean that studies—and even preliminary findings—often get tremendously broad dissemination within incredibly short periods. "I try very hard to favor breaking news in the *News-Blast*," reports Howie Schaffer, who oversees the *PEN Weekly NewsBlast*.

> The cycle of news is evolving. The weeklies like *TIME* don't try to break news anymore; they try to have relevant analysis. The daily papers try not to get burned breaking news that they know may evolve significantly throughout the day. The e-newsletters try to beat the bloggers to the story . . . so everyone is trying to keep their content fresh.[32]

This speed of dissemination added to the sense of urgency and subsequent ripple effects surrounding the AFT report. "My students had that report in thirty-three minutes," one researcher reports.

> The time it took for me to get dressed and get to my office, they had the darn thing on the screen. That was unheard of, unheard of fifteen years ago. I mean [it used to be] you hear about this and you have to make a phone call, can you send me a copy, and they say oh when we get around to it and then two weeks later you get a piece, you get an envelope. [R10]

The speed with which research is disseminated means that some studies make an impact even before their final analysis is completed. Consider the NCES-funded study to compare the effectiveness of public and private schools using hierarchical linear modeling, as discussed in chapter 4 (Braun, Jenkins, and Grigg 2006b). The study was released on Friday, July 14, 2006. It was reported on the front page of the *New York Times* the next day. Within two weeks, Paul Peterson and Elena Llaudet of Harvard had released their rebuttal that not only critiqued the methodology of the original report, but also offered a reanalysis of the same data using different indicators and models and coming up with dramatically different results. "The reputation of academia is that it plods along indifferent to time lines and deadlines of the sort that people in schools or private employment have to cope with," wrote a skeptical Gerald Bracey. "But in the current politically charged education policy arena, things are different." Peterson's findings, he emphasized, were disseminated directly, largely via the Web, "not in a bona fide journal" (Bracey 2006, 61).

The NCES study had gone through months of internal reviews.[33] The rebuttal could not possibly have received the same scrutiny. Yet the rebuttal received about as much press attention as the original study. A month later, Peterson and Llaudet presented their paper at an academic conference, but by that point the paper had been revised. Indeed, they indicated that some of the tables presented were based on statistical analyses completed the day before the conference. The changes were substantial enough that one of the panel discussants was somewhat taken aback and expressed some uncertainty about whether her planned comments would still apply.[34]

Major news outlets face the decision about whether to follow suit or seem, in contrast, sluggish and out of date. As one researcher lamented,

> I think that what is happening is the age of the Internet has really hurt in this way. . . . When the media want to get the story out right away, as opposed to having the time to reflect. And I think that it makes it harder for them to be sophisticated and it makes it easier for them to say: "Okay, well here, let's take what these guys said, let's find some counter-quote, bam, done, published." [R13]

According to some, one of the factors that may have played a role in the front-page placement on the AFT story was that the union had granted it exclusive pre-release. It would be easy to think of the *Times'* interest in going this route as simply a desire to get a scoop. From the standpoint of the reporter, this can also be a vehicle for buying more time to make calls and get various reactions before rushing to get an article into print. The researcher quoted went on to say,

> And so you know the *New York Times.com* [for example] publishing tomorrow's story at 3:30 in the afternoon is wrong, I think. I mean, they kind of have to do it because that is what people demand. But it is sad because that is part of it. They feel this pressure. I don't want to go and say to the *New York Times, Washington Post, Wall Street Journal*, these guys are being derelict in their duties, because they are fighting for their survival. And they know that if they don't do it, people are going to see them as irrelevant and people want instant gratification rather than analysis. [R13]

Advocacy groups are not the only ones looking to get work out quickly without first submitting their research to the deliberative process of peer review. Some researchers, believing that their findings are important and timely, aggressively cultivate ties with the media. They then work hard to get word of their work out through op-eds, press releases, and press conferences, generating a sense of buzz about what they have found. When the researchers are linked to foundations, think tanks, or advocacy groups that put a high priority on dissemination, as mentioned in chapter 6, the result can be expensive and highly focused efforts to get the word out, sometimes hiring PR firms that sell themselves precisely based on their ability to garner attention in a media world in which many issues and groups are competing for attention.[35]

The result has been controversial within the education research community. Some have felt impelled by events to get drawn into the quick response mode. Kevin Welner and Alex Molnar explain:

> At a time when America's education policymakers have nominally embraced the idea of tying school reform to "scientifically based research," many of the nation's most influential reports are little more than junk science. A hodgepodge of private "think tanks" at both the state and national levels wield significant and very often undeserved influence in policy discussions by cranking out an array of well-funded and slickly produced—yet ideologically driven—research. (2007, 44).

Fearing that conservative foundations and think tanks were running circles around the truth in the competition to get their ideas and message out to the public, Welner and Molnar launched a Think Tank Review Project, to provide, for media and a general audience, expert reviews of think tank reports, assessments of think-tank reviews written by experts "in much the same fashion as would a reviewer for a scholarly, peer-reviewed journal" (Welner and Molnar 2007, 32). As a result, when Paul Peterson and Elena Llaudet launched their criticism of the NCES private versus public school study, they were almost as quickly subjected to a critical review on the project's Web site. Within less than a month, Chris and Sarah Lubienski posted their online dissection (Lubienski and Lubienski 2006c).

Rather than fight fire with fire, another alternative is to draw serious researchers back to the traditional mode of being more deliberative in disseminating their work and reasserting the value of scholarly peer review. In December 1999, for example, Edward Muir, a research associate at the AFT, criticized researchers and journalists for overreliance on non–peer-reviewed research. The examples he focused on all involved researchers whose work was regarded to be favorable to school choice and vouchers. He draws a distinction between social sciences and what Muir called the "so-called harder sciences," where "science journalists scan the leading journals for story ideas" and thereby encounter studies after they have had some time to engender critical commentary.

> While the announcement of a new cancer treatment might affect stock prices, it won't affect patients until the [FDA] review procedures, which are intrinsic to our concept of science, are concluded. This is not so in political science, where the results can be announced off the press and then put into practice by officials without any further review. (Muir 1999, 762)

Muir included an extended discussion of Jay Greene and Paul Peterson's early work on Milwaukee vouchers as an illustration of what he referred to as "the practice of providing the political debate with fodder that has not been properly tested." Greene and Peterson had written an op-ed piece, "School Choice Data Rescued from Bad Science," that appeared in the *Wall Street Journal* on August 14, 1996. They claimed that their research showed vouchers could "cut the gap between whites and minorities by one-half" and they dismissed earlier work by John Witte that had found little or no impact on students' test scores. This was the shot across the bow that started the battle of words between Peterson and Witte and, in many people's minds, set a tone of bitterness and polarization that endures. Muir summarized a number of subsequent studies that challenged the Greene and Peterson claims, noting: "All this rebutting occurred before a version of the [original] study was actually published more than two years later" (762).

Muir, unsurprisingly given his AFT affiliation, was critical of the research by Greene and Peterson. The thrust of his argument, however, was less about who was correct than about the fact that preliminary findings, not fully digested or externally reviewed, attracted substantial attention, whereas the rebuttal, and other serious scholarly research that had gone through double-blind peer review received almost none. According to his review, the Greene and Peterson findings were reported in more than thirty newspaper articles across the country. Rush Limbaugh covered it on his popular conservative radio show. It was mentioned on *The NewsHour with Jim Lehrer* on PBS. The authors cited it in testimony to Congress and the Wisconsin legislature. It was used in brochures by proponents of the 1998 voucher referendum in California. By way of contrast, Muir noted that not one of the ten articles published at about the same time in the *American Political Science Review*, the discipline's most prestigious journal, was referenced in any of the newspapers in the Lexis/Nexus database. Muir concluded with a dramatic denunciation

> against using the trappings of social science as totems of competence in political debate. . . . In fact, the application of the sobriquet "scientific" creates, in the general audience, a vision of research that has been tested and that is beyond reproach. As a community of scholars, we have developed

a number of norms and conventions that are an integral part of distinguishing good social science from pseudo-science. To present to the general public research that has not endured the scrutiny of peer review and whose statistical results have not been held to the standards established by the social scientific community, while all the time calling the work "political science," is a challenge to the basic nature of our enterprise as a community of scholars and citizens. (1999, 764)

One of the maxims of political infighting is to leave no charge unanswered, and that has expanded to the school choice debate. Predictably, Muir's essay drew a rebuttal from Greene and Peterson, which in turn drew a rejoinder from Muir, and a final response from Greene and Peterson, each with sly and biting titles (Greene and Peterson 2000a, 2000b; Muir 2000). Greene and Peterson characterized Muir's paper as reflective of an historical effort to "pillory, marginalize, and suppress" research on private alternatives to traditional public schools because it challenged a conventional wisdom "reinforced by the assiduous efforts of well-organized interest groups" (2000a, 221). This was before the AFT charter school study that has been the focal point of this book, but Greene and Peterson pointed to earlier AFT reports, by some of the same authors, that also were released to the press without peer review. They considered the possibility that Muir might have meant to restrict the admonition about bypassing peer review to scholars like them, leaving it open as an option to interest groups like the AFT.

But such an application of the rule would give interest groups the opportunity to release research reports without fear of prompt contradiction by scholars not associated with interest groups. Only after a prolonged period of peer review could alternative information be brought to bear on the issue under policy discussion. The net result would be to bias research available to the public in favor of well-established, vested interest groups that can hire their own research staff. (2000a, 222)

Greene and Peterson pointed out more examples of what they considered to be Muir's double standard. Their paper, they argued, had been reviewed by highly qualified peers, albeit those they selected and not through a formal double-blind process.

Of greater general import, they also challenged the core proposition that peer review should play a central gatekeeper role in vetting research before it is admitted into civic discourse, suggesting that this would be akin to institutionalizing censorship by status quo oriented elements within the established disciplines. Having the option to bypass peer review is critical, they wrote, to a truly free flow of ideas as well as to the public interest in getting information out in a timely fashion. Peer review "has its place," they concluded, because, despite the fact that it is "slow, tedious and may have the undesirable effect of giving priority to the familiar and acceptable rather than the new and controversial," the critiques that are generated often strengthen an article, and peer review can help editors and book publishers sort through the many submissions they receive. But it "should not be exercised in ways that will slow the exchange of ideas or suppress research that offends the sensibilities of the majority—or the interests of the well organized" (Greene and Peterson 2000a, 223).

It can be hard to penetrate the fire and smoke of rhetoric. Greene and Peterson went on to accuse Muir of trying to "demonize" them (2000a, 222; Muir accused them of waving "the bloody shirt of 'academic freedom' before the academic community." (2000, 225). Greene and Peterson retorted that Muir used "Orwellian" distinctions and criticized him for delivering "only a series of *ad hominem* attacks and a hodge-podge of unwarranted methodological criticism" (2000b, 229). Despite his paean to peer review, Muir uses a wide range of non–peer-reviewed outlets to express his position on education policy issues, including a column in *American Teacher*, an AFT publication. Despite his complaints about how the peer-review standard was used by Muir and others to criticize his work, Peterson later turned around and used the same cudgel to attack the credibility of the Lubienskis' analysis of public versus private school performance.[36]

In the final analysis, however, a serious issue was being joined. Academic journals have developed intricate mechanisms to make it more likely that quality will determine publication, rather than who you know and whether what you say is popular. Major journals use double-blind reviews, where the reviewer is not informed whose work she or he is commenting on and the submitter does not know who has reviewed it.[37] As seen in the previous chapter, major funders, including the federal government, also use at least semi-blind reviewing as part of their approval process.

The point is not that reviewers are omniscient or necessarily impartial, but that when pursued responsibly the exercise of peer-review filters out some of the grosser forms of favoritism, improves the product through the revision process, and adds an extra layer of legitimacy that comes from the collective exercise of oversight. Is this all a quaint notion in a time when policy decisions happen quickly and elected leaders want information now? Is peer review outmoded when rival forms of information dissemination operate so much more quickly and spread the word cheaply and broadly beyond the small and elite group that scrutinizes journals, frets over research design, and actually reads the footnotes and appendices? Are the costs of slowing down the flow of information—or biasing it toward the conventional wisdom, as Greene and Peterson allege—so great that the marginalization of peer review can be taken lightly or even welcomed?

In the minds of at least some education journalists the problem is not too much peer review, but too little. "You know, I pine for the sort of security that my colleagues who cover medicine have, where they can just say such and such is coming out in *JAMA* this week," one suggests [J4]. This journalist is a fan of education research, but also recognizes that some of what is published in education journals is poorly done, badly written, overly theoretical, or written and promoted by groups with a political ax to grind.

Researchers also see pros and cons to peer review. One notes a definite "downside to going public with stuff you just shot off your computer," but goes on to reflect on the fact that the alternative—to stay out of the public arena—may be unacceptable as well.

> If you go back to a disciplined public argument that is highly polarized with facts and you are doing serious research on a topic and you think you have facts to bring to bear, what is the responsible thing for you to do? Is it to file them away in your briefcase and keep your mouth shut while people are screaming back and forth across some divide? Or is it to say as best I can tell, here is what the truth is? And this ought to be dealt with and under certain conditions, that is the responsible thing to do. [R9]

When asked to evaluate how important to them are various alternate routes to disseminating their research, charter school researchers overall tend to favor more traditional academic channels such as journal articles, books, and scholarly conferences over the quick turnaround reports and electronic newsletters that have been controversial elements in the school choice debates (figure 7.7). Among those I interviewed, however, a small core raised serious challenges to the traditional academic peer review process of the kinds raised by Peterson and Greene in their debate with Muir. They argued that the scholarly peer review process was not only slow but also inherently biased against new ideas that challenged the intellectual status quo. These researchers were especially critical of education journals, which they considered highly parochial intellectually, with editors relying on a relatively small cadre of reviewers who enforced a bland, homogenous, and politically correct conception of the field. At least among those I interviewed, this skeptical stance was more prominent among researchers favorable to charters and choice, who believe that their academic counterparts are heavily biased against market-based alternatives. Ninety percent of choice skeptics said peer-review journals were a very important outlet for their research;[38] by contrast, only slightly more than a majority of researchers more favorable to charters and choice saw them in the same light.

Those who wish to see a more informed, democratic, and less ideologically polarized discourse about controversial policy issues often

Figure 7.7   Importance of Ways to Disseminate Research

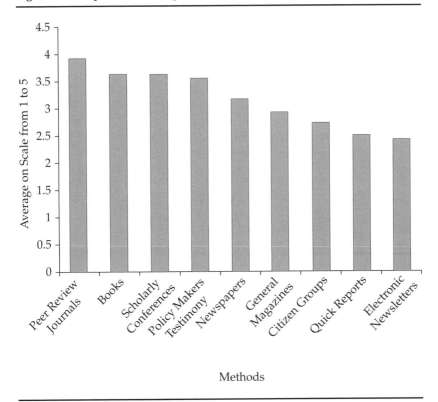

Source: Author's compilation.

place high expectations on the role of the traditional media, as conduits, filters, and interpreters for a public that oftentimes is inattentive and disengaged. Measured against those expectations, the print media's performance on the school choice and charter school debates is disappointing. They lack the space, time, expertise, and inclination to be the nation's tutor in complicated issues of research methodology. Neither, though, do they emerge as the villains in the story of research polarization. My analysis suggests that the media may too passively allow their coverage to be disproportionately influenced by a small coterie of researchers and organizations that aggressively market themselves for op-eds and citation. It supports neither that the charges that ideologically grounded editorial stances aggressively lead to one-sided news coverage, nor that reporters uniformly squeeze stories about research into a fixed template of competing claims. What the media might do better, and how realistic it is to expect that, are matters considered in chapter 8.

At least potentially, speedy and direct communication of research to the public could have a desirable democratizing effect: arming interested citizens with the kinds of information that might otherwise be monopolized by experts and elite interests able to hire experts to defend their cause. In practice, though, speedy and unfiltered dissemination can politicize the use of research in two ways. First, it promotes polarization, through a process in which research that aligns with major ideological cleavages is more likely to be pushed into the public realm. Second, it contributes to the erosion of the distinction between advocacy research and rigorous analysis that can withstand independent review.

Foundations and advocacy organizations with the most intense interests in broad political battles are also those most likely to fund supportive research and actively support dissemination campaigns designed to get the results in the hands of journalists and policy makers. The result is a selection bias in terms of what research gets attention, with studies that present mixed findings and make more moderate claims less likely to be carried into the stream of public discourse. The traditional media can play a role in muting this by taking on the responsibility to provide deeper and more discriminating coverage of research. Financial pressures, though, in large measure fueled by competition from the Web, mean that the traditional media are harder pressed than ever to provide the staffing and investment in longer-term reporting that this would require.

Degradation of the distinction between scholarship and advocacy, and blurring of the lines distinguishing institutions devoted to the former from those devoted to the latter, make it more difficult for even discerning journalists, politicians, and citizens to sort through the competing claims and distinguish stronger findings from weaker ones. Such interested but nonexpert audiences often rely on academia, broadly defined, to enforce quality controls, sort out the wheat from the chaff, and put an authoritative stamp of legitimacy on findings that have stood up to rigorous scrutiny and been replicated. Here, too, there are problems.

Chapter 8

Can the Ideal of Informed Democracy Be Revived?

Bad news and good news are intertwined in this story. The bad news is that the idealized vision of knowledge and democracy is once again shown to be naïve. The Progressives believed that expertise and democracy could be neatly apportioned, each to its own realm. Democracy—messy, emotional, symbol-laden, values-based—would be accorded the key roles of selecting leaders and setting broad priorities. Knowledge, and the research enterprise upon which it rests, would take over from there: experts would fashion policies and programs to maximize the democratically defined public good, oversee their implementation to ensure fidelity and efficiency, evaluate outputs and outcomes to feed new knowledge back into the process and continuously refine the collective effort. The AFT charter school flap makes it apparent that the lines between politics and research, between values and data, between theories and ideologies, are permeable and ill defined.

I say that the naïveté of the idealized vision has been revealed once again because, as we have seen, critics on both the right and the left have challenged the idealized vision before. Claims of knowledge, they have said, are socially constructed and typically erected with the specific function of protecting the institutional status quo. Privileged elites, in government and foundations, control the resources that determine which beliefs get rigorously tested and which are left unexamined. Elites, or those at the service of elites, control the various media that determine which claims are presented as evidence, which researchers are defined as experts, how much complexity the public is capable of processing or willing to countenance.

A good news side to our findings needs to be attended to as well. Compared to some other educational and social policy issues, charter schools present a tough case for those who would like to see a less politicized use of research in democratic decision-making. As discussed in chapter 3, the charter school issue was quickly framed in terms of privatization, and as a result took on added weight in the ideological war between those who favor markets and those who favor government as the primary vehicle through which to pursue the collective good. Despite this, I have argued throughout that charter school research is exhibiting an arc of illumination. Just as proponents of empirical research might have hoped, studies over time are sharpening our conceptualization, developing more precise measures, becoming better designed, and beginning to converge on a number of findings. The path is not straight. The increased convergence does not eliminate disagreement. The findings are contingent on setting and policy specifics. There is a large zone of uncertainty, still, around what we can say with any confidence. The trajectory of the research itself, however, is a positive one.

It is in the translation of research into public discourse, then, that caveats, contingencies, and cautions are abraded, and that findings are simplified and drawn to opposing poles. Why is this? Are research and politics like oil and water? Poured into the same beaker, do they necessarily separate into distinct layers? If so, is it always politics that sits on top? Is it possible—and consistent with the patterns of interaction revealed in this book—to envision a healthier relationship between knowledge and democracy? In this concluding chapter, I sift through the idiosyncrasies of the charter school story in order to offer some thoughts about broader forces at play, about whether and where causal responsibility should be assigned, and how we can acknowledge structural tensions that plague our aspirations without giving up hope for salvaging the vision of a more informed democracy.

Finding Leverage Points for Reform

The skirmishes around charter schools are not isolated. Rather, they reflect a broader conflict over the nature of science and how evidence can be used to obfuscate as well as enlighten. Chris Mooney has used the term *science abuse* to characterize politically or ideologically motivated uses of the language of science in ways that violate the dictates of science. The defining characteristic of science abuse is that it does not attack science directly—as when, during the Inquisition, Galileo was tried and found guilty of heresy. Instead, it co-opts science by charging that its opponents do science poorly or falsely asserting that evidence lies unambiguously on its side of a reigning debate. Mooney pins responsibility for the rise of science abuse primarily on the right—particularly conservative fundamentalists opposed to abortion, stem cell research, and the teaching of evolution, along with market-oriented conservatives seeking to undermine governmental involvement in a range of issues from regulating tobacco to reducing emissions that contribute to global warming. "When politicians use bad science to justify themselves rather than good science to make up their minds," Mooney writes, "we can safely assume that wrongheaded and even disastrous decisions lie ahead" (2005, 242).

Mooney does a service by highlighting what is at risk when politics is allowed to trump science. I am less inclined to assign the full load of causal responsibility to political tacticians on one side or the other. Charter school research, as we have seen, was drawn into the swirling waters of a much broader battle between those who believe government ultimately is the protector of democracy and the public good, and those who believe it is the protector of privilege and the status quo. Most scientific issues do not set off this tripwire of partisan engagement, and research in such arenas tends to be less visible and less fraught. Moreover, I argue, it was not a foregone conclusion even that charter schools would take on such heavy political baggage. The definition of the charter schools initiative as market-based rather than an experiment in public sector decentralization was a consequence of political positioning by conservative strategists who sought to convert the popularity of charters into a leading issue for vouchers, a more radical privatization scheme. Those on the left might have successfully contested this way of framing the issue. Most decided instead to fight the battle in these terms, as market versus government. It was as a result of this framing that pro-charter came to be seen as equivalent to pro-privatization. It was as a result of this framing that supporters of democratic and efficacious government were led to consider charter schooling a serious threat.

Once issues are defined in ways that map onto existing partisan cleavages, the stakes in the battle are substantially raised. They are raised so high that proponents on both sides are tempted to believe that any admission of uncertainty, any recognition of contingency, will be exploited by an enemy they fear and mistrust. In the hothouse environment of ideological warfare, too, speed of response is seen to be of the essence; deliberation is a potentially fatal weakness if while your side studies, the other acts. Good science depends on these very things: uncertainty and contingency and taking one's time to draw conclusions. It is this tension—both real and perceived—between the rules of engagement in partisan politics and the rules of engagement in the scientific enterprise that is the axis along which the events and dilemmas recounted in this book take shape.

Actors in this story feel themselves caught up in forces that constrain their options. Politicians who cite research selectively, based on endorsement through trusted networks, do so to communicate clearly with their supporters and to avoid being made to look confused or indecisive by crafty opponents. Researchers who want to make a positive difference in the world believe they must simplify their stories to be heard. Foundations that want to avoid getting ensnared in ideological quicksand believe they must avoid grant making in certain areas, leaving the ground more open for those that see engagement in such battles as central to their missions. Journalists who would like to cover research issues more deeply believe that the deep controversies among the leading researchers make it difficult for them to distinguish evidence from spin, leaving them little choice but to focus on the controversies and the personal battles.

Structural tensions between the dictates of politics and the processes of good science affect both the right and the left. Some on each side of the charter school debate have been too quick to rush preliminary findings into the public arena, too definitive and universal in their claims, and too quick to disparage the motivation and honesty of researchers with whose findings they disagree. That the challenges are structurally induced and that actors on both sides of the debate fall victim to the inducements to frame evidence based on political considerations, however, does not mean either that responsibility must be equally applied or that the phenomenon is so pervasive that nothing can be done. In making sense of the lessons of the charter school research debate, I find it helpful to draw a distinction between errors of commission and errors of omission. One segment in the pro-charter school coalition is intensely and ideologically committed to the view that government inevitably breeds bureaucratization, overregulation, special interest politics, inefficiency, and infringement on personal freedom. This segment favors markets over public provision of services across a wide range of policy arenas and does so with a fervor and conviction that does not require or seek independent confirmation through empirical analysis. Such free-marketers make up a small but disproportionately influential component of the overall charter school constituency. They see themselves as fighting a war and they are looking to win it. They strategically set out to ride charter schools as a warhorse in the battle for more extreme privatization, and self-consciously sought to build alternative institutions for funding, conducting, legitimating, and disseminating research supportive to their cause. Because their actions are deliberate, and because I believe those actions are eroding institutions and norms that are needed for a better-informed and more knowledge-based democratic discourse, I charge them with errors of commission. That some of them do so in the belief that the existing array of institutions are unfairly stacked against them helps account for, but does not excuse, their actions.

Most of the foot soldiers in the charter movement, however, are not fighting that particular war. They are educators, activists, and parents just trying to find new ways to deliver or receive good schooling. They have aligned with pro-market advocates to protect the fledgling school choice options they value and consider vulnerable. At the same time, they are available for enlistment into an effort to reframe the debate and to find a more civil, pragmatic, and open-minded approach to studying charter schools and drawing the right lessons from those investigations.

Others bear responsibility more for what they have failed to do. Some on the left, out of a fear that charter schools would prove to be a Trojan horse vehicle for a more radical assault on public schooling, reflexively attacked charter schools rather than adopting what might have been a more calibrated response. Some who favored charter schools as a vehicle for providing more decentralized, responsive, and diverse forms of public education acquiesced in portraying charter schools as an exemplar of market delivery and as a panacea for low test scores and the education gap. Some mainstream sources of funding, wary of controversy, frustrated with public school bureaucracies, reluctant to spend money on research that could go to direct services, have chosen to stand on the sidelines rather than invest in their own research agenda or working collaboratively to buttress the national knowledge-generating infrastructure. Major media, for various reasons to be detailed, have been reluctant to provide the in-depth coverage and more probing analysis that they could provide. Researchers excited by the thrill of engagement, and believing themselves to possess unique and critically important insights, have been too passive about letting others frame the debate and establish its tempo. They have lacked the confidence to defend the norms and practices of the research community in the face of charges that it is too deliberative, too careful, too inclined to ask for more study, too aware of what remains to be known.

Ultimately, too insistent a focus on the assignment of blame can distract us from finding the real leverage points for reform and building the constituency to act on what we learn. I believe that the institutions and values that sustain good research and the promise of a more informed democracy are under pressure. This pressure is less the effect of a deliberate assault than a by-product of inattention and structural factors. I suggest that there are some built-in tensions between, on the one hand, the enterprise of research and the norms and institutions that support it, and, on the other, the enterprise of democratic governance and its supporting institutions and norms. Such tensions are likely to be endemic, but they need not be debilitating. They are amplified, though, by changes in the broader American political landscape, which I will then go on to describe. It is against that backdrop that a sense of urgency is warranted and it is within the context of those broader factors that the reform proposals I then offer will need to make their mark.

Dueling Cultures: Research-Think Versus Political-Think

In his famous 1959 lecture, "The Two Cultures," scientist and novelist C. P. Snow argued that society was increasingly polarized into two competing ways of looking at the world, one oriented toward science and one toward the humanities. Some of the patterns revealed in this book can similarly be understood as a reflection of two competing cultures. One—that of the researcher—tends to add complexities and resist final closure. The other—that of the political actor—tends to demand straightforward and easily communicated lessons that will lead to some kind of action. These dueling cultures do not exist in pure and separately distilled forms. Plenty of political actors appreciate science and wrestle with complexity. Plenty of researchers are eager to change the world and grow impatient with fellow researchers who split hairs and hedge bets. The two cultures exist as propensities. They are grounded in the different roles that scientists and politicians play, the tasks they confront, the incentives embedded in the institutions in which they operate, and the kinds of decisions they are expected to make. Difficulties in communication, as a result, are not simple matters of obstinate and perverse refusal to meet on common ground.

Table 8.1 identifies five dimensions in which researchers and political actors tend to differ in the way they think about evidence and action. The first dimension relates to time. Good research is often slow research. There are several reasons for this, lassitude not among them. One of the least understood is the need to allow time for new policies to mature. As the research discussed in chapter 5 suggests, individual charter schools may need time to learn the ropes and institutionalize routines; chartering bodies and governmental oversight regimes may need time to learn what information they need to demand, what pitfalls to watch out for. This maturation process is not unique to charter schools; it has analogues in virtually all policies and programs that are not incremental. The need for policy to mature does not mean that researchers cannot begin studying new policies right away. They can and they should. It does mean that they must withhold final judgment until wrinkles are worked out, and that they must allow for the possibility that early enthusiasms and successes might prove difficult to sustain. Researchers also need time because new policies often require new sources of data, and developing data collection methods and putting them into the field cannot be instantaneous.

Political actors may understand these matters, but their roles require them to march to a different beat. "Well you know, I think policy makers don't have that many opportunities to act on particular things," one researcher explains. "The window of opportunity on a particular policy issue may be pretty small and it is episodic." Political actors, as a result, have to be ready to act, and when they act they need to have whatever research is available at hand. "And so politicians are always thinking, 'Now.' They are not thinking, 'Oh, we will deal with this in eight years'" [R8].

A second dimension involves how we should think about and best pursue societal learning, whether to focus on one study at a time or the

Table 8.1   Researcher-Think Versus Political-Think

Dimension	Researchers	Political Actors
Time	Get it right	Need now
Multiple studies	Cumulation	Which ONE is right?
Causality	Fundamentally problematic in a multi-causal world; demands sophisticated research design and theoretically informed inference	Straightforward: sequence or correlation plus a credible story
Abstraction	Required to find general patterns	Artificial. Denies complexity of real life
Simplification	Via abstraction	Via "get the gist"

Source: Author's compilation.

gradual accumulation of evidence. Researchers tend to think of the scientific process as a collective enterprise. Each researcher may dream of conducting the definitive study—the one that has such strong data, such a strong design, such a clear and meaningful theoretical basis, that it leads even a skeptical audience to conclude "well, now we've settled that"—but most understand that the process of knowledge-production is cumulative. The best studies do not announce themselves as the best upon their release. They prove the best because they stand up to scrutiny, replication, and reanalysis. As demonstrated in chapter 5, the convergence occurring within the charter school research literature is not based on any single new study that instantly made the earlier ones obsolete. Some anticipated that the official multilevel analysis of NAEP data contracted for by the Department of Education (Braun, Jenkins, and Grigg 2006a) would play this role, but rather than put an end to debate it simply became one more bit of fodder for the debate. Because no study of a complex phenomenon can be definitive, this should have been expected from the start. Most political actors, however, do not have the time or inclination to sift through multiple studies, assign them varying degrees of credibility based on their technical strengths, and draw inferences about where the balance of research appears to lie. Because one of the important demands of their role is to convince others, they are anxious to be armed with so-called killer studies:[1] those so strong and compelling that they appear to settle issues once and for all.

A third dimension on which research-think and political-think diverge relates to establishing causality. Building a convincing case about causality is perhaps the most vexing and perplexing challenge researchers face. Arguably, this is more true about social research than physical research, more true about policy research than other social research, and more true about school choice and charter school research than much other policy research. Three factors bedevil efforts to establish causality: competing explanations, spurious correlation, and selective exposure. Most conditions that interest researchers are influenced by multiple factors. The more factors affecting the condition of interest, the more difficult it can be to apportion causality among them, and this is especially the case when not all the relevant causal factors are known. Spurious correlation—that two factors may tend to rise and fall in tandem, not because one causes the other, but because they are jointly influenced by a third unidentified variable—is also always on the minds of researchers. Selective exposure refers to the fact that individuals and populations typically are not randomly subjected to conditions but are differentially exposed, sometimes based on choice (whether to enroll in a charter school) and sometimes based on externally imposed constraints (whether one lives in a neighborhood with concentrated poverty). Sorting out and assigning relative causality can be more challenging in the social than physical sciences, because multicausality tends to be more common, because the intentionality of the subjects—that human beings can behave differently based on what they know and think—introduces complications, and because true experiments as a strategy for dealing with selection bias are more difficult to mount. The challenges are greater in charter school research than in many other areas of social behavior because children's propensity to learn is so complex, because the outcomes of ultimate interest in schooling (students' success in life as workers, family members, and citizens) may take years to become manifest, and because one of the core characteristics of charter schools—that families choose them— makes controlling for selection bias inherently problematic.

Political actors for the most part understand these complexities about causal inference at least in rough terms. However, where researchers make their careers by being sensitive to these nuances, political actors make theirs by laying bets about likely causality and making confident claims attached to convincing narratives. If test scores were higher (or lower) in charter schools than in traditional public schools, researchers would immediately understand that this might be an artifact of selection bias. For them to fail to acknowledge that possibility would mean they were not doing their job correctly—just as one might criticize a doctor who, when told that a patient is suffering stomach distress, did not think to ask about what and where the patient had last eaten. A political actor with a stake in either supporting (or opposing) charter schools, on the other hand, would be quick to grab the finding and use it. Failure to do so would be seen by both allies and opponents as a sign of amateurishness or inattention.

Abstraction is the fourth dimension on which researchers and political actors tend to think in different terms. Researchers study particular cases, but most rewards within the field derive from their ability to relate concrete cases to broader categories and ideas. A study of six charter schools in Cleveland gains value to the extent that the researcher can explain what type of charter schools each one is an example of and how Cleveland is and is not like other cities. Each step up the ladder of abstraction is a step toward a more general finding with broader implications. Political actors more commonly are pulled in the opposite direction, toward specificity. In mobilizing an audience, it is the anecdotes and illustrations that are seen to have power: the story about how Johnny or Denisha thrived in this or that particular charter school is more inspiring than a summary of a 200-school study in which charter school students scored, on average, 0.3 standard deviations better than comparable children in traditional public schools. Political actors in their governance roles, particularly decision makers at the local level, also deal often with concretes. The issue in front of a chartering board, for example, is not whether charter schools in general are good, but whether this or that particular proposal is well considered and whether this or that sponsoring organization has the track record to prove it can deliver on its promises.

A final distinction is based on simplification. Simplification is necessary in human interactions. It is not a bad thing. As social psychologists have realized, all people work with cognitive limitations. We simply cannot attend to and process all the information to which we are potentially exposed (Jones 1995; Kahneman, Slovic, and Tversky 1982; Simon 1985). Researchers and political actors arguably have different overall tolerances for complexity and tend to resort to different devices when simplification is required.

Researchers are socialized into a worldview in which complications are sometimes associated with sophistication. When they do feel a need to simplify, their first recourse is often to do so abstractly. Rational choice theorists, for instance, may be content to model how nations respond to security threats by imagining two- or three-actor games with a limited set of tactical options, recognizing that political leaders operate in much more complex environments. Political actors simplify by reaching for the familiar; they strive to just capture the gist and connect with their audience's preconceptions.

Political-think does not necessarily promote polarization. Attention to the near term and an emphasis on the concrete, for example, under some situations are highly conducive to pragmatic solutions and compromise. Research-think does not necessarily promote usable knowledge. Tolerance of complexity and recourse to abstraction under some circumstances can induce paralysis in decision making or adoption of generalized policy interventions that disregard local particulars. When an issue like charter schooling, framed in terms of the relative merits of markets versus governments, is injected into a national political context marked by intense partisanship and polarization among activist elites, however, the tensions between the two approaches become more obvious and corrosive.

Polarizing Forces in Contemporary American Politics

"In the nation's vaunted legislative body, the moderate center is on life support."

—Jacob S. Hacker and Paul Pierson (2005, 7)

Scholars interested in American public opinion and political behavior have identified broad forces that are thinning out the moderate core of politicians in both major political parties, leaving the dance of national politics to be much more polarized than ever before, and much more polarized than the American public actually is. To understand the pressures on research to support ideological positions and the ways in which the boundaries between research and politics may be eroding, we must look at two important institutional changes. One is partisan polarization. The other is the growing tendency of politicians to craft arguments to evade or shape public opinion rather than to shape their positions to fit centrist public views as the median voter model would have predicted.

Partisan polarization is the decline in the proportion of moderates among party elites and the growing ideological distance between the parties. Beginning in the late 1960s or early 1970s, liberal Republicans and conservative Democrats became more and more of an oddity, making the parties simultaneously more ideologically homogeneous internally and heterogeneous externally. This showed up in the substantial dwindling of cross-party alignments in House and Senate roll call votes.

This polarization between the parties was not driven by polarization within the American public. Most Americans hold moderate or mixed positions on important policy issues. By moderate, I mean that they occupy the center on the conventional left-right continuum, eschewing, for example, politicians and positions that would bring about either nonincremental increases or nonincremental decreases in America's reliance on markets versus government. By mixed, I mean that they simultaneously hold conservative positions on some issues and liberal positions on others. For example, some Americans favor a stronger public-sector role in regulating pollution that could affect global warming but, at the same time, might be receptive to arguments for private deferred taxable college investment accounts as a supplement or alternative to government loans or grants to make higher education more affordable. Mass public opinion changed very little from the 1960s into the 1990s. The average voter became slightly more conservative, but the center of gravity remained rather evenly divided between the left and the right, with most Americans holding to a moderate position.

This creates something of a puzzle. Politicians, after all, are assumed to cater to the public because of their eagerness to be reelected (Mayhew 1975). Why would they play to the ideological poles if that were not where most voters are? When parties run candidates who appeal to their hardcore activists, theory and history predict they will be punished on election day. This is a lesson often illustrated with references to Barry Goldwater in 1964 and George McGovern in 1972. Goldwater was a strongly conservative candidate who appealed to the right wing of the Republican party and was beaten in the electoral vote by 486 to 52. McGovern was a liberal Democrat who excited the left wing, anti-Vietnamese war activists in the Democratic party and lost by 520 to 17.

The answer may lie in broad structural changes that have both allowed and encouraged politicians to play to the poles instead of the polls. Part of the pull to the extremes may come from the importance of campaign funding. To the extent that parties and politicians rely on big donors to even begin to compete, they must tailor their messages with the interests of those donors in minds. In addition, a combination of demographic shifts and gerrymandering of legislative boundaries has tended to create more homogeneous electoral districts even when the overall population has more mixed or moderate views. With fewer competitive elections, candidates in either safe Democratic or safe Republican districts have less incentive to adopt moderate positions. As the general elections became less important (because their results were more pre-ordained), the internal processes by which the parties select their candidates became proportionally more important (Hacker and Pierson 2005).

Party politics has always been disproportionately influenced by those who are more ideologically intense and pure, but changes in primaries (such as the move from open elections to caucuses attended only by party insiders) exacerbate this. "The implications are significant: the combination of fewer legislators outside their party's ideological mainstream and growing policy differences between the parties on social issues and economic issues increased the costs of compromising the policy goals of partisans" (Jacobs and Shapiro 2000, 32). To maintain the loyalty of ideologically purist elements among their parties' activists, elected leaders are frequently forced to adopt more one-dimensional and extreme positions than the average citizens might prefer. Hacker and Pierson remark on this:

> Unconcerned about challenges from the other side of the aisle, protected by the resources of the party (and fearful of losing the favors of powerful groups and leaders), most members of Congress today find it far better to be a loyalist than a maverick. And so most voters sit on the sidelines watching a political blood sport that plays with little concern for what the moderate center of opinion thinks—except as that moderate center represents a modest obstacle to be avoided. (2005, 9)

Politicians who place themselves to the right or left of the median voter position are not irrationally risking defeat, in other words. They may instead be rationally following the new map and new rules for what election entails. "Increasingly, parties and candidates view politics not as persuasion but rather as the mobilization of already-committed voters," writes William Galston in his analysis of polarization in education debates. "Mobilizing requires focusing on, and intensifying, key differences between political adversaries. This discourages compromise and civility while rewarding extreme positions, passionately presented and intransigently defended" (2005, 64). At the same time, they are feeling more free to disregard the median voter, party activists have become more ideologically extreme. Public opinion surveys reveal that the differences between moderate voters and more partisan voters were growing. "In 1964, the distance between the ideological feelings of the average American and those of the strong Republican and strong Democrat was about 16 points; by the mid-1990s, the distance had grown 40 percent to about 23 points" (Jacobs and Shapiro 2000, 35–36).

To explain how politicians may adhere to extreme positions while retaining credibility with more moderate audiences, Jacobs and Shapiro introduce the concept of crafted talk. This refers to the use of words and presentations carefully honed to create the appearance of responsiveness. "Intent on lowering the potential electoral costs of subordinating voters' presentations to their policy goals, politicians use polls and focus groups not to move their positions closer to the public's but just the opposite: to find the most effective means *to move public opinion closer to their own* desired policies (Jacobs and Shapiro 2000, xv, emphasis in the original). Politicians place considerable political stock in changing public opinion, but they rarely count on directly persuading the public of the merits of their position by grabbing the public's attention and by walking it through detailed and complex reasoning" (Jacobs and Shapiro 2000, 49–50).

As Jacobs and Shapiro portray it, politicians both create and are enmeshed within a dysfunctional set of assumptions about the "public's capacity for reasoned and critical thought" (2000, 50). Believing that the average citizen is ill-informed and gullible, politicians rationalize adopting simplistic, symbol-loaded, and ploddingly repetitive positions with the assumption that if they do not do this their competitors will.

A Modest Agenda

What should be done? This is no simple matter of rooting out the bad guys or getting researchers to behave themselves. The connection between the dynamics of the charter school debate and complex factors such as the structure of academia, changes in research funding, the political economy of the media, and the broad landscape of American electoral politics makes that clear. Taking on broader constraints like these is intimidating, and the likelihood of success depends on the premise that there ultimately is a constituency—either latent or creatable—that will rally around a vision of a more pragmatic and informed democratic discourse. What is called for is a long-term strategy, anchored by an idealistic vision but modest in its expectations for immediate and dramatic change, and therefore less vulnerable to disillusionment when the challenges prove intractable. With that in mind I conclude with some general principles and steps worth considering.

Reframe the Charter School Debate: Learning from the Pragmatism of Localized Politics

One of the striking things about charter school politics is the difference in the way the issue plays out politically at the local and national levels. At the national level, charter school politics is a surrogate battleground for the broad ideological war between proponents of government and proponents of markets. Framed thus, the stakes are high. Conservative ideologues consider the superiority of markets over government a core belief and value. If charter schools represent market principles, any claim that they are ineffective, or costly, or socially destructive must be challenged head-on and with all guns blazing. Liberal ideologues see the model of the common public school as sacrosanct and see charter schools as a Trojan horse designed to weaken public institutions and prepare the way for a more full-fledged assault.

Local politics around charter schools can also be intense, but it usually lacks this all-or-nothing, winner-take-all profile. At the local level, charter schooling is less a symbolic abstraction that stands in opposition to an idea of public education and more a set of specific charter school providers, often with track records and constituencies already in place. At the local level, the traditional public school system is not a stand-in for heroic visions of democracy and the public good, but rather a familiar institution with a particular history of successes and failures.

Part of the reason for this lies in differences in the nature of national and local politics and governance (Henig and Stone 2008). The charter school issue is much less freighted and volatile when it is left to unfold on its own terms in specific school districts and communities. National politicians need to hold together disparate coalitions, and abstract models help them to organize their appeals in ways that crystallize a commitment to action at the same time that they obscure the differences in situation, values, and particularities that would otherwise introduce disharmony in the ranks. Congress passes laws designed to exert leverage in a particular direction but leave the details to be worked out within the rule-making process and then, subsequently, at the state and local level where the flesh of specifics must be added to the national policy skeleton. Local actors operate in a more concrete arena in which context, personalities, and parochial idiosyncrasies loom large. Local decision makers have to pay more attention to policy detail because they are charged with responsibility for providing that detail. The president and Congress are in a position to ignore it. Local decision making is more sensitive to context because local decision makers are immersed in a relatively fixed and familiar environment, and it impinges on them in inescapable ways.

One way to moderate the politicization of charter school research, then, might be to push the issue further down the ladder of federalism. National leaders could acknowledge that charter schools are one of many possible tools for reform whose value can vary mightily by context and specifics, and that decisions about whether to employ charter schools might best be left to local prerogative. It may sound unbearably idealistic to imagine national leaders admitting that they do not hold all the answers and agreeing on their own initiative to shrink their own portfolio of decision-making responsibilities. Two points are worth recalling here. First, education in general has only recently become a highly nationalized issue. One reason national parties in the past have been content to leave education policy to states and locals under the reserved powers concept was that education was recognized as a political hot potato, around which passions can run high and politicians' fingers easily get burned. The confluence of events that led both national parties to think that education could be a winner issue for them (McGuinn 2006) might not be as permanent as some believe. Second, and more specifically, it is arguable today that neither national party has turned the charter school issue to its benefit. Republicans initially embraced charter schools in the expectation that this could be a powerful vehicle for counteracting Democrats' traditional advantage on the issue of education policy. By accepting it at least in principle, Democrats kept Republicans from being able to claim sole credit for the movement's popularity. Now that research on test scores shows that charter schools are neither panacea nor disaster, there are incentives on both sides to adopt a friendly but more arm's-length stance.

Is denationalization of the charter school debate the only way to reframe it in less ideologically polarizing terms? Is it possible to inject pragmatism into the national level discourse of charter schools, as opposed to pushing it down to the more naturally pragmatic levels of the federal system? Possibly. We have seen that governors who become presidents sometimes carry their more pragmatic issue-framing with them onto the national stage. Bill Clinton embraced charter schools and, by doing so, succeeded to some extent in reframing them as a mode of public sector reform rather than a first large step down a slippery slope to privatization. George W. Bush exhibited his pragmatism around the issue of standards and testing more than charter schools. Previously, a national push towards standards was seen in ideological terms as an assault on conservatives' visions of states rights. Bush withstood this and helped to make that particular debate one in which party alignments were not sharply defined. Organizations representing state and local officials—the National Governors Association, Conference of State Legislatures, League of Cities, U.S. Conference of Mayors, Council of Great City Schools, and the like—are a less muscular and unified voice than in their heyday in the 1970s (Haider 1974). With national alignments such that neither party currently holds a strong and secure control, it is possible that these organizations can find new influence in shaping the terms of national debate. Finally, the increased emphasis on test scores and outcomes measures that both gave birth to and drew new momentum from NCLB could force a new element of pragmatism into national education politics and the charter school debate, since it raises the prospects that future presidents and Congresses might be held accountable for a bottom line, and accordingly limited in their ability to rely on symbolic appeals.

Research and Advocacy: Avoid the Temptation to Meet in the Middle

The enterprise of research and the enterprise of politics nurture and reward different ways of thinking and problem solving. Each has something to offer to society and each has something to offer to the other. How, then, best to realize the potential complementarities without allowing one to dominate the other? One answer would be to bring the two into closer alignment. Policy researchers could be trained to think more like political actors and encouraged to frame their research questions in terms that facilitate their incorporation into the spheres of politics and governance. Public officials and their staffs could be encouraged to delve deeper into the research process, to develop their own understanding of research design, quantitative analysis, methodological debates.[2]

Much of what is going on today can be understood at least in part as the result of efforts to draw the worlds of research and policy closer together. The curriculums of many schools of public policy and public affairs already reflect this aspiration, with faculty including practitioners as well as scholars and with students taught to synthesize research into one-page policy memos. The growth of think tanks and private consulting firms that depend on government contracts provides political leaders with access to research expertise that can be more timely, more focused, less theoretical, and less unpredictable than could be found reliably within the more cosseted niches of academe. The increased attention by foundations to issues of dissemination and applications of research makes today's foundation-funded research less esoteric and more immediate in its implications. The emergence of researcher-raconteurs who are skillful and enthusiastic about translating research findings into compelling narratives makes it easier for the media to present expert options without having to slog through long-winded interviews about arcane debates that are fascinating to scholars but opaque to everyone else. The expansion of Web-based and electronic delivery mechanisms for disseminating research eliminates the delay and filtering imposed by academic journals with their own rhythm and own standards of what constitutes significance.

This meeting-in-the-middle phenomenon comes with attendant costs. Some of the very characteristics of academia most frustrating to the political world evolved in part because of the way they support research as an independent, collective, cumulative, open-ended enterprise of knowledge creation and testing. By independent, I mean that the selection of research questions and the development of theories and arguments are not fully determined by the most powerful and the most wealthy. By collective and cumulative, I mean that the value of individual researchers and studies depends on how they reinforce or unsettle an existing body of literature comprising shared concepts, provisional hypotheses, comparable measures, tested and replicable methods of analysis. By open-ended, I mean two things. First, that incentives to build on existing foundations are counter-balanced by incentives to find something new, to challenge conventional wisdom, to shake things up. Second, that the time horizon for knowledge creation is measured over decades—not days, weeks, or election cycles.

It is frequently noted—and true—that the culture of many academic institutions actively discourages young scholars from engaging too directly and visibly in the fashionable issues of the moment. Untenured professors who publish an opinion piece in the *New York Times* or make the rounds of the Sunday television news programs are politely congratulated but simultaneously reminded to focus their attention on more scholarly pursuits. It is said, only half in jest, that chances of earning tenure are inversely correlated with the number of copies one's first book sells. Frustrating as this is to outsiders, who would like to see academia more engaged in the issues of the day, this is the flip side of the independence that keeps the research enterprise half a step off the beat set by dominant cliques and dominating ideas.

The expectation within academia is that each new study be situated in the context of its predecessors, that its terms and measurements be precisely defined and carefully calibrated by reference to works by others. This can seem tedious and off-putting to political actors anxious to get to what they see as the policy-relevant bottom line. This expectation also functions, however, to moderate the temptation to treat each new study as terra nova, new ground that warrants immediate reconsideration of existing notions and policies. That academic disciplines still dominate universities frustrates policy makers, who see them as one-dimensional lenses ill suited for understanding the multifaceted problems represented in the real world. The disciplines, though, also have a beneficial focusing effect. They narrow the range of definitions, assumptions, methods, research questions, and standards of excellence in ways that reinforce the collective and cumulative aspects of the research enterprise. Peer review in academic journals plays a similar role. As critics assert, and as discussed in chapter 6, peer review not only slows down the process of dissemination, it also potentially plays a conservative role by empowering more established scholars to screen out new research and ideas that may challenge their dominance. At the same time, these processes weed out the frivolous, force new studies to account for their findings against the backdrop of what has gone before, and assert an institutionalized pressure to speak a common language. Tenure—what many consider an archaic institution that ensures stagnation—also provides both independence and a safer jumping off point for taking intellectual risks. Finally, the crusty standards for promotion within the academic hierarchy, which outsiders see as reinforcing insularity, tend to be harnessed to criteria that weigh long-term contributions over short-term popularity. A favored instrument in many departments for judging worthiness of promotion to full professor status is the citation index. Because it measures the impact of journal articles and books (which themselves can take years to get into circulation) by references to them in subsequent waves of publications (with their own inherent delays), it necessarily interprets merit as having a long half-life.

It is tempting to think that breaking the walls between academic research and applied policy making will allow us to blend the best of both worlds. In reflecting on the case of charter school research, I'm drawn to a different conclusion. Despite a few highly visible studies that have dominated the public face of research, the accumulation and convergence of insights mapped in chapter 5 depended more on a series of lower-visibility studies written less for policy makers than for other researchers. From a societal point of view, more might be gained by maintaining the distinctions between academic, applied, and advocacy research, just as a musical chorus depends on blending of distinct voices rather than recruiting a group of singers each reasonably able to sing high and low notes. That does not mean there should be no discourse between researchers and political actors. There needs to be. The institutions that distinguish them should be differentiated, however, not eroded. Rather than seeking overlapping ways of thinking, we should cultivate the differences and then build mechanisms with the specific task of bridging, an issue to which I shall return.

Redefining Policy Relevance: Do Not Mistake Political Time for Policy Time

By the mid-1970s, some proponents of a more research-based public policy process were beginning to become alarmed. Despite the production of many studies, social science did not appear to be making much of an imprint on what policy makers did. A small subfield developed of people interested in the issue of research utilization. Why was research not used more directly? Some of the popular answers had to do with timing. The research either took too long to be useful or the findings were released at a time when decision makers were focusing on other matters.

Since then, as we have seen, efforts to speed the flow of research into the policy process have been initiated by both the research and the policy communities. Researchers have streamlined the transition from computer output to dissemination, taking advantage of Web sites, electronic newsletters, op-eds, participating in issues forums with political leaders, and the like. Political actors—advocates and public officials—have accelerated the process by moving more toward a "work for hire" model, employing research firms and consultants to give them the research they want, when they want it, on their own terms. Foundations and media have supported this decrease in the time it takes for results to get from the researchers' brains to the policy makers' ears. Foundations do so by making dissemination a major focus of their grant making and oversight. The media do this by encouraging researchers to discuss preliminary results whenever an issue comes across a reporter's radar screen.

The pressure for fast, simple, and confident conclusions, however, is generated by the needs of politicians—not necessarily the needs of the polity. There is a difference, for example, between political time and policy time. Political time is defined by election cycles, scheduled reauthorization debates, and the need to respond to short-term crises or sudden shifts in public attention. A consideration of the history of public policy suggests that societal learning about complex problems and large-scale policy responses takes place on a much more gradual curve. The issues on the table in today's debates about vouchers, charter schools, and school choice more generally are in many key respects the same issues that were presented—with urgency—ten and fifteen and twenty years ago. The arc of learning within the charter school arena suggests that research time unfolds at a pace too deliberate for those focused on short-term political openings. It also suggests that pace may be much more acceptable if judged against the longer-term needs of a polity wrestling with conditions and policies that must be continuously revisited, reconsidered, and re-engineered. Arguably, we would now be better off if we had then set a research agenda designed to provide better answers today, rather than rush various findings into the public discourse too soon—before the phenomenon had come into clear focus, before the range of variability had been recognized, before the longitudinal data had been collected.

Dispense with the Mystique of the Killer Study

In an effort to make policy research more accessible, researchers unintentionally contribute to the politicization of research. By speeding the transmission of findings into public discourse, bypassing peer review, glossing over the technical details, and boiling down interpretation into sound-bites delivered without caveats, researchers have missed a chance to explain and defend some of the characteristics of the scientific enterprise that constitute the core of its long-term value. The more recent emphasis on scientific rigor in one sense represents a needed correction of this course. It, too, overpromises. Emphasizing the importance of strong research design and good data, it has overemphasized the potential for the killer study. The term *killer application* emerged in the software industry as a way to characterize wildly popular new computer programs that not only sell well but also redefine the market and lift the underlying hardware to new levels of credibility. In the context of charter school research, the prospect of a killer study encourages public and private funders to concentrate available resources on one or two truly superior—and highly expensive—studies in the expectation that these can answer central questions once and for all.

This is likely to be an empty promise, a view that gets some support from the recent history surrounding the HLM charter school study. During the years between its initiation and its final release, people held great hopes for this study, a nationwide, multilevel study using the known and respected NAEP data. Many anticipated it as the kind of watershed project that would resolve the question of whether differences in public and charter school performance were attributable to differences in the populations they served.[3] Its ultimate release, however, caused little more than a ripple. Indeed, its authors and sponsoring agency contributed to this muted response, taking great pains to emphasize how inappropriate it would be to draw bold conclusions from it (Cavanagh and Robelen 2006; Robelen 2006).[4]

One recent study sought to identify the most influential studies in the field of education policy by surveying prominent experts from within media, policy-making agencies, think tanks, universities, professional organizations, advocacy groups and foundations (Swanson and Barlage 2006). The report seems to accept the notion of the killer study. Its findings, however, in my view support the alternative view of research as a collective enterprise that comprises multiple studies and lines of thinking. Despite the fact that the survey specifically asked respondents to identify influential studies, respondents often cited broad databases or collections of work rather than individual reports or collections. The report, nonetheless, sought to distinguish what it called blockbuster studies: "truly exemplary studies apart from the rest . . . that have fundamentally shaped the course of debate and action in education policy during the past ten years" (28). Of all those listed, the ones that clearly rose to the top were "furthest removed from the traditional conception of a discrete study"—that is, NAEP and the Trends in International Mathematics and Science Study (TIMMS).

Knowledge development in the charter school arena has been a process of learning by accretion. It is only as more studies are accumulated—conducted in different settings, at different times, focusing on different consequences, distinguishing among different types of charter schools, using differing measures and research designs—that we have begun to get a handle on the phenomenon. No single randomized field trial, no matter how well conducted, could have settled the question of how charter schools perform under changing circumstances. No national study, no matter how comprehensive the database, could have resolved the question of whether a more developed charter school alternative would tip the dynamics sharply in the direction feared by loyalists to the traditional public school system or envisioned by those who imagine a radically reformed system that is more flexible, responsive, and effective. We can, of course, ramp up our vision of what the killer study might look like. We could add hundreds of RFTs looking at different kinds of charters in different legal, demographic, and competitive contexts, sustained over time; or the development of a national student level database tracking students wherever they attend school and combining data on family background, previous performance, residential circumstance; and so on down the line. Such an imagined superstudy would be hugely expensive. The political and logistical obstacles to fielding it would reveal it to be imaginary indeed. At least as important, it is doubtful such a strategy would settle more questions than we could expect from a rival approach.

In place of the elusive killer study, I believe we would be better served if funders and the scholarly community self-consciously adopted a more pluralistic conception of the research enterprise. Maintaining pressure to raise the quality of the median study, this approach suggests a more-the-merrier objective. Conceiving of research as a collective and cumulative process, it favors strategically lowering the marginal costs of research, distributing funding more broadly, and increasing cross-fertilization among subsectors of research and creating mechanisms to more efficiently identify those that warrant heightened visibility and support.

Fund the Architectural Core of the Research Enterprise

The public good aspects of research clash with the culture of instrumentality that has affected funding sources both public and private. What makes research most valuable to democracy over the long haul is uncertainty about what it may find. Research that merely confirms the conventional wisdom is not without value, but its value is limited. Research that really carries a payoff is research that surprises us, that shows us something we did not know or that forces us to reconsider something we thought we knew.

Funding agencies and the personnel who inhabit them typically have a more narrow mission on their minds. Federal agencies, to the extent that they are accountable to political appointees, are encouraged to think in terms of research products that reinforce the administration's mission. Foundations have become more instrumental in the ways they conceive of research, too (Bacchetti and Ehrlich 2007; Lagemann and de Forest 2007). The first generation of foundations invested in enterprises like the National Bureau of Economic Research, the Social Science Research Council, and various university centers and programs of public policy and urban affairs; they operated less with an expectation of specific near-term benefits and more in the belief that they could catalyze broad changes in the nation's infrastructure of knowledge gathering, application, and dissemination in ways that would have substantial, but long-term and unpredictable, results. Today's newer foundations—and even the leadership of the more mature foundations—seem eager to be able to trace the lines of their impact and they discipline themselves to stay on mission. To the extent that resouces previously may have been frittered away, this kind of focus may be all to the good. We can reasonably expect both government, as the formal champion of the public good, and foundations, as vehicles charged with meeting social needs in return for tax and other benefits accorded them, to also take into account the need to sustain a core infrastructure for research that will be used in unpredictable ways.

The federal government in particular should focus more on building the infrastructure of the research enterprise, even if this entails doing less funding of specific studies. The principal strategy is to focus on data systems. Good national data systems lower the marginal cost of research by lowering data collection expenses, making it more feasible for many researchers and research organizations to conduct studies formulated around research questions of their own devising. Good national data systems—because they encourage researchers to use the same measures rather than those that are idiosyncratic and ad hoc—facilitate tests of reliability of findings and assessments of the degree to which findings may be systematically different in different settings. Good longitudinal data systems make it possible to isolate the effects of policy interventions and distinguish these from background trends. Finally, good national data make case study research more valuable by making it easier to determine how the settings of cases—the particular school, or district, or state in which the research takes place—fits within the universe of other settings to which we might want to generalize.

The federal government needs to focus on this role because it is in a unique position to carry it out. Federally funded data efforts have been influential in the history of school choice research, charter school research, and educational research in general. Several of the truly classic studies comparing public and private schools, for example, drew on the High School and Beyond (HS&B) data that followed a national sample of 1980 seniors and sophomores. Both cohorts were surveyed every two years through 1986, and the 1980 sophomore class was also surveyed again in 1992 (Bryk, Lee, and Holland 1993; Chubb and Moe 1990; Coleman and Hoffer 1987). The broader National Educational Longitudinal Study (NELS) followed a cohort of students who were in the eighth grade in 1988, surveying them every two years since that time. Significantly, neither HS&B nor NELS were designed specifically to focus on school choice issues. Significantly also, these data sets have proven invaluable in studying a range of issues not related to choice (such as school size, class size, and the effects of teacher professionalism). NAEP is another national data set that was not designed with a specific research project in mind, but which, as we have seen, has been front-and-center in addressing issues about charter schools. That NAEP was not designed for the research questions for which it is sometimes used plays a role in the controversy over how to interpret studies using that data. The dollar-for-dollar research pay-off for data systems like these is huge, however, and (I believe) ultimately much more defensible than would be efforts to craft, de novo, more precisely appropriate data for specific analyses.

The federal role should not depend on the national government collecting its own data. We have seen that individual state data systems, based on student level data and capable of tracking students as they move from school to school, have been especially important in advancing understanding about the consequences of charter schools. The nation's research enterprise will be well served if other states follow the lead established by states such as Florida, Texas, and North Carolina. The federal government cannot legally, politically, or logistically take over the task of maintaining a student-level longitudinal data system. It can provide funding and other incentives to encourage states to do so, and it can influence the states to adopt broadly compatible indicators (to promote comparability across states) and to adopt policies that make it easier for researchers to gain access to such data (while protecting student confidentiality).

Foundations—even the behemoths among them—cannot afford to fund the nation's data core. There are roles they can play in supporting the infrastructure of research nonetheless. Most foundations define their data needs rather narrowly as they relate to specific projects or mission themes. That is understandable and fine. When they do fund research for their specific needs, however, foundations could be more alert to the positive ripple effects that could occur if they structure their data collection and analysis to exploit and complement, as much as possible, the broader national research enterprise. Some foundations have a local focus, and within their sphere of influence the resources they bring to bear are substantial. Consider, for example, the case of a local foundation that may be providing support to several charter schools or considering whether to do so. It might decide to fund research to assess whether that set of schools is having intended impacts on students' test scores and long-term success. The lure of the funding it controls is likely to generate high levels of cooperation from the schools in question, making it conceivable that such a study could get unusual access to teachers, parents, and students and develop rich and original indicators as a result. Pursued on its own terms, such research might tell the foundation quite a bit about the small set of schools under its microscope. At the same time, it would shed relatively little light on the general phenomenon of chartering or even on what aspects of those charter schools account for the findings. Framing the research more broadly to include other charters or traditional public schools, or using some more generally available measures or survey instruments, would reduce some of the richness of the study but might vastly increase spillover benefits. Such a study might make it more possible to isolate generalizable lessons, might make it more likely that others could replicate the study in other places or schools, and might encourage the district and other charter schools to open their doors to research.

A corollary to this point is that both public and private funders should begin to discourage sector-specific data collection in favor of efforts that incorporate charter schools, traditional public schools, and, where possible, private schools as well. Such cross-sector data bases are a more effective investment. One, they can answer a broader range of research questions. Two, they make it more possible to determine when desirable consequences are sector-specific or more generalizable. A structured preference for studies that incorporate multiple sectors is also in keeping with the earlier suggestion to reframe the charter school debate so that it focuses less on a bifurcated notion of markets versus government. Most of the pressing research questions in education involve factors that at least in principle can vary within and across sectors: the role, for example, of variation in teacher skills, class and school size, length of school day and year, school-based decision making, ability-based grouping, and the like. Research framed around these questions but using samples that include charter and noncharter schools will have a broader constituency and will be less likely to ignite the partisan passions than studies framed to answer the question of whether one sector is better than the others.[5]

Identify and Disseminate the Best Research: Prospects for Media Reform and the Need for a Peak Journal

I have argued that the core problems of politicization of research emerge at the dissemination stage, which seems to put the media in a critical role. The media overall, though, appears to me to reflect broader phenomena as much as shape them. It would be very good indeed if the major media could raise the status of their education staffs, devote more space to in-depth coverage, publish more pieces that synthesize existing knowledge on an issue rather than reacting to a short-term burst of interest (what one journalist refers to as "it-happened-yesterday stories" [J6]) or a single report.

The major print and electronic media are in poor position to respond in more than incremental ways, though, unless other actors lead the way. They face a hostile economic climate marked by sharp competition and a skeptical investment community, as discussed in chapter 7. It is possible that they underestimate the consumer demand for deeper coverage. Investors, if anything, are sending the opposite signal. The pressure is on to cut staff, not expand it, to generate less original content, not more.

There are some reasons, nevertheless, to think that the media can do more and better. Education coverage evolved for many years as a low-status beat on which novice reporters paid their dues sitting through long and dull school board meetings to write short summaries as a community information service. Structural changes in the nature of education policy, however, are raising its visibility and perceived importance. No Child Left Behind signals that education is now a national issue, one on which presidential and congressional candidates need to have positions and things to say. Education issues may still lack the buzz and drama of those such as national security, of course. Reporters covering the beat, though, now at least have a chance to make a mark and media covering the issues have a chance to win national awards.

Somewhat paradoxically, too, there is a chance that the pressure to compete with blogs and other electronic news sources may put at least some of the major media in position to cover issues such as state and local education policy more deeply than they could when their only outlet was valuable and limited newsprint columns or on-air slots. The major networks, newspapers, and news magazines are investing substantially in their Web presence and some of these operations are beginning to show promise as sources of advertising revenue. It is not yet clear what the formula will be for the content of these Web versions. Some existing examples primarily replicate their regular coverage. Others are experimenting with new and more niche oriented features. Even if there is not enough demand for in-depth coverage of education issues to warrant bumping other items from a space constrained newsprint window, there may be enough interest to justify intense coverage in the more readily expandable virtual media world.

That said, the best hope for better media coverage of education research probably rests on the behavior of others. Foundations could play a helpful role. Media rationales for the thin coverage they currently provide boil down to economic concerns about staff allocations and audience interest. Some foundations already take it upon themselves to provide funds for more in-depth coverage of specific issues that matter to them and that media have been able or unwilling to fully fund with their own resources. Listeners to National Public Radio, for instance, are familiar with the fact that some types of news coverage have received special funding from donors whose interests align with those of the station. Local foundations could consider supporting local media coverage of education policy research, perhaps with a special emphasis on coverage that considers how research undertaken elsewhere does and does not have connotation on the local scene. Specific activities might include funds for local journalists to take short courses in research methodology and to attend national conferences that may not have clear promise of generating near-term stories but which would build background knowledge and exposure to enrich subsequent coverage.

The scholarly community has a role here that it can play as well. Some of the journalists with whom I spoke openly wished that they could—like their counterparts in health and medical reporting—rely on a high-profile, high status peer-reviewed journal—such as the *New England Journal of Medicine* or the *Journal of the American Medical Association*—to authoritatively steer them to studies most worthy of attention and best able to withstand critical scrutiny. Rather than welcoming the growing tendency of researchers to release studies quickly via Web sites and press releases, the journalists felt that this put them in a tougher position, that it made it all the more difficult for them to separate the slick from the significant and exposed them to risks if they accord attention to a study that might be subsequently discredited. Currently, the journal world in education is overflowing, uneven in quality, and overly fragmented by substantive focus and methodological orientation. Those outside the education research community could benefit from a stronger and more authoritative signaling mechanism to help them find the best theoretical and empirical work in the field.

Creating a peak journal—whether a new publication or a reconstituted version of an existing one—is no simple matter. There are important questions about who could and should sponsor such an effort should it occur. The American Education Research Association (AERA) already sponsors five journals. Their quality is mixed, their focus varies,[6] and they compete not only with one another but also with a number of others. Conceivably, AERA could reconfigure its offerings in such a way to raise one above the others as the flagship voice on education policy research. Some of the most valuable charter school research, however, has been carried out by discipline-based scholars who may have professional incentives to prefer publishing in their discipline-based journals. To attract these scholars as a first choice for releasing their best work, a peak journal on educational policy might have to be housed outside of AERA and offer both a high profile sponsoring body and an advisory board that included top economists, political scientists, sociologists, and the like. Alternatively, the journal—or a section of it—could offer a "best of the rest" approach, reprinting the best articles from other venues or inviting revisions written with a broader audience in mind.

The scholarly community of education researchers most likely lacks the coordinating capacity or institutional framework to initiate such a journal on its own. A consortium of major foundations and a strong publishing company, however, could take the lead. One model might be *Education Next*, a journal with high production values featuring relatively short articles by prominent researchers and written in nonacademic prose. These features allowed *Education Next*, introduced in 2001, to rapidly attract attention and an audience. According to one recent survey, *Education Next* is the most influential journal in education (Swanson and Barlage 2006). It has, however, probably been too closely associated with conservative funders, scholars, and ideas to serve as an objective arbiter of what constitutes the best research and thinking in the field. Certainly, on issues of school choice, its editors and editorial board—which include Paul Peterson, Chester Finn, Caroline Hoxby, John Chubb, and Terry Moe—is too tightly clustered around the strong pro-voucher position to have genuine credibility as an independent voice. *Education Next* demonstrates, though, that there is room for a major new entrant that, if properly conceived and if supported by the right core of top-notch scholars, could serve in such a role.

Researcher Heal Thyself

I've argued that the demands and dictates of politics make it problematic whether good research will trump weaker studies. I have also argued that research has—despite the personalized, polarized, and politicized use of it in the public charter school debate—been converging on some general new understandings of the phenomenon that highlight how much its impact depends on such particulars as types, time, and place. What this suggests is that the core challenges have less to do with the production of research than with the ways that research gets taken up within public forums.

Researchers have some responsibility in remedying this. Ironically, they need to do so by framing their claims about the importance of research more realistically, which means more modestly. At the same time we sound the call for improved research designs and investment in the infrastructure of data, we need to be educating the media, funders, policy makers, and public more about the limitations of research. When policy makers say they need the information and they need it now, we must sometimes be ready to tell them honestly that it does not yet exist. When funders or the media say they need a sharp and definitive and broadly stated lesson, we sometimes need to hold our ground and say that available evidence permits only tentative, contingent, and qualified conclusions.

To some, this might sound like a recipe for irrelevance. Researchers, however, should more confidently challenge the notion of relevance dominated by politicians' near-term needs. Moreover, failing honestly to present the challenges and complexities of research carries its own risks of irrelevance as well. The current course of action has been eroding the impact of good research by erasing the distinction between, on the one hand, strong methodology and nuanced findings, and, on the other, compelling talk. It is exhilarating for researchers to be on the public stage and to feel themselves a part of serious discussions about serious matters. Arguably, we would be better off bearing politicians' irritation with our tentativeness and disdain for our deliberateness than losing touch with the norms and procedures that over the long run set research apart and give it what authority it deserves.

Final Thoughts: Expect More from Policy Makers and Citizens

Some of the core debates in democratic theory boil down to this. Should we shrink our expectations of democracy so that they better fit the limitations of our citizens? Or should we hold to a high ideal of democratic decision making and use all means at hand to help develop a citizenry that is up to the challenge? There are many variants of this debate. For example, at the time the nation was founded, a key issue revolved around expectations about man's moral compass. Some argued that humans were inherently self-interested and motivated to pursue wealth and power. Others believed humans capable of public-spirit and personal sacrifice in the pursuit of a public good. Some of the most important institutions adopted in the Constitution—particularly the separation of powers, federalism, the Bill of Rights—reflected the more cynical, or perhaps more realistic, view. More attention was devoted to limiting likely abuses of authority than to creating a government with the capacity to act effectively in maximizing the majority's will.

The key questions invoked in this book have less to do with moral compass than cognition. Is the average citizen capable of wrestling with complex issues of research and evidence as they bear on public policy? If not, one intellectually coherent response would be that associated with the Progressives. That is, constrain the role of citizenship to the simple task of voting the rascals in and out but buffer the deliberations about specific policies and programs so that those with knowledge can proceed without interference from politics which is partisan, emotional, parochial, and nonrational. The opposite response can be just as coherent. Consider appeals to science and evidence to be elitist tools for manipulating the public and instead elevate institutions of direct democracy that respond to the intuitive common sense of the average Joe.

It is somewhat ironic that in the era of No Child Left Behind—when leaders are quick to assert that all students can be academically proficient and that expecting anything less is soft bigotry—we find it easy to lower the bar for public discourse. Schools and teachers are told to set high standards and accept no excuses. Foundations, the media, and politicians, however, operate at times as if there is an imperative to bring the presentation of research and evidence down to the level of simple bullet points, authoritative findings, and unambiguous lessons.

The irony is heightened by the fact that those calling for higher standards in education often reflexively argue that government's legitimate role in prescribing a public education policy is the responsibility to create an informed citizenry. Proponents of deliberative democracy argue that a disengaged and uninformed citizenry is as much a reflection of the institutions within which public discourse takes place as it is an indicator of fixed limitations on what the public can hear and digest. The extent to which this is so is ultimately an empirical question. Observing that politicians who present nuanced and scholarly arguments are often dismissed as eggheads, and that newspapers or newscasts that delve into complicated issues in depth are muscled out of markets by competitors with infotainment for sale, is not enough to resolve it. There is persuasive evidence that over the long haul and in the aggregate the American public exhibits stability, moderation, and rational consistency in its political voice. That this can occur even if many citizens are erratic and ill-informed is a comforting reminder that deliberative democracy need not depend on unrealistic expectations that all citizens match some idealized standard. Shifting the center of gravity of public discourse toward a higher level of sophistication seems within grasp, and seems likely also to generate positive results.

Appendix 1

List of Those Interviewed

Jeanne Allen, Center for Education Reform

Richard Colvin, Hechinger Institute on Education and Media

David Ferrero, Gates Foundation

David Figlio, University of Florida

Chester Finn, Fordham Foundation

Bruce Fuller, University of California, Berkeley

Dan Goldhaber, University of Washington

Jay Greene, University of Arkansas; Manhattan Institute

Eric Hanushek, Stanford University

Rick Hess, American Enterprise Institute

Paul Hill, Center on Reinventing Public Education, University of Washington

William Howell, University of Chicago

Helen Ladd, Duke University

Hank Levin, Teachers College, Columbia University

Tom Loveless, Brookings Institution

Chris Lubienski, University of Illinois at Urbana-Champaign

Bruno Manno, Annie E. Casey Foundation

Jay Mathews, *Washington Post*

Gary Miron, The Evaluation Center, Western Michigan University

Terry Moe, Stanford University

F. Howard Nelson, American Federation of Teachers

Daniel Okrent, formerly public editor, *New York Times*

Janice Petrovich, The Ford Foundation

Gary Putka, *Wall Street Journal*

Jonah Rockoff, Columbia University

Bella Rosenberg, American Federation of Teachers

Andrew Rotherham, Education Sector

Jesse Rothstein, Princeton University

Richard Rothstein, Economic Policy Institute

Diana Jean Schemo, *New York Times*

Mark Schneider, Commissioner of the National Center for Education Statistics; State University of New York at Stony Brook (on leave)

Kathy Smith, Walton Family Fund

Marshall (Mike) Smith, William and Flora Hewlett Foundation

Greg Toppo, *USA Today*

Amy Stuart Wells, Teachers College, Columbia University

John Witte, University of Wisconsin-Madison

Appendix 2

Diana Jean Schemo, "Charter Schools Trail in Results, U.S. Data Reveals," *New York Times* (Late Edition, East Coast), August 17, 2004, p. A1

The first national comparison of test scores among children in charter schools and regular public schools shows charter school students often doing worse than comparable students in regular public schools.

The findings, buried in mountains of data the Education Department released without public announcement, dealt a blow to supporters of the charter school movement, including the Bush administration.

The data shows fourth graders attending charter schools performing about half a year behind students in other public schools in both reading and math. Put another way, only 25 percent of the fourth graders attending charters were proficient in reading and math, against 30 percent who were proficient in reading, and 32 percent in math, at traditional public schools.

Because charter schools are concentrated in cities, often in poor neighborhoods, the researchers also compared urban charters to traditional schools in cities. They looked at low-income children in both settings, and broke down the results by race and ethnicity as well. In virtually all instances, the charter students did worse than their counterparts in regular public schools.

Charters are expected to grow exponentially under the new federal education law, No Child Left Behind, which holds out conversion to charter schools as one solution for chronically failing traditional schools.

"The scores are low, dismayingly low," said Chester E. Finn Jr., a supporter of charters and president of the Thomas B. Fordham Foundation, who was among those who asked the administration to do the comparison.

Mr. Finn, an assistant secretary of education in the Reagan administration, said the quality of charter schools across the country varied widely, and he predicted that the results would make those overseeing charters demand more in the way of performance.

"A little more tough love is needed for these schools," Mr. Finn said. "Somebody needs to be watching over their shoulders."

Mr. Finn and other backers of charter schools contended, however, that the findings should be considered as "baseline data," and could reflect the predominance of children in these schools who turned to charters after having had severe problems at their neighborhood schools.

The results, based on the 2003 National Assessment of Educational Progress, commonly known as the nation's report card, were unearthed from online data by researchers at the American Federation of Teachers, which provided them to The New York Times. The organization has historically supported charter schools but has produced research in recent years raising doubts about the expansion of charter schools.

Charters are self-governing public schools, often run by private companies, which operate outside the authority of local school boards, and have greater flexibility than traditional public schools in areas of policy, hiring and teaching techniques.

Federal officials said they did not intend to hide the performance of charter schools, and denied any political motivation for failing to publicly disclose that the data were available. "I guess that was poor publicity on our part," said Robert Lerner, the federal commissioner for education statistics. Mr. Lerner said further analysis was needed to put the data in its proper context.

But others were skeptical, saying the results proved that such schools were not a cure-all. "There's just a huge distance between the sunny claims of the charter school advocates and the reality," said Bella Rosenberg, a special assistant to the president of the American Federation of Teachers. "There's a very strong accountability issue here."

Of the nation's 88,000 public schools, 3,000 are charters, educating more than 600,000 students. But their ranks are expected to grow as No Child Left Behind identifies thousands of schools for possible closing because of poor test scores.

Once hailed as a kind of free-market solution offering parents an escape from moribund public schools, elements of the charter school movement have prompted growing concern in recent years. Around the country, more than 80 charter schools were forced to close, largely because of questionable financial dealings and poor performance, said Luis Huerta, a professor at Columbia University Teachers College. In California, the state's largest charter school operator has just announced the closing of at least 60 campuses, The Los Angeles Times reported on Monday, stranding 10,000 children just weeks before the start of the school year.

The math and reading tests were given to a nationally representative sample of about 6,000 fourth graders at 167 charter schools in February 2003. Some 3,200 eighth graders at charter schools also took the exams, an insufficient number to make national comparisons.

The results are not out of line with earlier local and state studies of charter school performance, which generally have shown charters doing no better than traditional public schools. But they offered the first nationally representative comparison of children attending both types of schools, and are expected to influence public debate.

Amy Stuart Wells, a sociology professor at Columbia University Teachers College, called the new data "really, really important."

"It confirms what a lot of people who study charter schools have been worried about," she said. "There is a lack of accountability. They're really uneven in terms of quality."

Detractors have historically accused charters of skimming the best students, those whose parents are most committed, from the poorest schools. But supporters of charter schools said the data confirmed earlier research suggesting that charters take on children who were already performing below average. "We're doing so much to help kids that are so much farther behind, and who typically weren't even continuing in school," said Jeanne Allen, president of the Center for Education Reform, in Washington, which represents charter schools. She said the results reflect only "a point in time," and said nothing about the progress of students in charter schools.

That, she said, could be measured only by tracking the performance of charters in future tests. For the moment, however, the National Assessment Governing Board has no plans to survey charters again.

One previous study, however, suggests that tracking students over time might present findings more favorable to the charter movement. Tom Loveless, director of the Brown Center on Education Policy at the Brookings Institution, who conducted a two-year study of 569 charter schools in 10 states found that while charter school students typically score lower on state tests, over time they progress at faster rates than students in traditional public schools.

The new test scores on charter schools went online last November, along with state-by-state results from the national assessment. Though other results were announced at a news conference, with a report highlighting the findings, federal officials never mentioned that the charter school data were publicly available.

Researchers at the American Federation of Teachers were able to gain access to the scores from the national assessment's Web site only indirectly: by gathering results based on how schools identified themselves in response to a question.

In a significant departure from earlier releases of test scores, Mr.

Lerner said the charter school findings would be formally shown only as part of a larger analysis that would adjust results for the characteristics of charter schools and their students.

In the 1990's, the National Assessment Governing Board had rejected requests from states for such analyses, with Mr. Finn, then a member of the board, contending that explanatory reports would compromise the credibility of the assessment results by trying to blame demographic and other outside factors for poor performance.

But Mr. Lerner said he thought such an analysis was necessary to put the charter school test scores in context. He called the raw comparison of test scores "the beginning of something important," and said, "What one has to do is adjust for many different variables to get a sense of what the effects of charter schools are."

Appendix 3

"Charter School Evaluation Reported by *The New York Times* Fails to Meet Professional Standards"

We, the undersigned members of the research community, are dismayed by the prominent, largely uncritical coverage given by *The New York Times* to a study of charter schools by the American Federation of Teachers (AFT). According to the paper's lead news story on August 17, the analysis shows "charter school students often doing worse than comparable students in regular public schools."

The study in question does not meet current professional research standards. As a result, it tells us nothing about whether charter schools are succeeding. The following considerations are key:

Data Quality. The study is based on data from the 2003 National Assessment of Educational Progress (NAEP). Often referred to as the Nation's Report Card, NAEP provides a valuable snapshot of student performance nationwide at a single point in time. But since only limited family background information is currently available for the 2003 NAEP, the study does not provide reliable information on the effectiveness of any particular type of school.

Only One Set of Test Scores. Because only one year of information is available for charter schools from NAEP, the study provides test scores for only one point in time. But without better background information, accurately measuring school effectiveness requires information on student performance from at least two points in time.

Limited Background Information. Because of limited NAEP information on family background, the study does not take into account such key characteristics of students known to affect their performance as parental education, household income, and the quality of learning resources in the home.

Unsophisticated Analysis. When analyzing charter schools' effects on student performance, the study considers differences in only one family background characteristic at a time. To obtain accurate estimates, all available background characteristics must be considered simultaneously.

What NAEP *Can* Tell Us. NAEP data do show that charter schools tend to serve a relatively disadvantaged population. As compared with traditional public schools, a higher proportion of students in charter schools are eligible for the federal free or reduced-price lunch program, are from minority backgrounds, and attend a school located in a central city.

Journalistic Responsibility. The news media has an obligation to assess carefully any research sponsored by interest groups engaged in policy debates. Such studies need to be vetted by independent scholars, as is commonly done in coverage of research on the biological and physical sciences.

Further Research. To date, we lack definitive evidence on the effectiveness of charter schools, in part because they are so new and so varied. Fortunately, higher-quality research on charter schools is already underway. Still more needs to be done before jumping to conclusions about the merits of one of the nation's most prominent education reform strategies.

Julian R. Betts
*University of California,
San Diego*

John E. Brandl
University of Minnesota

David E. Campbell
University of Notre Dame

Mary Beth Celio
University of Washington

James G. Cibulka
University of Kentucky

Gregory J. Cizek
*University of North
Carolina, Chapel Hill*

David N. Figlio
University of Florida

David J. Francis
University of Houston

Howard L. Fuller
Marquette University

Charles Glenn
Boston University

Jay P. Greene
Manhattan Institute

Eric A. Hanushek
Stanford University

James J. Heckman
University of Chicago

Paul T. Hill
University of Washington

William G. Howell
Harvard University

Caroline M. Hoxby
Harvard University

Tom Loveless
The Brookings Institution

Robert Maranto
Villanova University

Terry M. Moe
Stanford University

Thomas J. Nechyba
Duke University

Paul E. Peterson
Harvard University

Michael Podgursky
*University of Missouri,
Columbia*

Margaret E. Raymond
Stanford University

Jonah Rockoff
Columbia University

Simeon Slovacek
California State University, Los Angeles

Tim R. Sass
Florida State University

Paul Teske
University of Colorado, Denver

Richard K. Vedder
Ohio University

Herbert J. Walberg
University of Illinois, Chicago

Martin R. West
Harvard University

Patrick J. Wolf
Georgetown University

Notes

Chapter 1

1. The full text of the article is reproduced in appendix 2.
2. Sometimes referred to as scholarships.
3. Special programs within schools, or incorporating whole schools, that offer a special curriculum or emphasis designed to attract students from across the district. Magnets schools initially emerged as a tool for racially integrating schools without mandatory busing.
4. Programs, usually enacted at the state level, that make it possible for students in one district to attend public schools in another district that may offer a better or more appropriate program.
5. The advertisement is reproduced in appendix 2.
6. Quoted in John Horgan's December 18, 2005, *New York Times* review of the book *The Republican War on Science,* by Chris Mooney.
7. Kevin Smith (2005) quoting Jay Greene, Paul Peterson, and Jiangtao Du (1996).
8. Smith quoting David Berliner and Bruce Biddle (1995).
9. I'll have more to say about the Witte-Peterson spat and the *Journal's* coverage of it in chapter 4.
10. To select a group that did not overly represent one side or another, I initially scored potential interviewees as either being strongly or moderately pro- or anti- or being mixed or unidentifiable on that dimension and selected those to approach so as to keep the overall group broadly representative. Along the way I added a few interviewees not on the original list, because of suggestions I received from other respondents. In one case, I subsequently decided that a researcher I expected to be moderately pro-choice and charter school should probably be counted in the skeptic camp and in analysis later in the book that person is so coded.
11. The interviews with funders tended to be more unstructured. This was because their organizational contexts and direct involvement with charter school research differed quite a bit, and I found it more productive to probe deeply on some questions than to force the interviews into a constraining format.
12. An advocate, as coded here, implies someone associated with an organization that promotes particular policy positions and may be either a supporter or opponent of charter schools.

Chapter 2

1   Accessed November 11, 2004, at http://www.ed.gov/about/offices/list/ies/index.html.
2. Initially a department, education was promptly demoted to bureau status until 1979 (Vinovskis 2002).
3. Most of the others dealt with such issues as employment income transfers, health, and counseling.
4. More precisely, variations in school inputs did not account for much variance in student test scores once family background and class peers are taken into account.
5. As is often the case with rich and influential concepts, the notion of deliberate democracy is complex and the term is used with many variants. It includes some very practical efforts to construct forums in which citizens are given a chance to digest available data and analyses and engage in structured discussions, with evidence that participants' views, at the end of such deliberations, vary in meaningful and desirable ways from the results of conventional public opinion polling (for example, Fishkin 1991; see also the Kettering Foundation publications at http://www.kettering.org/readingroom). It also includes more theoretical discussions of the specific core norms, processes, and rules of engagement that might be required for healthy and truly democratic discourse (Gutmann 1987; Gutmann and Thompson 1996; Macedo 1999).

Chapter 3

1. Comments offered in anticipation of release of the National Center for Education (NCES) hierarchical linear modeling report on charters.
2. The figures are provided by Robert Smith, AERA director of meetings.
3. For an excellent biography of this complex and important leader see Richard Kahlenberg (2007).
4. This section draws from an earlier formulation in Jeffrey Henig (2006).
5. Accessed at http://www.presidency.ucsb.edu/showplatforms.php?platindex=R1980
6. Support for the bill came from a coalition of strange bedfellows, including Republican governor Tommy Thompson, State Representative Annette "Polly" Williams, a Democratic, African American single parent of four children who twice chaired Jesse Jackson's presidential campaigns in that state, and Howard Fuller, an African American community activist, who in 1987 had proposed creating a separate school district in the predominantly black portion of the city (Hess 2002). Williams and Fuller came around to vouchers out of frustration with the failure of the local system to respond to the black community's demand for high quality schools in their neighborhoods. Integration, as implemented in the city, they felt had been structured more for the benefit of the city's white population (Henig 1994). Their interest in vouchers, then, came less out of a commitment to market ideals than the desire to grab onto a plan—politically feasible be-

cause it had Republican support at the state level—that could shake things up and deliver some immediate benefits to their constituency.

7. According to the National Committee for Responsive Philanthropy, a nonprofit organization that has kept a critical eye focused on conservative foundations, Harry Bradley "was a right-wing political activist affiliated with the John Birch Society." The foundation, which received its endowment from the sale of the Allen-Bradley Corporation to Rockwell International, has treated Milwaukee as a "laboratory" for projects furthering its vision that the "good society is a free society" (Krehely, House, and Kernan 2004, 61).

8. As Hess observed, PAVE "was intended as a stopgap measure, offering educational options to low-income families, stabilizing enrollment at Milwaukee's secular schools, and cultivating a political constituency for the voucher program, while proponents sought to expand the MCPC to include religious schools" (Hess 2002, 88).

9. Media Transparency Profile, Grants by source: http://www.mediatransparency.org. Bradley also provided some funding to Paul Peterson, whose claimed findings that the vouchers were substantially raising student test scores is the subject of a controversy I discuss further in the next chapter. The role of other conservative foundations, including Olin and the Walton Family fund, which in 2000 and again in 2001 gave grants of more than $20 million to support a private voucher program in New York City, is discussed in greater detail in chapter 6.

10. Enrollment data from http://www.schoolchoiceinfo.org.

11. Tuition tax credits allow families to deduct some proportion of their private school expenses from the state taxes they otherwise would owe.

12. Unlike at least some voucher plans, too, charters did not stir fears of a violation of the historic separation of church and state.

13. Despite the fact that this phrase was often attributed to him, it turns out that the character may never have said it in precisely these words. For a debunking of the common perception, see http://www.snopes.com/radiotv/tv/dragnet.htm.

14. Charters are not prohibited from soliciting other forms of private support, and indeed many depend rather heavily on philanthropic support.

15. Accessed January 11, 2006, at http://www.americandecency.org/stern/index.htm.

Chapter 4

1. See, for example, "Muzzling Those Pesky Scientists," an editorial in the *New York Times* (December 11, 2006), decrying the Bush administration's plan to force staff scientists within the EPA to draft their recommendations jointly with politically appointed members rather than separately issuing a scientific appraisal as had been done in the past.

2. This is not to say that the main reason Wisconsin initially capped the size of the program was a shared commitment to Campbell's visions of collective learning. Anyone trying to understand why the state introduced the

program in a way that ensured that there would be some eligible families not served—making a control group feasible—would do better to turn to explanations based in political compromise and cost.

3. Peterson criticized Witte's reliance on statistical controls for family background, arguing instead for a gold standard design based on randomization of subjects into experimental and control groups. Taking advantage of the lottery aspects of the voucher program, which applied when there was too little room in a school to accept all applicants, he compared students who were awarded vouchers to students who applied for them but did not receive them because of the luck of the draw.

4. In an interesting and somewhat surprising coda to this story, Witte and Peterson were in 2006 working together, both on the oversight board of a new Milwaukee voucher study.

5. At least until recently. The Wisconsin legislature has cooperated in the initiation of the new Milwaukee study (see note 4), partly, according to Witte, because be had "been badgering them for years that there are no data on a $80 million program" (email communication).

6. At least within the rarefied atmosphere of the school choice research community.

7. Accessed at http://www.nber.org/info.html.

8. The NBER functions more as a supplement than alternative to traditional journal publication. Hoxby had originally made her study available through NBER in 1994, six years before it was published in a major peer-reviewed economics journal. Later in the book I consider more extensively the issue of peer-review journals and alterative outlets for disseminating research and controversy over whether getting research out more quickly increases its social usefulness or undermines its credibility.

9. Accessed at http://www.aft.org/about/index.htm.

10. This language is from NAGB, Resolution on Reporting State-Level NAEP Results (March 5, 1994) as cited in Nelson, Rosenberg, and Van Meter (2004, 2).

11. Fourth grade Hispanic children in charter schools averaged 200 to the 199 of those in other public schools.

12. For example: "Students' Scores Rise in Math, Not in Reading" (November 14, 2003); "As Testing Rises, 9th Grade Becomes Pivotal" (January 18, 2004); "A Miracle Revisited: Measuring Success; Gains in Houston Schools: How Real Are They?" (December 3, 2003); "Students' Scores Rise in Math, Not in Reading" (November 14, 2003); "Graduation Study Suggests That Some States Sharply Understate High School Dropout Rates" (September 17, 2003); "Test Shows Students' Gains In Math Falter by Grade 12" (August 3, 2001).

13. For example: "Education Group Calls for Revised Law" (October 16, 2003); "The 2002 Election: Education; G.O.P. Foresees Expansion Of Its Themes on Schooling" (November 10, 2002).

14. For example: "Officials Say School Choice Often Just Isn't an Option" (December 22, 2001); "Voucher Study Indicates No Steady Gains in Learning" (December 9, 2001); "Voucher threat improves Florida schools, study says; Critics attack report, say state's failing grade was motivation" (February 16, 2001).

15. For example, a February 2004 article she co-wrote with Sam Dillon quoted

AFT sources criticizing Secretary of Education Rod Paige for remarks he had made likening the NEA to a terrorist organization.

16. The total word count, not including the table, is 1264. AFT appears at word 370. This equates to 29.3 percent.

17. According to Schemo, "I saw it pretty much that way, and felt I easily could have written two separate stories following each angle. But I wasn't sure readers had the appetite for two separate stories, so I tried to write as economically as possible and cover all the territory in a single story."

18. As explained, there was more than one version of the Hoxby paper. The first is dated September. *Edweek* and the *New York Post* received copies in time to run articles on September 8.

19. These were all those for whom data was available, and Hoxby indicated that those missing tended to be from very small schools and brand new schools. Where fourth-grade scores were not available, she used fifth- and third-grade scores.

20. CNN, "Charter School Successes," September 14, 2004.

21. A Web version was released on December 15, 2005. The printed documented is dated May 2005 (National Center for Education Statistics 2004).

22. This largely confirmed an earlier finding by Chris and Sara Lubienski, who used essentially the same data (but looking only at mathematics) and methodology. The Lubienski study created a stir, but, without the imprimatur of NCES sponsorship, lacked some of the public impact that accompanied the later study (2006a).

23. The *Times*, perhaps made a bit gun shy by the criticism it had received for, in the eyes of charter proponents, over-hyping the AFT report, opted this time for a very modest headline: "Public Schools Close to Private In U.S. Study."

24. Peterson and Llaudet criticized the use of eligibility for various federal programs—Title I, free and reduced lunch, programs for those with limited English and for those with disabilities—as indicators of the different background students bring to schools. They argued that, because private schools might be less likely to participate in these programs, these indicators would systematically underestimate the level of disadvantage among the populations they served. They criticized the use of student absenteeism and the presence of a computer and number of books in the home, arguing that these might be the result of school policies rather than independent characteristics the children bring with them to the schools. If private schools, for example, succeed in part by convincing families to purchase more books for their children, Peterson and Llaudet argued that treating the books as an independent variable could systematically underestimate the schools' effects. See Lubienski and Lubienski (2006c) for a critique of their reasoning and the variables they used.

Chapter 5

1. See also Ron Zimmer and Richard Buddin (2006) for California, Tim Sass (2006) for Florida, and Gary Miron and Christopher Nelson (2002) for Michigan.

2. Bifulco and Ladd found Hispanic enrollment slightly lower in North Carolina charter schools. Sass found it slightly higher in Florida. Buckley and Schneider, in the District of Columbia, found that overall charter schools were slightly underserving Hispanic populations, but "this overall pattern hides a critical fact," they noted. "A few charter schools were focused on the specific needs of Hispanic students."

3. There is anecdotal evidence that this occurs in at least some charter schools. One choice researcher reported to me that a relation was an office administrator at a California charter school, and that she met children in the hallways to remind them to have their families fill out the paperwork, called parents at home, and even helped parents fill out the forms.

4. As the example of Los Milagros suggests, schools may signal the types of students they are searching for by such devices as the names they select. For a fuller investigation of the ways in which charter schools can selectively market themselves to specific types of families, see Lubienski (2003).

5. These thirteen studies involved nine states. For eight states, the available studies showed higher proportions of blacks in charter schools. In Michigan, one study found a higher concentration of blacks but two did not.

6. These studies involved Connecticut, Michigan, Texas, and Wisconsin. In Michigan and Texas, other studies in the set Carnoy and his colleagues reviewed did not find an overconcentration of Hispanics and in Texas found it small.

7. These involved the District of Columbia, Michigan, and Texas. In Michigan and Texas, the overrepresentation was marginal. Other studies in the same state did not find the poor overrepresented.

8. Accessed at http://www.wvsarts.org. Note that, despite the ambiguity resident in the terms, *special talents* and *special skills* in this case refer to characteristics most often considered to be obstacles to schooling.

9. Carpenter's definition of *targeted* schools includes those aimed at *gifted* students, but his breakdown suggests that this is a small proportion (less than 1 percent overall).

10. For a summary of state provisions regarding enrollment preferences, see the report prepared by the Education Commission of the States (accessed at http://mb2.ecs.org/reports/Report.aspx?id=79%20).

11. There are a number of reasons why, in theory, this could be the case. Traditional public school systems might be more aggressive about pursuing additional funding from federal and state sources. Parents in the traditional system might be more aggressive about pursuing legal rights to support services associated with disability status. Charter schools might be wary of legal and bureaucratic entanglements that get triggered by the enrollment of children with disabilities.

12. Richard Kahlenberg, in reviewing an earlier draft of this chapter, suggested it presents a false dichotomy between the old focus on segregation-fragmentation and the new focus on measurable outcomes. He argues that one major reason to be concerned about economic segregation "is not just that it fragments society, but more to the point, that high poverty schools don't produce positive educational outcomes" (Personal communication).

I think he is correct that racial and economic integration can be understood as a vehicle for increasing academic outcomes, but I do not think that this captures the dominant framing of the issue or the way it has been understood by most of the political actors driving education policy.

13. Author's calculations.

14. For perhaps the most comprehensive review of the alternative research designs and their relative strengths and limitations, see Julian Betts and Paul Hill (2006). See also Bryan Hassel and Michelle Terrell (2006).

15. Although sophistication can produce more valid analysis, it can also make things more complicated. The selection of variables and operations makes such analysis more vulnerable to discretionary judgments made by the researchers. In the highly politicized environment, the AFT feared that the administration would influence the researchers in ways that would make the results seem more favorable to charter schools.

16. The notation "when perfectly carried out" should be taken seriously. In practice, social policy experiments almost always confront a range of challenges that make it nearly impossible to maintain the experimental conditions in all key respects (Greenberg, Linksz, and Mandell 2003). See Patrick McKewan and Rob Olson (forthcoming) for a discussion of some of the complexities of relying on charter schools' lotteries to provide truly random samples.

17. Chester Finn, reflecting on the lessons The Fordham Foundation had learned through its experience sponsoring charter schools in Ohio, admits: "It's far harder than theorists thought to actually close a mediocre (or even bad) school. I plead guilty to having helped to propagate a naïve doctrine here. Unless its students face imminent danger or someone has fled to Bermuda with the payroll, shuttering a school is a tricky business. Parents and kids usually like their school, no matter its low test scores and torpid curriculum, and don't want it closed any more than do the clients of a surplus district school." *The Education Gadfly,* May 24, 2007 (accessed at http://www.edexcellence.net/foundation/gadfly/index.cfm#3415).

18. The transcript is available online at http://abcnews.go.com/2020/Stossel/story?id=1500338.

19. Accessed June 8, 2007, at http://www.edisonschools.com/charter-schools/school-design-curriculum.

20. Accessed June 8, 2007, at http://www.kipp.org/01/whatisakippschool.cfm.

21. For the arguments and evidence on social capital formation as it relates to charters and school choice, see Scott Franklin Abernathy (2005) and Buckley and Schneider (2007).

22. They argued that democratic majorities necessarily generate regulations to ensure that their policies are followed throughout the system, and that these regulations, in turn, constrain principals and teachers in ways that prevent them from becoming as effective as they might otherwise be. For equally bleak assessments, see Andrew Coulson (1999) and Myron Lieberman (1993). Chubb, now a vice president in Edison Schools, may have changed some of his views about the rigidity of public systems. In accounting for the failure of Edison-run Philadelphia schools to outpace the

test score performance of other schools in the city, Chubb emphasized that the presence of Edison and other private providers may have worked to raise the level of performance for the system overall (Viadero 2006).

23. Accessed at http://taxonomy.pbwiki.com.

Chapter 6

1. Media Transparency, a Web site with extensive information about grant giving by conservative foundations identifies eleven grants totaling $2,335,588 from Olin to Peterson or his Program on Education Policy and Governance at Harvard between 1994 and 2004. For years, the Olin Foundation was a dominant force in building the ideas beyond the emergent right. "Part Medici, part venture capitalist," as characterized by the *New York Times*, before it deliberately spent out its endowment and closed its doors in 2005, the foundation had "spent three decades financing the intellectual rise of the right and exciting the envy of the left" (DeParle 2005; DiMaggio and Anheier 1990).

2. Hendrie (2005). The book was published jointly by Teachers College Press and the Economic Policy Institute (EPI). EPI is an independent, nonprofit, nonpartisan research institute that focuses on "the impact of economic trends and policies on working people in the United States and around the world." The organization does receive substantial funding (29 percent) from unions and the president of the AFT sits on its board. Most of its funding comes from foundations (59 percent). Teachers' unions in total provide less than 8 percent of the organizations funding. Lawrence Mishel, EPI president and a co-author on the book, explains: "It is not appropriate to label EPI by our funding any more than it would to label AEI 'business-backed' (or Heritage, CATO or Brookings for that matter)." The union support "is not connected to particular projects and the teacher unions neither knew about our charter school research before it was released (nor obviously were they able to review it)" (email communication, May 28, 2007).

3. For good accounts on the emergence of think tanks and their current roles, see Andrew Rich (2005), James Smith (1991), and David M. Ricci (1993).

4. Accessed at http://ncrp1.mediastudio.tv/about_us/history.asp.

5. Accessed at http://www.mediatransparency.org/recipientgrants.php?recipientID=63.

6. The memo was leaked to columnist Jack Anderson, who revealed its existence in his column. Some of the background, as well as the full text of the memo, can be found at http://www.mediatransparency.org/storyprinterfriendly.php?storyID=22.

7. In the memo, Powell shows sensitivity to the risks of interfering with academic freedom and compromising the integrity and valued autonomy of universities. His emphasis is not on purging leftists or their ideas but on ensuring some broader representation of views on college campuses.

8. This, among other things, runs seminars for congressional staffers, provides young students internships with conservative organizations, and

sponsors the Pro-Market Network News, "to facilitate communication between market-oriented professionals, policy centers, government offices, education institutes, and other organizations." Background and description from http://www.mediatransparency.org/recipientprofile.php?recipientID:413. The quotation is attributed to the Pro-Market Network News but no specific issue, date, or page number is identified.

9. Its mission is "to support the achievement of a freer society by discovering and facilitating the development of talented, productive students, scholars, and other intellectuals who share an interest in liberty and who demonstrate the potential to help change the current climate of opinion to one more congenial to the principles and practice of freedom" (accessed at http://www.theihs.org/about/).

10. Even A3, the respondent quoted here, emphasizes that, despite the need for funds, projects that would "compromise various standards" are often off limits. In saying that money is everything, A3 explains, "I merely meant that it is everything in the sense that without rocket fuel, rockets don't go."

11. Soft money refers to the fact that the organization relies on competitive grants and contracts, and that employees' positions depend upon the ability to keep generating this external support.

12. To select a group that did not overly represent one side or another, I initially scored them from –2 to +2 with 0 for a small number of researchers whose findings had sometimes been interpreted as favorable and sometimes unfavorable. For the figure here, I collapsed the milder and stronger leanings and, drawing on the additional information I gained through the interviews themselves, I forced the mixed group into the positive or negative camp into which they best fit.

13. Research refers to "systematic study directed toward fuller scientific knowledge or understanding." Research can be classified as basic ("directed toward fuller knowledge or understanding of the fundamental aspects of a phenomenon" without specific uses in mind) or applied ("systematic study to gain knowledge or understanding necessary to determine the means by which a recognized and specific need may be met"). Development refers to the "systematic application of knowledge or understanding, directed toward the production of useful materials, devices, and systems or methods" (Meeks 2005).

14. There are no regular systematic data on state and local spending for research and development. A 1998 survey estimated that states then spent about $2.5 billion from their own revenue sources. This was only about $1.20 of every $100 spent by state and federal government combined. State R&D spending, though, had been increasing more rapidly than federal over the previous three decades, so it is reasonable to expect that this ratio might be somewhat higher today (Jankowski 1999).

15. All program areas within NSF orient their decisions around the two criteria of merit and impacts, and rely on reviews by experts to evaluate proposals and advise on whether they should receive funding. Some programs use a panel of experts who review all proposals; some rely on an external group of reviewers, selected for each proposal based on their specific expertise, and some rely on a combination of both. A partial exception

is NSF's Small Grants for Exploratory Research (SGER) program. SGER—called sugar—grants are meant to support innovative research on untested, novel ideas or respond quickly to unanticipated needs, such as Hurricane Katrina. In these cases, Congress has actually prohibited the use of expert reviewers, presumably to speed the process and because experts might impose conventional expectations that are inhospitable to innovation and quickly assembled projects, but the proportion of their budget that can be used for SGER grants is small and program officers still must defend their recommendations with reference to the merit and impact standards.

16. Intellectual merit relates to such questions as "How important is the proposed activity to advancing knowledge and understanding within its own field or across different fields? How well qualified is the proposer (individual or team) to conduct the project? To what extent does the proposed activity suggest and explore creative and original concepts? How well conceived and organized is the proposed activity? Is there sufficient access to resources?" Broader impacts refers to such questions as: "How well does the activity advance discovery and understanding while promoting teaching, training, and learning? How well does the proposed activity broaden the participation of underrepresented groups (for example, gender, ethnicity, disability, geographic, and the like)? To what extent will it enhance the infrastructure for research and education, such as facilities, instrumentation, networks, and partnerships? Will the results be disseminated broadly to enhance scientific and technological understanding? What may be the benefits of the proposed activity to society?" (accessed at http://www.nsf.gov/about/how.jsp).

17. For more on the political dynamics surrounding the formation of IES and its mission, see Andrew Rudalevige (2007).

18. Accessed at http://ies.ed.gov/director/board.asp. According to the IES's first biennial report to Congress, its current system for peer review that "is similar in many ways to the process of peer review at the National Institutes of Health. A key provision is intended to put distance between, on the one hand, the program officers and administrators within the Institute who administer grant programs, work with grantees, and disseminate the results of research, and, on the other hand, those who are responsible for the peer review of applications for funding under those grant programs. To that end, an office for peer review and standards was created and staffed within the office of the deputy director for science of the Institute. That office selects peer reviewers, determines review criteria, manages competitions, provides feedback to applicants, and generates scores for applications that determine scientific merit for funding decisions. This office also handles peer review of all Institute reports" (U.S. Department of Education 2005a).

19. Education Research Request for Applications. CFDA Number: 84.305. Release Date: April 7, 2006. See http://ies.ed.gov/funding.

20. The question did not distinguish between federal government support and support that might conceivably come from states or districts, but the accompanying discussion made it clear that the researchers almost exclu-

sively thought about National Science Foundation or the United States
Department of Education when asked about government support for research.

21. Institutional support refers to funds made available (for research assistants, travel, data collection, and so on) by their employer, as a largely discretionary pot of money not tied to specific projects and for which only
minimal clearance was required.

22. Some grants listed in a separate grants award database (accessed at
http://www.ed.gov/fund/data/award/grntawd.html) did not appear
in the biennial report. Those coded as research were extracted and added
to the initial list. When there were direct conflicts (for example, in the characterization of the grant), the information in the biennial report was given
precedence.

23. Most of these had start dates of 2000 or later, but some (fewer than 10 percent) were begun during the 1990s with the two oldest going back to 1994
and 1995.

24. I am a member of this advisory committee.

25. The AFT, sensing that the findings would essentially confirm its earlier
analysis, kept pressure on the Department to release the findings. The department took the position that the study was being held up because of
the need for careful review. When it was finally released, the Commissioner of Education Statistics made it clear that he wished the study had
not been done under its auspices. When asked why it was released any-
way, he noted that the AFT would have had a field day attacking them for
political motivation had they held it up any longer.

26. The top five were Westat, American Institute of Research, RTI International, Education Testing Service, and Mathematica.

27. The searches were restricted to programs on education, education and human resources, education and workforce, education research, educational
research initiatives.

28. The fact that four of the grants went to one research team (Mark Schneider
and colleagues) and that two were small dissertation grants highlights the
fact that NSF has not been a major funder in this area.

29. Another factor may be the straightforward one that other aspects of education may simply seem more critically important. NSF's directorate for
Education and Human Resources, for example, historically has placed its
major emphasis on the teaching of math and science.

30. Accessed at http://www.taxpayer.net/awards/goldenfleece/about.htm
#original.

31. The defining aspects of RFTs is that they include pre- and postpolicy measures of outcomes on the group or groups that receives the policy in question and a control group—randomly selected from among the potential recipients—that does not. For a discussion of the arguments for RFTs and
the factors leading to the IES efforts in this regard, see Frederick Mosteller
and Robert Boruch (2002).

32. There is a flip side to this phenomenon. When researchers do see a way to
study school choice with an RFT design, they may be more likely to pursue federal funding. One researcher, who felt IES turned down a poten-

tially valuable study precisely because it lacked an RTF format, went on to observe: "Now if I can get the random design in with the solid credentials, I think it will be a piece of cake" [R10].

33. Accessed at http://www.fordfound.org/about/mission2.cfm.

34. Many proponents of market-based strategies see what I am calling mainstream foundations as ideologically hostile to their agenda and just as activist in pursuing a left-wing set of objectives as the conservative foundations are in pursuing a right-wing one. There is some merit in their assertion that the large mainstream foundations have a more progressive tilt and wariness toward privatization approaches. Later in the book I add a distinction between mainstream foundations and a small set of activist progressive ones, but these are not a significant part of the charter school research story.

35. Accessed at http://fconline.fdncenter.org. Most of the analyses are based on data downloaded from this site in June 2006.

36. The Foundation Center's database allows one to select grants that specify research as a grant subject. Using this as a search parameter reduced the number to 792 grants. One of the limitations of the data, however, as Greene points out, is that the coding can be influenced by the sometimes idiosyncratic ways in which foundations categorize the information they submit. Greene (2005) suggests that the Foundation Center data relies totally on the foundation codes and is therefore unreliable. In communication, Foundation Center sources indicate that they re-code data To make it less likely that I would fail to include research-related grants simply because research was not indicated specifically as the type of support, I used a text search function to identify those grants in which the term *research* appeared anywhere in the FC entry. My thanks to Neil Eckardt, research assistant on this project, who did most of the heavy lifting in terms of assembling this data file.

37. Reported in the education blog mrs panstreppon 2006 at http://www.tpmcafe.com/blog/mrs_panstreppon/2006/mar/15/is_arianna_a_ringer.

38. I coded foundations as conservative if either of two conditions applied: one, they were identified as active conservative foundations by the National Committee for Responsive Philanthropy, a liberal watchdog group, or, two, they provided at least one education research grant to an organization in the State Policy Network, a decentralized collection of conservative think tanks that were established to promote market-based policies. I coded funders as progressive if either of two conditions applied: they were identified as progressive foundations by Andrew Rich (2005); or they provided at least one grant to a small group of markedly progressive organizations—Poverty and Race Research Action Council; Campaign for Fiscal Equity; Economic Policy Institute; Cross City Coalition, or any group with *lesbian* and *gay* in its name. This process identified fifteen conservative foundations and fourteen progressive foundations. All others were coded as mainstream.

39. This is not to say that such collusion never occurs; just that the broader systemic forces are enough to have these consequences even when we presume good motivations and ethical behavior all around.

Chapter 7

1. John F. Burns, "Taken at Gunpoint, U.S. Journalist and His Interpreter Are Missing in Iraq," *New York Times* (Late Edition, East Coast), August 17, 2004, p. A.10.
2. Eric Lichtblau, "C.I.A. Officer Denounces Agency and Sept. 11 Report," *New York Times* (Late Edition, East Coast), August 17, 2004, p. A.14 .
3. Dean E. Murphy, "Study Finds Climate Shift Threatens California," *New York Times* (Late Edition, East Coast), August 17, 2004, p. A.18.
4. *The Washington Post* did not attend to the issue until September 11, when it ran an editorial, by a former journalist employed by the KIPP Foundation, which funds charter schools, suggesting that the AFT report failed to point to the very dramatic successes of some charter schools (Schorr 2004). Some newspapers covered the story over the week that followed. Most of these carefully counterbalanced the AFT's interpretation with responses by charter school proponents, challenging the report's claims. *USA Today's* story, for example, led with this sentence: "A new analysis that shows students at charter schools perform worse than their peers in public school is worrisome, experts said Tuesday, but critics argued that the report is hardly a fair look at whether charter schools help kids improve" (Kelly and Szabo 2004, B13).
5. Two of the most important and influential books about the politics of agenda setting disagree, for example, on this point. John Kingdon, in *Agendas, Alternatives, and Public Policies,* attributes a significantly stronger independent role to media than do Frank Baumgartner and Bryan Jones in *Agendas and Instability in American Politics* (Baumgartner and Jones 1993; Kingdon 1995).
6. People for the American Way obtained original documents relating to the contract with Ketchum, the public relations and marketing firm, through a Freedom of Information request and has made these available online (accessed at http://interactive.pfaw.org/ketchum).
7. On these points, Benjamin Page cites Shanto Iyengar (1991), Iyengar and Donald Kinder (1987), Maxwell McCombs and Donald Shaw (1972), and Page, Robert Shapiro, and Glenn Dempsey (1987).
8. Based on a search of citations and abstracts in ProQuest current and historical databases using the search terms "Charter schools," or "School choice" or "School voucher." The precise total is 4,335. Coverage includes editorials, opinion pieces, letters to the editor, and book reviews.
9. The spike in choice articles overall in that year is largely attributable to coverage of a California voucher referendum on November 1993. The *Los Angeles Times* accounted for 60 percent of the articles in the five newspapers that year.
10. The longer list of articles in the two papers was trimmed based on two criteria—use of experts and evaluative content. Any article or commentary citing or written by well-known, highly visible authors in the school choice field was automatically included. Next, article titles were reviewed to weed out those in which keywords appeared in the abstract (or citation) only. This generated a smaller but still sizable list of 685 articles (*New York*

Times = 463; *Wall Street Journal* = 223). The abstracts for these 685 articles were then read and coded by two research assistants based upon whether there was explicit reference made to the evaluation of school choice, charter schools, or vouchers. Articles with reference to individual schools or districts were included only if they were related to the evaluation of school choice initiatives as a general policy approach. A key rule of thumb for inclusion was whether the article in would be useful for someone trying to answer the basic questions: Does school choice work? Is it good or bad? This reduced the number of articles to ninety-eight. For these the coders read full text, and, after eliminating several that were essentially duplicates or letters written by citizens that did not bring or refer to empirical evidence in taking evaluative positions, we were left with a sample of eighty-eight articles that explicitly cited experts or referred to empirical evidence in ways that were conducive to drawing conclusions about whether charter schools are working.

11. The *Boston Globe* and the *Los Angeles Times*, in that order, had the highest number of articles, followed by the *New York Times*, the *Washington Post*, and the *Wall Street Journal*.

12. The *Los Angeles Times* had a spike of coverage in 1993 driven by the state's referendum on vouchers that year, for example.

13. One reader of an earlier draft of this book suggested that it may be unfair to insinuate that the *Journal* underplayed the report, since the AFT had "packaged and hand-delivered" its findings to the *Times*. It is reasonable to expect the paper to be reticent about playing up a story on which it had been scooped by a rival. The divergence in coverage in this instance, though, is rather extreme. It is worth noting, too, that the *Times'* special access came about because another major paper had turned the story down.

14. The term *articles* here includes editorial comments and opinion pieces. Later in the chapter I discuss the difference between news articles and opinion pieces.

15. Thanks to Neil Eckardt and Jonah Lieberman for their excellent support for this part of the analysis.

16. A score of 0 could result from a disagreement between a coder who saw it as positive and another who saw it as negative, but these kinds of disagreement were relatively rare, and scores of 0 usually reflect agreement that the article is mixed or neutral. A combined score of +.5 was recoded as a +1; a combined score of -.5 was recoded as a -1.

17. A second reason for coding headlines as well as content has more to do with issues of methodology. In studies of the American political agenda, researchers have been able to get a reasonably accurate picture of changes in issue definition by coding article headlines or short abstracts for content and valence (Baumgartner and Jones 1993). Questions remain as to whether headlines alone provide enough information to accurately and reliably gauge whether the body of the article provides a richer and perhaps even different message than the title alone. By coding this entire set of articles both ways—not only for the positive and negative tone, but also for other aspects to be discussed—it should be possible to see if there is substantial agreement. One possibility is that headlines, because they pro-

vide less information, are simply more difficult to code in one direction or the other; if that is the case we should see more scores of 0 among the headline than content codes across both newspapers.

18. A strong and consistent finding of an ideological stance in principle could reflect ownership's ability to steer news coverage. Matthew Gentzkow and Jesse Shapiro, however, present strong evidence that newspaper slant may be driven more by consumer demand than owners' ideological pre-dispositions. Newspaper that have more conservative readers present a conservative slant; those with more liberal readers present a more liberal slant (2006).

19. Methodologically, this suggests that research on media and on policy agendas (for example, the influential work by Baumgartner and Jones) that relies on headline coding can be risky. That is not to say that the risk always trumps the greater ease of coding headlines, and the prospect of increasing the number of articles coded as a result. For one thing, as suggested in discussing the inattentive reader, sometimes the case can be made that it is the headlines that may be most important. For another, other types of articles may be easier to code based on headlines than the research-focused ones considered here. Finally, even with these same articles and coders, other aspects of the articles did not generate as great a disparity between the headline and content codes. For instance, in coding whether the article primarily dealt with charters, or vouchers or the general concept of school choice, coding based on titles and content was the same in seventy-eight of eighty-eight cases.

20. Scores of 0 more often result from articles that present contrasting perspectives on the research (noting that studies and researchers disagree) than from articles that characterize the research itself as presenting mixed or neutral results.

21. I count an expert as featured if they either provided an evaluative quote or wrote one of the op-eds or letters to the editor.

22. Op-eds do not necessarily come in uninvited. Occasionally those responsible for the opinion pieces solicit a piece by a known expert or stakeholder. I am not able, here, to distinguish those that are invited to those that come in over the transom.

23. Richard Rothstein presents something of a special case. During this period, he was a regular columnist for the *Times*. This table includes two columns that he wrote in that role; these are not self-initiated in quite the same way as those of the others.

24. CBS News/*New York Times* Poll (2006). Some of this suspicion toward the media reflects a general cynicism. For example, in the same poll, 59 percent of respondents said they thought the Bush administration told the truth only sometimes or hardly ever. Despite the fact that so many expressed doubts about truth telling, 69 percent said they thought the news media reports are "generally accurate."

25. New technologies have allowed a phenomenon referred to as citizen journalism to emerge on the Web. In this instance, some citizens may act as amateur journalists opening new channels of information and opinion to others.

26. Along with the Hechinger Institute, the Education Writers' Association, a professional organization with more than 1,000 members, tries to address this deficit. For example, since 2005, it has helped to sponsor an annual education research and statistics "boot camp" including "hands-on training on how to work with data and lessons on how to read education research and to tell good statistics from bad" (accessed at http://www.ewa.org).

27. The phenomenon is not limited to newspapers. "With the advent of cable, satellite and broadband technology," television journalist Ted Koppel argues, "today's marketplace has become so overcrowded that network news divisions are increasingly vulnerable to the dictatorship of the demographic. Now, every division of every network is expected to make a profit. And so we have entered the age of boutique journalism" (2006, Section 4, 16).

28. Information on dissemination from Howie Schaffer, PEN Public Outreach Director (email correspondence, February 17, 2007).

29. Email correspondence with Michael Petrilli, February 18, 2007.

30. Email correspondence with Andrew Rotherham, February 17, 2007.

31. These counts are as of February 17, 2007.

32. Email correspondence with Howie Shaffer, February 21, 2007.

33. Enough so that choice critics concluded that the Department of Education was trying to bury the report.

34. There is nothing wrong with revising one's work to make it better. As much as possible, it is best to capture as much of that process of correction, clarification, and improvement within the pre-publication period. Academic conferences are actually a good place to work these things through. The problem, in this instance, in my judgment, is the decision to have aggressively injected the preliminary findings into the public arena before this cleaning up process had taken place. Researchers may undertake this because they sincerely believe the issues are too important and too urgent to wait. I believe some researchers systematically overestimate this time pressure, or accede too easily to entreaties to meet the time pressures imposed by political dynamics, a point I elaborate on in the next chapter.

35. As an example, it is literally the case that as I was writing this paragraph I received an email distribution from one social science research organization, announcing some studies and asking me to respond to a "two-minute survey" designed to help them better target information to me. Among the features of their new Web site that I was asked to evaluate were policy briefs, fast facts, and summaries and overviews of reports.

36. In a special appendix to their paper criticizing the NCES public versus private school study, Peterson and Llaudet wrote of the Lubienskis that "although their [earlier] study has not been published in a peer-review journal, it has received prominent, favorable coverage in prestige news outlets" (2006, 35). At the time, Peterson and Llaudet offered that characterization, the Lubienskis had in fact submitted their findings to academic journals. One piece had been submitted months before to *American Educational Research Journal*, was accepted shortly after Peterson and Llaudet made their argument, and has subsequently appeared in print (Lubienski and Lubienski 2006b). Another is scheduled for publication in 2007.

37.   There are wrinkles and can be blemishes on this process. Often reviewers can make inferences about whose work they are reading, based on the pattern of citations, the data being used, and so on. Still, these usually are just inferences. Some journals will reveal their reviewers after an article has been accepted if the reviewer consents to this. Sometimes, of course, journals make mistakes, such as sending articles with authors' names still attached or discoverable.

38.   The score equivalent is a 4 or 5.

Chapter 8

1.   I return to this concept of killer studies later.

2.   Michael Malbin argued for this more than twenty-five years ago, suggesting that assumptions necessarily made by researchers inevitably bias interpretations and that the failure by Congress to understand and probe these assumptions puts the institution in the position of using research as a fig leaf that masks tough debates about values and choices (1980).

3.   When news of the AFT charter school study first broke, Robert Lerner, the commissioner of Education Statistics, suggested that the HLM study-in-waiting would provide much stronger and potentially different results. As reported in the *New York Times*, Lerner indicated that NCES would be releasing "a larger analysis that would adjust results for the characteristics of charter schools and their students." He characterized the AFT "raw comparison of test scores" as "the beginning of something important,"' and said, "What one has to do is adjust for many different variables to get a sense of what the effects of charter schools are" (Schemo 2004a, A1).

4.   Arguably, the NCES efforts to downplay the significance of the study's findings was in part attributable to their perceived political volatility. Although not a killer study in the sense I discuss here, my expectation is that this report will stand as a major contribution to the literature and our understanding of what charter schools can and cannot be expected to accomplish.

5.   This does not mean that controversial findings that bear on broad questions of sector benefits will not emerge. In principle, for example, we might learn that longer school years produced better results wherever they are adopted, but that traditional systems are politically unable to put them into place. We might learn that when traditional public schools provide more autonomy to principals they combine the positive aspects of charter schools with the more institutionalized oversight that can reduce levels of outright malfeasance and improve democratic accountability. It is also possible that we will discover that sector itself matters less than many other factors, and divert attention more profitably toward addressing these instead of high-energy battles that serve national-level party activists better than they do local communities looking for pragmatic solutions to concrete needs.

6.   These are: *The American Educational Research Journal*, which emphasizes "original empirical and theoretical studies and analyses in education. . . .

from a wide variety of academic disciplines and substantive fields"; *Educational Evaluation and Policy Analysis,* which publishes "scholarly articles concerned with important issues in the formulation, implementation, and evaluation of education policy"; *Educational Researcher,* which contains a Features Section that "publishes articles that report, synthesize, review, or analyze scholarly inquiry" bearing on "the interpretation, implication, or significance to research work in education"; and a Research News and Comment section that offers articles analyzing "trends, policies, utilization, and controversies concerning educational research"; *Journal of Educational and Behavioral Statistics,* which focuses on "original statistical methods useful for the applied statistician working in educational or behavioral research"; and *Review of Educational Research,* "a forum for reviews of previously published work" (accessed at http://www.aera.net/publications).

References

Abernathy, Scott Franklin. 2005. *School Choice and the Future of American Democracy*. Ann Arbor, Mich.: University of Michigan Press.

AFT. 2004. *AFT's Closer Look*, August 27, 2004. Washington: American Federation of Teachers. Accessed at http://www.aft.org/pubs-reports/closer_look/082704.htm.

Alexander, Karl L., Doris R. Entwisle, and Linda Steffel Olson. 2001. "Schools, Achievement, and Inequality: A Seasonal Perspective." *Educational Evaluation and Policy Analysis* 23(2): 171–91.

Anrig, Greg. 2007. *The Conservatives Have No Clothes: Why Right-Wing Ideas Keep Failing*. New York: John Wiley & Sons.

Axelrod, Robert M. 1984. *The Evolution of Cooperation* New York: Basic Books.

Bacchetti, Ray, and Thomas Ehrlich. 2007. "Foundations and Education: Introduction." In *Reconnecting Education and Foundations*, edited by Ray Bacchetti and Thomas Ehrlich. New York: John Wiley & Sons.

Bachrach, Peter, and Morton S. Baratz. 1963. "Decisions and Nondecisions: An Analytical Framework." *The American Political Science Review* 57(3): 632–42.

Banfield, Edward C. 1980. "Policy Science as Metaphysical Madness." In *Bureaucrats, Policy Analysts, Statesmen: Who Leads?*, edited by R. A. Goldwin. Washington: American Enterprise Institute.

Baumgartner, Frank R., and Bryan D. Jones. 1993. *Agendas and Instability in American Politics*. Chicago, Ill.: University of Chicago Press.

Berelson, Bernard R., Paul F. Lazarsfeld, and William N. McPhee. 1954. *Voting: A Study of Opinion Formation in a Presidential Campaign*. Chicago, Ill.: University of Chicago Press.

Berliner, David C., and Bruce J. Biddle. 1995. *The Manufactured Crisis*. New York: Longman.

Betts, Julian, and Paul Hill. 2006. "Key Issues in Studying Charter Schools and Achievement: A Review and Suggestions for National Guidelines." National Charter Schools Research Project. Accessed at http://www.ncsrp.org/cs/csr/view/csr_pubs/5.

Betts, Julian, Y. Emily Tang, and Andrew C. Zau. 2007. "Madness in the Method? A Critical Analysis of Popular Methods of Estimating the Effect of Charter Schools on Achievement." Unpublished paper presented at the annual meetings of the American Educational Research Association, Chicago, Ill., April 2007.

Bifulco, Robert, and Helen F. Ladd. 2004. "The Impacts of Charter Schools on Student Achievement: Evidence from North Carolina." Working Papers Series SAN04-01. Durham, N.C.: Terry Stanford Institute of Public Policy, Duke University.

———. 2005. "Results from the Tar Heel State." *Educaion Next* 4(Fall): 60–66.

Booker, Kevin, Ron Zimmer, and Richard Buddin. 2005. *The Effect of Charter Schools on School Peer Composition.* Santa Monica, Calif.: Rand.

Booker, Kevin, Scott Gilpatric, Timothy Gronberg, and Dennis Jansen. 2005. "The Effect of Charter Schools on Traditional Public School Students in Texas: Are Children Who Stay Behind Left Behind?" New York: National Center for the Study of Privatization in Education.

Bracey, Gerald. 2006. "Public or Private?" *Principal Leadership* 7(3): 60-62.

Braun, Henry , Frank Jenkins, and Wendy Grigg. 2006a. *A Closer Look at Charter Schools Using Hierarchical Linear Modeling.* Washington: U.S. Department of Education, National Center for Education Statistics, Institute of Education.

———. 2006b. *Comparing Private Schools and Public Schools Using Hierarchical Linear Modeling.* NCES 2006-461. Washington: U.S. Department of Education, National Center for Education Statistics, Institute of Education Sciences.

Brown, Heath, Jeffrey R. Henig, Thomas T. Holyoke, and Natalie Lacireno-Paquet. 2005. "The Influence of Founder Type on Charter School Structures and Operations." *American Journal of Education* 111(4): 487–522.

Bryk, Anthony S., Valerie E. Lee, and Peter B. Holland. 1993. *Catholic Schools and the Common Good.* Cambridge, Mass.: Harvard University Press.

Bryk, Anthony S., Penny Sebring, David Kerbow, Sharon Rollow, and John Easton. 1998. *Charting Chicago School Reform: Democratic Localism as a Lever for Change.* Boulder, Colo.: Westview.

Buckley, Jack, and Mark Schneider. 2006. "Are Charter School Parents More Satisfied With Schools? Evidence from Washington, D.C." *Peabody Journal of Education* 81(1): 57–78.

———. 2007. *Charter Schools: Hope or Hype?* Princeton, N.J.: Princeton University Press.

Butler, Stuart M. 1985. *Privatizing Federal Spending: A Strategy to Eliminate the Deficit.* New York: Universe Books.

Campanile, Carl. 2006. "Smarter Charter Kids." *New York Post,* July 20, 2006. Accessed at http://www.bwcf.org/NYPost20060720.htm.

Campbell, Angus, Phillip E. Converse, Warren E. Miller, and Donald E. Stokes. 1960. *The American Voter.* New York: John Wiley & Sons.

Carey, Benedict. 2006. "A Shocker: Partisan Thought Is Unconscious." *New York Times,* January 24, 2006: 1.

Carnoy, Martin, Rebecca Jacobsen, Lawrence Mishel, and Richard Rothstein. 2005. *The Charter School Dust-Up: Examining the Evidence on Enrollment and Achievement.* New York: Teachers College Press.

Carpenter, Dick M. II. 2005. *Playing to Type? Mapping the Charter School Landscape.* Washington: Thomas B. Fordham Institute.

Casey, Leo. 2005. "Triumphant Managerialism and the Strategy of Intellectual Non-engagement and Avoidance." December 16, 2005. Accessed at http://edwize.org.

Cavanagh, Sean, and Erik W. Robelen. 2006. "NCES Calls for Sticking to the Stats Study of Charter Scores Latest to Be Questioned." *Education Week* 26(1): 1.

CBS News/*New York Times.* 2006. "The State of the Media." Accessed at http://www.cbsnews.com/htdocs/pdf/020306POLL.pdf.

Center for Education Reform (CER). 2004. *Weekly Newswire Library*. Accessed at http://www.edreform.com/index.cfm?fuseAction=document&document ID=1860.

———. 2006. *CER Quick Fact*. Bethesda, Md.: The Center for Education Reform. Accessed at http://www.edreform.com/index.cfm?fuseAction=document &documentID=1964.

———. 2007. *CER Quick Facts*. Bethesda, Md.: The Center for Education Reform. Accessed at http://www.edreform.com/index.cfm?fuseAction=document&documentID=2632.

Chubb, John E., and Terry M. Moe. 1990. *Politics, Markets, and America's Schools*. Washington: Brookings Institution Press.

Chute, Eleanor. 2005. "Cyber Schools Spring Up in State." *Pittsburgh Post-Gazette*, May 8, 2005. Accessed at http://www.post-gazette.com/pg/05128/ 500990-85.stm.

Cobb, Casey D., and Gene V. Glass. 1999. "Ethnic Segregation in Arizona Charter Schools." *Education Policy Analysis Archives* 7(1): 1–36.

Cohen, David K., and Eleanor Farrar. 1977. "Power to the Parents? The Story of Educational Vouchers." *The Public Interest* 48(Summer): 72–97.

Coleman, James S., and Thomas Hoffer. 1987. *Public, Catholic, and Private Schools: The Importance of Community*. New York: Basic Books.

Converse, Phillip E. 1964. "The Nature of Belief Systems in Mass Publics." In *Ideology and Discontent*, edited by David E. Apter. New York: Free Press.

Coulson, Andrew J. 1999. *Market Education: The Unknown History*. New Brunswick, N.J.: Transaction Publishers.

Cradler, Jon, and Ruthmary Cradler. 2002. "Federal Programs Suggest an Expanded Role for Technology." *Learning & Leading with Technology* 30(2): 46–57.

Cross, Christopher T. 2006. "The Changing Role of the U.S. Department of Education: Looking Back, Looking Ahead." Transcribed interview, October 18, 2006. Accessed at http://www.edweek.org/chat/transcript.10.18.2006 .html.

Davis, Bob. 1996. "Class Warfare: Dueling Professors Have Milwaukee Dazed Over School Vouchers—Studies on Private Education Result in a Public Spat About Varied Conclusions—Candidates Debate the Point." *Wall Street Journal*, October 11, 1996: A1.

DeParle, Jason. 2005. "Goals Reached, Donor on Right Closes Up Shop." *New York Times*, May 29, 2005: A1.

DiMaggio, Paul J., and Helmut K. Anheier. 1990. "The Sociology of Nonprofit Organizations and Sectors." *Annual Review of Sociology* 16:137–59.

District of Columbia Public Charter School Board. 2006. *School Performance Report 2006*. Washington: District of Columbia Public Charter School Board. Accessed at http://www.dcpubliccharter.com/publications/docs/SPR2006 Book.pdf.

Dryzek, John S. 1989. "Policy Sciences of Democracy." *Polity* 22(1): 97–118.

Education Gadfly. 2004. Unsigned review of "A Straightforward Comparison of Charter Schools and Regular Public Schools in the United States," by Caroline M. Hoxby. Accessed at http://www.edexcellence.net/foundation/ gadfly/issue.cfm?id=162&editions.

Elacqua, Gregory. 2005. "School Choice in Chile: An Analysis of Parental Preferences and Search Behavior." National Center for the Study of Privatization and Education, Working Paper #97. Accessed at http://www.ncspe.org.

Epstein, Keith. 2005. "Philanthropy, Inc.: How Today's Corporate Donors Want Their Gifts to Help the Bottom Line." *Stanford Social Innovation Review* 3(Summer): 20–27.

Erikson, Robert S., Michael B. MacKuen, and James A. Stimson. 2002. *The Macro Polity*. New York: Cambridge University Press.

Finn, Jr., Chester E., Gregg Vanourek, and Bruno V. Manno. 2000. *Charter Schools in Action*. Princeton, N.J.: Princeton University Press.

Fishkin, James. 1991. *Democracy and Deliberation: new Directions for Democratic Reform*. New Haven, Conn.: Yale University Press.

Fiske, Edward B. 2004. "Letter: On Charter Studies' Use of Family Background." *Education Week* 24(6): 33.

Fliegel, Seymour. 1993. *Miracle in East Harlem*. New York: Times Books.

Friedman, Milton. 1955. "The Role of Government in Education." In *Economics and the Public Interest*, edited by Robert A. Solo. New Brunswick, N.J.: Rutgers University Press.

———. 1962. *Capitalism and Freedom*. Chicago, Ill.: University of Chicago Press.

———. 1995. "Public Schools: Make Them Private." *Washington Post*, February 19, 1995: C9.

Gentzkow, Matthew, and Jesse M. Shapiro. 2006. "What Drives Media Slant?: Evidence from U.S. Daily Newspapers." NBER Working Paper 12707. Cambridge, Mass.: National Bureau of Economic Research.

Gittell, Marilyn. 1971. "The Potential for Change: Community Roles." *Journal of Negro Education* 40(3): 216–24.

Goldring, Ellen B., and Rina Shapira. 1993. "Choice, Empowerment, and Involvement: What Satisfies Parents?" *Educational Evaluation and Policy Analysis* 15(4): 396–409.

Goodnough, Abby. 2000. "Clinton Seeks Some Control of Charter Schools." *New York Times*, May 5, 2000: A24.

Greenberg, David, Donna Linksz, and Marvin Mandell. 2003. *Social Experimentation and Public Policymaking*. Washington: Urban Institute Press.

Greene, Jay P. 2005. "Buckets into the Sea: Why Philanthropy Isn't Changing Schools and How it Could." In *With the Best of Intentions: How Philanthropy is Reshaping K-12 Education*, edited by Frederick M. Hess. Cambridge, Mass.: Harvard Education Press.

Greene, Jay P., and Paul E. Peterson. 2000a. "Should Public Discussion of Political Science Research Be Controlled? Why Interest Group Recommendations on the Proper Procedures for Reporting Research Should Be Treated with Skepticism." *PS: Political Science and Politics* 33(2): 220–4.

———. 2000b. "If the Peer Review Attack Fails, Attack Something Else." *PS: Political Science and Politics* 33(2): 229–31.

Greene, Jay, Paul Peterson, and Jiangtao Du. 1996. "The Effectiveness of School Choice in Milwaukee: A Secondary Analysis of Data From the Program's Evaluation." Paper read at American Political Science Association Annual Meeting. San Francisco, Calif., August 29–September 1, 1996.

Greifner, Laura. 2006. "Help for the Summer." *Education Week* 25(44): 28-31.

Gutmann, Amy. 1987. *Democratic Education*. Princeton, N.J.: Princeton University Press.

Gutmann, Amy, and Dennis Thompson. 1996. *Democracy and Disagreement*. Cambridge, Mass.: Harvard University Press.

Hacker, Jacob S., and Paul Pierson. 2005. *Off Center: the Republican Revolution & the Erosion of American Democracy*. New Haven, Conn.: Yale University Press.

Haider, Donald. 1974. *When Governments Come to Washington*. New York: The Free Press.

Hanushek, Eric A., John F. Kain, Steven G. Rivkin, and Gregory F. Branch. 2005. "Charter School Quality and Parental Decision Making with School Choice." NBER Working Paper 11252. Cambridge, Mass.: National Bureau of Economic Research.

Hassel, Bryan C., and Michelle Godard Terrell. 2006. *Charter School Achievement: What We Know*. Third edition. National Alliance for Public Charter Schools. Accessed at http://www.uscharterschools.org/contact/publication/detail/1554/.

Hassel, Bryan C., and Thomas Toch. 2006. "Big Box: How the Heirs of the Wal-Mart Fortune Have Fueled the Charter School Movement." *Connecting the Dots Series*. Washington: The Education Sector. Accessed at http://www.educationsector.org/usr_doc/CTDWalton.pdf.

Hassel, Bryan C., and Amy Way. 2005. "Choosing to Fund School Choice." In *With the Best of Intentions: How Philanthropy is Reshaping K-12 Education*, edited by Frederick M. Hess. Cambridge, Mass.: Harvard Education Press.

Hastings, Justine S., Thomas J. Kane, and Douglas O. Staiger. 2005. "Parental Preferences and School Competition: Evidence from a Public School Choice Program." NBER Working Paper 11805. Cambridge, Mass.: National Bureau of Economic Research.

Hendrie, Caroline. 2005. "Book Faults Achievement in Charter Schools: Authors Stir New Debate by Revisiting 'Dust-Up' Over 2003 NAEP Scores." *Education Week* 24(30): 3.

Henig, Jeffrey R. 1994. *Rethinking School Choice: Limits of the Market Metaphor*. Princeton, N.J.: Princeton University Press.

———. 1999. "School Choice Outcomes." In *School Choice and Social Controversy*, edited by Stephen D. Sugarman and Frank R. Kemerer. Washington: Brookings Institution Press.

———. 2005. "Understanding the Political Conflict over School Choice." In *Getting Choice Right: Ensuring Equity and Efficiency in Education Policy*, edited by Julian R. Betts and Tom Loveless. Washington: Brookings Institution Press.

———. 2006. "Education Policy and the Politics of Privatization Since 1980." Paper read at Annual Meeting of the New England Political Science Association. Portsmouth, N.H., May 5, 2006.

Henig, Jeffrey R., and Clarence N. Stone. Forthcoming. "Rethinking School Reform: The Distractions of Dogma and the Potential for a New Politics of Progressive Pragmatism." *American Journal of Education*.

Henig, Jeffrey R., Thomas T. Holyoke, Natalie Lacireno-Paquet, and Michele M. Moser. 2003. "Privatization, Politics, and Urban Services: The Political Behavior of Charter Schools." *Journal of Urban Affairs* 25(1): 37–54.

Herszenhorn, David. 2006. "A New York School That Teaches Teamwork by Camping." *New York Times*, March 20, 2006: B1.

Hess, Frederick M. 2002. *Revolution at the Margins: the Impact of Competition on Urban School Systems*. Washington: Brookings Institution Press.

———. 2006. "The Wrong Way to Argue for Charter Schools." *New York Daily News*, June 25, 2006. Accessed at http://www.aei.org/publications/filter .all,pubID.24594/pub_detail.asp.

Hess, Frederick M., and Laura LoGerfo. 2006. "Chicanas from Outer Space." *The National Review*, May 8, 2006. Accessed at http://article.national review.com/?q=ZDYwOGExMmUxOWY0ZDgxNGQxMGEwZjg4NTNhM zQ2M2M=.

Hilsenrath, Jon E. 2005. "Making Waves: Novel Way to Assess School Competition Stirs Academic Row to Do So, Harvard Economist Counts Streams in Cities; A Princetonian Takes Issue." *Wall Street Journal*, October 24, 2005: A1.

Howell, William G., editor. 2005. *Besieged: School Boards and the Future of Education Politics*. Washington: Brookings Institution Press.

Howell, William G., and Paul E. Peterson. 2002. *The Education Gap: Vouchers and Urban Schools*. Washington: Brookings Institution Press.

Howell, William G., Paul E. Peterson, and Martin R. West. 2004. "Dog Eats AFT Homework." *Wall Street Journal*, August 18, 2004: A10.

Hoxby, Caroline M. 2000. "Does Competition Among Public Schools Benefit Students and Taxpayers?" *The American Economic Review* 90(5): 1209–39.

———. 2001. "Rising Tide." *Education Next* 1(4): 70-74.

———. 2004. "Chalk It Up." Op-ed. *Wall Street Journal*, September 29, 2004: A18.

———. 2005a. "Competition Among Public Schools: A Reply to Rothstein." NBER Working Paper 11216. Cambridge, Mass.: National Bureau of Economic Research. Accessed at http://www.nber.org/papers/w11216.

———. 2005b. "Do Charter Schools Help Their Students?" *Manhattan Institute, Civic Bulletin* 38.(February): 1–5. Accessed at http://www.manhattan-institute .org/pdf/cb_38.pdf.

Hoxby, Caroline M., and Jonah E. Rockoff. 2004. "The Impact of Charter Schools on Student Achievement." Accessed at http://www.economics.harvard .edu/faculty/hoxby/papers.html.

Huerta, Luis A., Maria-Fernanda Gonzalez, and Chad d'Entremont. 2006. "Cyber and Home School Charter Schools: Adopting Policy to New Forms of Schooling." *Peabody Journal of Education* 81(1): 103–39.

Illich, Ivan. 1971. *Deschooling Society*. New York: Harper & Row.

Iyengar, Shanto. 1990. "Framing Responsibility for Political Issues: The Case of Poverty." *Political Behavior* 12(1): 19–40.

———. 1991. *Is Anyone Responsible? How Television Frames Political Issues*. Chicago, Ill.: University of Chicago Press.

Iyengar, Shanto, and Donald R. Kinder. 1987. *News That Matters: Television and American Opinion*. Chicago, Ill.: University of Chicago Press.

Jacob, Brian, and Jens Ludwig. 2005. "Can the Federal Government Improve Education Research?" In *Brookings Papers on Education Policy: 2005*, edited by D. Ravitch. Washington: Brookings Institution Press.

Jacobs, Lawrence R., and Robert Y. Shapiro. 2000. *Politicians Don't Slander: Polit-*

ical Manipulation and the Loss of Democratic Responsiveness. Chicago, Ill.: University of Chicago.

Jankowski, John E. 1999. *What is the State Government Role in the R&D Enterprise?* Arlington, Va.: National Science Foundation, Division of Science Resources Studies.

Jencks, Christopher. 1966. "Is the Public School Obsolete?" *The Public Interest* 2(Winter):18–27.

Jenkins-Smith, Hank. 1990. *Democratic Politics and Policy Analysis*. Pacific Grove, Calif.: Brooks Cole Publishing.

Jones, Bryan D. 1995. *Reconceiving Decision-Making in Democratic Politics: Attention, Choice, and Public Policy*. Chicago, Ill.: University of Chicago.

Kahlenberg, Richard D. 2001. *All Together Now: Creating Middle-class Schools through Public School Choice*. Washington: Brookings Institution.

———. 2007. *Tough Liberal: Albert Shanker and the Battles Over Schools, Unions, Race, and Democracy*. New York: Columbia University Press.

Kahneman, Daniel, and Amos Tversky, editors. 2000. *Choices, Values, and Frames*. London and New York: Cambridge University Press and Russell Sage Foundation.

Kahneman, Daniel, Paul Slovic, and Amos Tversky. 1982. *Judgment Under Uncertainty: Heuristics and Biases*. New York: Cambridge University Press.

Kanigel, Robert. 1997. *The One Best Way: Frederick Winslow Turner and the Enigma of Efficiency*. New York: Viking.

Kelly, Dennis, and Liz Szabo. 2004. "Charter School Performance Study Stirs Debate." *USA Today*, August 18, 2004: B13.

Kelman, Steven. 1981. "Cost-Benefit Analysis: An Ethical Critique." *Regulation* 5(1): 33–40.

Kingdon, John W. 1995. *Agendas, Alternatives, and Public Policies*, 2nd edition. Boston, Mass.: Little, Brown.

Koppel, Ted. 2006. "And Now, a Word for Our Demographic." *New York Times*, January 29, 2006: Section 4, 16.

Krehely, Jeff, Meaghan House, and Emily Kernan. 2004. *Axis of Ideology: Conservative Foundations and Public Policy*. Washington: National Committee for Responsive Philanthropy.

Krueger, Alan B., and Pei Zhu. 2004. "Another Look at the New York City School Voucher Experiment." *The American Behavioral Scientist* 47(5): 658–99.

Kuklinski, James H., and Norman L. Hurley. 1994. "On Hearing and Interpreting Political Messages: A Cautionary Tale of Citizen Cue-Taking." *Journal of Politics* 56(3): 729–51.

Lacireno-Paquet, Natalie. 2006. "Charter School Enrollments in Context: An Exploration of Organization and Policy Influences." *Peabody Journal of Education* 81(1): 79–102.

Lacireno-Paquet, Natalie, Thomas T. Holyoke, Jeffrey R. Henig, and Michele M. Moser. 2002. "Creaming versus Cropping: Charter School Enrollment Practices in Response to Market Incentives." *Educational Evaluation and Policy Analysis* 24(2)(Summer): 145–58.

Lagemann, Ellen Condliffe. 2000. *An Elusive Science: The Troubling History of Education Research*. Chicago, Ill.: University of Chicago.

Lagemann, Ellen Condliffe, and Jennifer de Forest. 2007. "What Might Andrew Carnegie Want to Tell Bill Gates: Reflections on the Hundredth Anniversary of The Carnegie Foundation for the Advancement of Teaching." In *Reconnecting Education and Foundations*, edited by Ray Bacchetti and Thomas Ehrlich. New York: John Wiley & Sons.

Lesk, Michael. 1997. "How Much Information Is There In the World?" Accessed at http://www.lesk.com/mlesk/ksg97/ksg.html.

Lieberman, Myron. 1993. *Public Education: An Autopsy*. Cambridge, Mass.: Harvard University Press.

Loveless, Tom. 2005. "How Program Officers at Education Philanthropies View Education." In *With the Best of Intentions*, edited by Frederick M. Hess. Cambridge, Mass.: Harvard Education Press.

Lubienski, Christopher. 2003. "School Competition and Promotion: Substantive and Symbolic Differentiation in Local Education Markets." New York: Columbia University, Teachers College, National Center for the Study of Privatization in Education.

———. 2004. "Charter School Innovation in Theory and Practice: Autonomy, R&D, and Curricular Conformity." In *Taking Account of Charter Schools*, edited by Katrina E. Bulkley and Priscilla Wohlstetter. New York: Teachers College Press.

Lubienski, Christopher, and Sarah Theule Lubienski. 2006a. *Charter, Private, Public Schools and Academic Achievement: New Evidence from NAEP Mathematics Data*. New York: National Center for the Study of Privatization in Education.

———. 2006b. "School Sector and Academic Achievement: A Multi-Level Analysis of NAEP Mathematics Data." *American Educational Research Journal* 43(4): 651–98.

———. 2006c. "Think Tank Review of 'On the Public-Private School Achievement Debate.'" *Education Policy Research Unit, Think Tank Review*. Accessed at http://www.asu.edu/educ/epsl/EPRU/ttreviews/EPSL-0608-207-EPRU .pdf.

Lynn, Laurence E., Jr. 1978. The Question of Relevance. In *Knowledge and Policy: The Uncertain Connection*, edited by Laurence E. Lynn, Jr. Washington: National Academy of Sciences Press.

MacDonald, Heather. 1996. "The Billions of Dollars that Made Things Worse." *City Journal* (Autumn 1996). Accessed at http://www.city-journal.org/ html/6_4_a1.html.

Macedo, Stephen, editor. 1999. *Deliberative Politics: Essays on Democracy and Disagreement*. New York: Oxford University Press.

Malbin, Michael J. 1980. "Congress, Policy Analysis, and Natural Gas Deregulation: A Parable About Fig Leaves." In *Bureaucrats, Policy Analysis, Statesmen: Who Leads?*, edited by Robert A. Goldwin. Washington: American Enterprise Institute.

Maranto, Robert, and April Gresham. 1999. "The Wild West of Education Reform: Arizona's Charter Schools." In *School Choice in the Real World*, edited by Robert Maranto, Scott Milliman, Frederick Hess, and April Gresham. Boulder, Colo.: Westview.

Mayhew, David. 1975. *Congress: The Electoral Connection*. New Haven, Conn.: Yale University Press.

McCombs, Maxwell E., and Donald L. Shaw. 1972. "The Agenda-Setting Function of Mass Media." *Public Opinion Quarterly* 36(2):176–87.

McGuinn, Patrick. 2006. *No Child Left Behind and the Transformation of Federal Education Policy 1965–2005.* Lawrence, Kan.: University Press of Kansas.

McKewan, Patrick, and Rob Olson. Forthcoming. "Admission Lotteries in Charter Schools." In *Getting and Using Real Evidence About Charter Schools,* edited by Paul Hill and Julian Betts. Washington: Brookings Institute Press.

McNeil, Michele. 2006. "States Giving Performance Pay by Doling Out Bonuses." *Education Week* 26(2): 30.

Meeks, Ronald L. 2005. *Federal Funds for Research and Development: Fiscal Years 2002, 2003, and 2004,* Volume 52. NSF 05-307. Arlington, Va.: National Science Foundation, Division of Science Resources Statistics.

Mervis, Jeffrey. 2006. "Senate Panel Chair Asks Why NSF Funds Social Sciences." *Science* 312(5775): 829–45.

Micklethwhaite, John, and Adrian Wooldridge. 2004. *The Right Nation: Conservative Power in America.* New York: Penguin.

Mindlin, Alex. 2004. "Requiem for a Much-Beloved School." *New York Times,* July 4, 2004: Section 14, 4.

Mintrom, Michael. 2000a. *Leveraging Local Innovation: The Case of Michigan's Charter Schools.* East Lansing, Mich.: Michigan State University Department of Education.

———. 2000b. *Policy Entrepreneurs and School Choice.* Washington: Georgetown University Press.

Miron, Gary, and Christopher Nelson. 2002. *What's Public About Charter Schools: Lessons Learned About Choice and Accountability.* Thousand Oaks, Calif.: Corwin Press.

Moe, Terry M. 2001. *Schools, Vouchers, and the American Public.* Washington: Brookings Institute Press.

Mooney, Chris. 2005. *The Republican War on Science.* New York: Basic Books.

Mosteller, Frederick, and Robert Boruch, eds. 2002. *Evidence Matters: Randomized Trials in Education Research.* Washington: Brookings Institute Press.

Moynihan, Daniel Patrick. 1969. *Maximum Feasible Misunderstanding: Community Action in the War on Poverty.* New York: The Free Press.

mrs panstreppon's Blog. 2006. "Is Arianna a Ringer?" March 15, 2006. [cited July 15, 2006]. Accessed at http://www.tpmcafe.com/blog/mrs_panstreppon/2006/mar/15/is_arianna_a_ringer.

Muir, Edward. 1999. "They Blinded Me with Political Science: On the Use of Nonpeer Reviewed Research in Education Policy." *PS: Political Science and Politics* 32(4): 762–4.

———. 2000. "Social Science Should Be a Process, Not a Bloody Shirt." *PS: Political Science and Politics* 33(2): 235–7.

Nathan, Joe. 1999. *Charter Schools: Creating Hope and Opportunity for American Education.* San Francisco, Calif.: Jossey-Bass Publishers.

———. 2002. "Minnesota and the Charter School Idea." In *The Charter School Landscape,* edited by Sandra Vergari. Pittsburgh, Penn.: University of Pittsburgh Press.

National Center for Education Statistics (NCES). 2004. *The Nation's Report Card.*

America's Charter Schools: Results from the NAEP 2003 Pilot Study. Washington: U.S. Department of Education, National Center for Education Statistics.

National Committee for Responsive Philanthropy (NCRP). 2004. *Axis of Ideology: Conservative Foundations and Public Policy.* Washington: National Committee for Responsive Philanthropy.

National Education Association. 1998. "NEA Charter Schools Take Initiative." *NEA Today*, April 1998. Accessed at http://findarticles.com/p/articles/mi_qa3617/is_199804/ai_n8807872.

National School Board Association. 2003. *Keep Public Education Public: Why Vouchers are a Bad Ideas.* Alexandria, Va.: National School Board Association. Accessed at http://www.nsba.org/site/docs/33800/33743.pdf

Nelson, F. Howard, and Tiffany Miller. 2004. "A Closer Look at Caroline Hoxby's 'A Straightforward Comparison of Charter Schools and Regular Public Schools in the United States'." Washington: American Federation of Teachers.

Nelson, F. Howard, Bella Rosenberg, and Nancy Van Meter. 2004. *Charter School Achievement on the 2003 National Assessment of Educational Progress.* Washington: American Federation of Teachers.

New York Sun. 2006. "The Arbiter of Choice." Editorial. August 2, 2006. Accessed at http://www.nysun.com/article/37152.

Orfield, Gary. 1969. *The Reconstruction of Southern Education.* New York: John Wiley & Sons.

Page, Benjamin I. 1996. "The Mass Media as Political Actors." *PS: Political Science and Politics* 29(1): 20–24.

Page, Benjamin I., and Robert Y. Shapiro. 1992. *The Rational Public: Fifty Years of Trends in Americans' Policy Preferences.* Chicago, Ill.: University of Chicago Press.

Page, Benjamin I., Robert Y. Shapiro, and Glenn R. Dempsey. 1987. "What Moves Public Opinion?" *American Political Science Review* 81(1): 23–43.

Peterson, Paul E., and Elena Llaudet. 2006. "On the Public-Private School Achievement Debate." Paper presented at the Annual Meetings of the American Political Science Association, August 31-September 3, 2006, Philadelphia, Penn.

Petrilli, Michael J. 2006. "Review: Key Issues in Studying Charter Schools and Achievement: A Review and Suggestions for National Guidelines." *The Education Gadfly*, June 15, 2006. Accessed at http://www.edexcellence.net/foundation/gadfly/issue.cfm?edition=&id=246#2891.

Pew Research Center for the People and the Press. 1998. "Deconstructing Distrust: How Americans View Government." April 17, 1998. Accessed at http://people-press.org/reports/print.php3?ReportID=92.

Project for Excellence in Journalism. 2007. *The State of the News Media: An Annual Report on American Journalism.* Washington: Pew Research Center. Accessed at http://www.stateofthenewsmedia.org/2007.

Revkin, Andrew C. 2006. "Climate Expert Says NASA Tried to Silence Him." *New York Times*, January 29, 2006: A1.

Rhoads, Stephen. 1985. *The Economist's View of the World.* New York: Cambridge University Press.

Ricci, David M. 1993. *The Transformation of American Politics: The New Washington and the Rise of Think Tanks.* New Haven, Conn.: Yale University Press.

Rich, Andrew. 2004. *Think Tanks, Public Policy, and the Politics of Expertise.* New York: Cambridge University Press.

———. 2005. "War of Ideas: Why Mainstream and Liberal Foundations and the Think Tanks They Support Are Losing in the War of Ideas in American Politics." *Stanford Social Innovation Review* Spring(2005): 18–25. Accessed at http://www.ssireview.org/images/articles/2005SP_feature_rich.pdf.

Robelen, Eric W. 2006. "Reanalysis of NAEP Scores Finds Charter Schools Lagging Study Initiated by NCES Revisits Data Underlying Controversy in 2004." *Education Week* 26(1): 26.

Rochefort, David A., and Roger W. Cobb, editors. 1994. *The Politics of Problem Definition: Shaping the Policy Agenda.* Lawrence, Kan.: University Press of Kansas.

Rofes, Eric. 2000. "Teachers as Communitarians: A Charter School Cooperative in Minnesota." In *Inside Charter Schools: The Paradox of Radical Decentralization,* edited by Bruce Fuller. Cambridge, Mass.: Harvard University Press.

Rose, Lowell C., and Alec M. Gallup. 2003. "The 35th Annual Phi Delta Kappa/Gallup Poll of the Public's Attitudes Toward the Public Schools." *Phi Delta Kappan* 85(1): 41–52.

Rotherham, Andrew. 2005. "The Pros & Cons of Charter School Closures." In *Hopes, Fears, & Reality" A Balanced Look at American Charter schools in 2005,* edited by R. J. Lake and P. T. Hill. Seattle, Wash.: National Charter School Research Project.

Rothstein, Jesse. 2005. "Does Competition Among Public Schools Benefit Students and Taxpayers? A Comment on Hoxby (2000)." NBER Working Paper 11215. Cambridge, Mass.: National Bureau of Economic Research.

Rothstein, Richard. 2004. *Class and Schools: Using Social, Economic, and Educational Reform to Close the Black-White Achievement Gap.* Washington: Economic Policy Institute.

Roy, Joydeep, and Lawrence Mishel. 2005. *Advantage None: Re-examining Hoxby's Finding of Charter School Benefits.* Washington: Economic Policy Institute.

Rudalevige, Andrew. 2007. "'Truth vs. Partnership': Structure and Science in Federal Education Research. Paper read at The Politics of Knowledge: Why Research Does(or Does Not) Influence Education Policy." Paper presented at the American Enterprise Institute. Washington, D.C., May 21, 2007.

Saba, Jennifer. 2006. "Merrill Lynch Raises Alarm on Health of Newspaper Industry." *Editor & Publisher,* May 26, 2006. Accessed at http://www.editorandpublisher.com/eandp/news/article_display.jsp?vnu_content_id=1002576581.

Sass, Tim R. 2006. "Charter Schools and Student Achievement in Florida." *Education Finance and Policy* 1(1): 91–122.

Schemo, Diana Jean. 2004a. "Charter Schools Trail in Results, U.S. Data Reveals." *New York Times,* August 17, 2004: A1.

———. 2004b. "A Second Report Shows Charter School Students Not Performing as Well as Other Students." *New York Times,* December 16, 2004: A36.

———. 2006. "Public Schools Close to Private in U.S. Study." *New York Times,* July 15, 2006: A1.

Schnaiberg, Lynn. 2000. "Charter Schools: Choice, Diversity May Be At Odds." *Education Week* 19(35): 1.

Schneider, Mark, and Jack Buckley. 2002. "What Do Parents Want from Schools?

Evidence from the Internet." *Educational Evaluation and Policy Analysis* 24(2): 133–44.

Schneider, Mark, Paul Teske, and Melissa Marschall. 2000. *Choosing Schools: Consumer Choice and the Quality of American Schools.* Princeton, N.J.: Princeton University Press.

Schorr, Jonathan. 2004. "Charter Schools: Still Proving What Works." *Washington Post*, September 11, 2004: A21.

Seelye, Katherine. 2006a. "Times to Reduce Page Size and Close a Plant in 2008." *New York Times*, July 18, 2006: C5.

———. 2006b. "Newspaper Circulation Falls Sharply." *New York Times*, October 31, 2006: C1.

Severo, Richard. 2005. "William Proxmire, Maverick Democratic Senator From Wisconsin, Is Dead at 90." *New York Times*, December 16, 2005: B13.

Shreeve, James. 2004. *The Genome War: How Craig Venter Tried to Capture the Code of Life and Save the World.* New York: Alfred A. Knopf.

Simon, Herbert A. 1985. "Human Nature in Politics: The Dialogue of Psychology and Political Science." *American Political Science Review* 79(2): 293–304.

Simon, William E. 1978. *Time for Truth.* New York: Readers Digest Association.

Smith, James A. 1991. *The Idea Brokers.* New York: The Free Press.

Smith, Kevin. 2005. "Data Don't Matter? Academic Research and School Choice." *Perspectives on Politics* 3(2): 285–99.

Smith, Vernon H., Robert D. Barr, and Daniel J. Burke. 1976. *Alternatives in Education: Freedom to Choose.* New York: Phi Delta Kappa International.

Stephan, Stephen A. 1935. "Prospects and Possibilities: The New Deal and the New Social Research." *Social Forces* 13(4): 515–21.

Swanson, Christopher B., and Janelle Barlage. 2006. *Influence: A Study of the Factors Shaping Education Policy.* Arlington, Va.: Education Research Center.

Teske, Paul, and Robert Reichardt. 2006. "Doing Their Homework: How Charter School Parents Make Their Choices." In *Hopes, Fears, & Reality: A Balanced look at American Charter Schools in 2006*, edited by P. T. Hill and R. J. Lake. Seattle, Wash.: National Charter School Research Project.

the polling company, inc. No date. "National and Statewide Surveys on Charter Schools: Executive Summary and Key Findings." Unpublished document.

Tierney, John. 2006. "Spinning a Bad Report Card." *New York Times*, July 18, 2006: A21.

Toppo, Greg. 2005. "Education Dept. Funds Need Monitoring." *USA Today*, September 3, 2005. Accessed at http://www.usatoday.com/education/2005-09-03-education-funding_x.htm.

Tyack, David. 1974. *The One Best System.* Cambridge, Mass.: Harvard University Press.

U.S. Department of Education. 2005a. *Biennial Report: Grants, Cooperative Agreements, and Contracts over $100,000 Receiving Funding FY 2002 through FY2004.* Washington: Institute of Education Sciences. Accessed at http://ies.ed.gov/about/reports/annual/otherplanrpts.html.

———. 2005b. *Review of Department Identified Contracts and Grants for Public Relations Services.* Final Inspection Report. Washington: U.S. Department of Education, Office of the Inspector General. Accessed at http://www.ed.gov/about/offices/list/oig/aireports/13f0012.pdf.

Viadero, Debra. 2006. "Study: EMO Schools Don't Outscore Other Phila. Schools." *Education Week* 25(32): 15.

Vinovskis, Maris. 2000. "Teachers Unions and Educational Research." In *Conflicting Missions?: Teachers Unions and Educational Reform*, edited by Tom Loveless. Washington: Brookings Institution.

———. 2002. "Missing in Practice? Development and Evaluation at the U.S. Department of Education." In *Evidence Matters: Randomized Trials in Education Research*, edited by Frederick Mosteller and Robert Boruch. Washington: Brookings Institution Press.

Viteritti, Joseph P. 2005. "School Choice: How an Abstract Idea Became a Political Reality." In *Brookings Papers on Education Policy 2005*, edited by Diane Ravitch. Washington: Brookings Institution Press.

Watson, James D. 1968. *The Double Helix; A Personal Account of the Discovery of the Structure of DNA*. New York: Atheneum.

Weiher, Gregory R., and Kent L. Tedin. 2002. "Does Choice Lead to Racially Distinctive Schools? Charter Schools and Household Preferences." *Journal of Policy Analysis and Management* 21(1): 79–92.

Welner, Kevin G., and Alex Molnar. 2007. "Truthiness in Education." *Education Week* 26(25): 44.

White, Andrew Dickson. 1890. "The Government of American Cities." *Forum* 4(December): 213-6.

Wildavsky, Aaron. 1987. *Speaking Truth to Power*. New Brunswick, N.J.: Transaction Publishers.

Witte, John F., Jr. 2000. *The Market Approach to Education*. Princeton, N.J.: Princeton University Press.

Witte, John, David Weimer, Arnold Shober, and Paul Schlomer. 2007. "The Performance of Charter Schools in Wisconsin." *Journal of Policy Analysis and Management* 26(3): 567–88.

Zimmer, Ron, and Richard Buddin. 2006. *Making Sense of Charter Schools*. Santa Monica, Calif.: Rand.

Index

Numbers in **boldface** refer to figures and tables.